REDBONE CHRONICLES

VOLUME 1 NUMBER 1, FEBRUARY 2007

A Compilation of publishing's by the

Redbone Heritage Foundation

2004-2015

Edited by Backintyme Publishing

COVER ART: Wi-jun-jon-The Pigeon's Egg Head Going to Washington: Return to his home. Two views of Wi-jun-jon, first, on his way to Washington wearing Native American dress and carrying a calumet, then, on his return to his village wearing a uniform with top hat and carrying a fan and an umbrella. Currier & Ives. Caitlin, George, 1796-1872, artist.

Backintyme

**History of the
U.S. Color Line**

Published by Backintyme Publishing

Crofton, Kentucky, U.S.A.

Copyright @ 2016 by Backintyme

Backintyme Publishing

1341 Grapevine Rd.

Crofton, KY 422117

270-985-8568

Website: http://backintyme.biz

Email:backintyme@mehrapublishing.com

Printed in the United States of America

February 2016

ISBN: 978-0-939479-10-8

Library of Congress Control Number: 2016933921

For 200 years Redbones have been Louisiana's mystery people; for 400 years, America's mystery tribe. They left the east coast, principally Maryland, Virginia, Kentucky, Tennessee, North Carolina, South Carolina and other locales, in search of new land and freedom from discrimination in the west. In the early 1800s, the southwestern part of Louisiana, joining Spanish owned Texas, was a No Man's Land and just the kind of place these people of mixed racial heritage were seeking. Being on the border between two countries provided the option of border crossing when it was to their advantage to do so.

Redbones were everywhere discriminated against because of their mysterious ethnic origins, and hew of their skin. Settling in this territory; they formed loosely organized communities that were bound together by their determination to protect each other from the discriminatory practices of the dominant culture.

A large part of the defensive posture these early settlers assumed was secrecy about their past and especially their heritage. This secrecy, perhaps a conspiracy of secrecy, eventually led to true forgetting and loss of family and cultural history. Modern day Redbones are taking advantage of the opportunities to uncover that past brought about by the electronic revolution. They are trying to uncover their hidden past and to develop comfort in sharing it with their offspring and with the dominant culture. This effort is beyond the capacity of one person working alone. The task is intellectually challenging and emotionally difficult. A not-for-profit corporation has been formed to assist and support individual efforts in accomplishing these difficult tasks

Dedication

IN MEMORY OF REDBONE HERITAGE FOUNDATION FOUNDERS, AND EDITORS OF THE REDBONE CHRONICLES 2004-2016.

LEFT DON C. MARLER (1933-2016) AND RIGHT GARY "MISHIHO" GABEHART (1943-2015). GREAT FRIENDS AND FOUNDING MEMBERS DON MARLER, AND CHICKASAW INDIAN AND REDBONE DESCENDANT GARY GABEHART. GREAT LEADERS AND ALLIES OF THE PEOPLE KNOWN AS REDBONE.

Contents

Native American Ancestry in Southern Mustee Communities

Native American Ancestry in Southern Mestee Communities

By Alvie Walts

There has been much controversy over the origins of the Melungeons, Brass Ankles, Redbones and other Mestee or "Mixed Blood" groups in the Southern United States. The purpose of this article is to focus on the Native American element in the Mestee groups of the Southern United States and how these tribes survived into modern day descendants.

In accounting for their heritage, some groups choose a Mediterranean origin while others say they were Native Americans. Some researchers will only focus on the African ancestry in these groups while others deny any African ancestry at all. Both positions on the African ancestry in these groups are historically, genetically and culturally incorrect and reflect a social stigma based on the American view of race and color. It is a prejudicial concept based on ideological, political and cultural views of America's slavery past and society's present, that were and are to separate ethnic populations in the nation. Culturally, the Jim Crow "one drop rule" is still very much alive with both liberal and conservative ideologues today and in many other Americans -- even if on an unconscious level.

The truth is not that simple. The truth is not "black and white", not in color, and not in race and not in the so-called "Tri racial" groups. All of these groups were of multi ethnic backgrounds of various degrees. All were humiliated, stereotyped, persecuted and were considered outcasts by the Anglo majority and African minority in the surrounding communities. All were of degrees of European, South Asian, Mediterranean, North African, Middle Eastern and Native American ancestry.

Figure 1 Photo: Mary Elizabeth Evans daughter of Samuel Evans Cherokee Saponi and Nancy Chavers Tuscarora in Jackson County Alabama Cherokee Saponi Tuscarora before 1894

Figure 2 Photo: Pamunkey Indian Family. Note this picture is associated with "Queen Anne of the Pamunkey"

There is no "Last of The Mohicans."

The Native American tribes along the Atlantic eastern coast of the United States were the first Native Americans to come in contact with Europeans and thereby suffered a loss in population to a great degree due to warfare and disease. Thousands of these people died due to European diseases to which they had no resistance. The tribes further west, such as the Cherokee in the mountains of North Carolina, were able to form a more gradual resistance, although disease must have taken its toll long before they ever saw their first European.

The Mohicans Are Walking Around Today.

As stated above, diseases such as small pox, and wars such as the King Phillip's War, inflicted much damage on the Native populations. The Native American tribes, out of necessity, absorbed Europeans, South Asians, Mediterranean and African people to compensate for this loss. The people assimilated were indentured servants, who grew tired of the servitude, runaway slaves, outlaws and later possibly Tories who were loyal to the British during the American Revolution. They formed alliances and intermarried with the Native American tribes who frequently lived on land that was deemed worthless to the other European settlers. Even more important they adopted the native culture of these groups to form separate Mestee populations. In time they became known by names such as Croatoan, Red Legs, Turks, Brass Ankles and Redbones. All were racial epitaphs given to them by the surrounding populations.

The Native American tribal elements of these people are of many diverse groups belonging to the Algonquin, Siouan and Iroquoian language groups. As the decimation began

Native American Ancestry in Southern Mestee Communities

Native Americans banded together to form new "tribes" or confederations such as the Saponi, a tribe that was formed from previous smaller tribes of Siouan speakers. However in time all would have had to inter-marry with the various Europeans, Africans and others in order to survive.

One of the first tribes to make contact with the Europeans was the Powhatan Empire, a confederation of Algonquin speaking tribes who first encountered the Europeans at the Jamestown settlement. The European diseases and constant warfare with the Europeans, took a massive toll on the Algonquin population. At the same time the new settlers were also showing their distrust of the colonial English government. The Bacon Rebellion was an uprising of new settlers, both poor Europeans and poor free Africans, against the English government. This uprising was a possible echo towards independence and the American Revolution; The Bacon Rebellion not only almost destroyed Jamestown but, once again, brought more destruction to the surrounding Native American communities. However, like the mountain men during the 1800's, the more friendly Native American communities must have looked inviting to this poor class of men who were fed up with the old world system of European tyranny. Many fled to the surrounding Native communities, intermarried with the local Native American women, and then formed separate multi-racial communities. These are the so-called "Tri-racial" communities. The most famous of these groups are the Melungeons, a people thought to be of Anglo, Native American and African ancestry, but have shown recently a large input of Mediterranean ancestry. Another famous group is now an organized Native American tribe. The Lumbee Tribe of North Carolina is the largest Native American tribe East of the Mississippi River. The Lumbee are descendants of the Cheraw and other Native American tribes and also of the runaway Anglo and African people of the early American frontier. The Lumbee also have described themselves as 'Portuguese" and from the number of English versions of Hispanic surnames in the tribe this very well may be the case. Another group is the Brass Ankles, who seem to be regrouping into several modern day Pee Dee Native American tribes in South Carolina. Still another large group that is seldom mentioned is the Houma Indians in Louisiana who are the descendants of French and mixed blood Indians in the Southern coast of Louisiana. The Redbones of Louisiana is yet another group that has been formed; they are from various admixtures of Anglo, Mediterranean,

Middle Eastern, Native American and African ancestry. Some of the Redbones have retained Native American cultural traits and they acknowledge their mixed ancestry.

All of these groups have various degrees of multi ethnic ancestry. All are descendants of Native American tribes that were decimated as a result of migration of Europeans.

Mestee Communities

Listed below are some of the tribes that are thought to have formed the Mestee communities and the modern day tribes of the same groups:

- Powhatan Tribal Groups, Virginia, Algonquin
- Pamunkey, a Powhatan tribe, Virginia, Algonquin
- Nansemond, a Powhatan tribe, Virginia, Algonquin
- Mattaponi, a Powhatan tribe, Virginia, Algonquin
- Chickahominy, a Powhatan tribe, Virginia, Algonquin
- Occaneechi Saponi, Virginia and North Carolina, Siouan
- Chowanoake, Virginia, North Carolina, Iroquoian
- Meherrin, Virginia and North Carolina, Iroquoian
- Catawba, North and South Carolina, Siouan
- Amonsoquath, Virginia, Iroquoian Nottoway, Virginia, Iroquoian Assateague, Virginia, Algonquin
- Tutelo, Virginia, Siouan
- Nantecoke, Maryland, Delaware, Virginia, Algonquin
- Southern Tuscarora, Virginia, Iroquoian Monacan, Virginia, Siouan
- Cheraw, Virginia, North/South Carolina, Siouan
- Nahyssan, Virginia, Siouan
- Cherokee, North Carolina, Iroquoian
- Modern Tribes Today:
- Powhatan Tribes, Virginia
- Meherrin Tribe, Virginia
- Monacan Tribe, Virginia
- Occaneechi Saponi Tribe, North Carolina
- Haliwa Saponi Tribe, North Carolina Catawba, South Carolina
- Eastern Cherokee, North Carolina Lumbee, North Carolina
- Cohari Tribe, North Carolina Waccamaw Tribe, North Carolina

In Conclusion

Modern DNA evidence shows that these tribes did not die out or become extinct as thought by some historians today. They survive, to a degree, in the modern day descendants of the so-called "Tri racial" communities or, if you will, the descendants of Mulattoes or in the Free

People of Color of early American history. They also survive, to a degree, in thousands of descendants of African and Anglo Americans in the United States.

Their survival no matter how small the number, is on a genetic and cultural level, a testament to these Native Americans along the Atlantic coast. Although they absorbed a vast amount of European, South Asian and African ancestry they have always described themselves as being from partial Indian ancestry. We are the descendants of these proud people, the remnant of once great nations who would not go quietly into the night and who imbedded their cultural identity into the fabric of many people and families in the Southern United States

Land, History, and a People Called "Redbones"

By Sammy Tippit

I was shocked when I received a phone call from my sister in May 2004. She said a man from Portugal had contacted her saying that he had evidence that he was our brother. What transpired during the next month would place me on a search for my roots and teach me about a mystery people in Central and Southwest Louisiana called "Redbones." After many conversations with the gentleman from Portugal and both of us submitting to DNA testing, I learned that he was not my brother. However, I was confronted for the first time in my life with my family history. I was backed into a corner and needed answers.

Answers were not far away, and I could have known my heritage many years earlier. My cousin, Jane Parker McManus, has researched and written extensively about our family. For many years, I had a copy of both her genealogical books on my family. Her mother and my father were brother and sister. Her book, A Backwards Glance, was full of pertinent information about my roots. Thus, Jane was the first person I contacted when my sister told me about the man from Portugal. She has been extremely helpful in assisting me to find the answers that I needed.

One of the most fascinating discoveries that I made as I began to research my heritage was that my grandmother was a descendent of a people who were derogatorily called "Redbones." I had not previously heard that name. My father became ill when I was a small child. I grew up in Baton Rouge, and his people lived deep in the pine forests of Central and Southwest Louisiana. His parents, Samuel C. Tippit and Eliza Bass Tippit, died before I was born. Thus, I knew nothing about them.

I gave my heart and life to Christ as a university student and surrendered my life to preach the gospel two days later at the Istrouma Baptist Church in Baton Rouge. I was licensed and ordained to the ministry in a Southern Baptist Church, which was a part of the Louisiana Baptist Convention. Because my family very seldom attended church, I often felt like an outsider among my new found Baptist friends. You can imagine how surprised I was to learn that my grandparents four and five generations earlier were some of the first members of Louisiana Baptist churches that would later become the Louisiana Baptist Convention.

After learning who my forefathers were, I researched everything that I could find on the internet about them. One of the first places with information was a website from the Amiable

Baptist Church near Glenmora. It stated that my three times great grandparents, John and Delaney Bass, were founding members of this historic church begun September 6, 1828.1 The website mentioned a man named Joseph Willis. I later learned that he was a man of mixed race who pioneered Baptist work in Louisiana.

I turned again to my cousin for information. She was kind enough to send me a copy of an original document stating that my four times great grandmother, Francis Smith Taylor Sweat, and her husband Gilbert Sweat gave the land for the first Baptist church west of the Mississippi River.2 Francis "Fanny" Sweat was the mother of Delaney Taylor Bass.3

Finding the Amiable Baptist Church website and having a copy of the donation of the land for the first Baptist Church west of the Mississippi River placed a sense of passion in my heart to know my roots. Because I did not grow up attending church, I knew little about Baptist history and church life in Louisiana. Suddenly, I discovered that my background was deeply rooted in the beginnings of Baptist work in Louisiana. The search for who I was turned into a passion to learn as much as possible. That passion led me to land transactions, a court case, and a rich and colorful history of Louisiana's mystery people called "Redbones" and their part in the formation of the Louisiana Baptist Convention which numbers today more than 700,000 members.

I will attempt to give a detailed description of those persons of "Redbone" background who were involved in this historic church, some- of the church history, the land donated, and the controversy that emerged among them. It was in my search for the location of the land that I came to understand the complex nature of the people called "Redbones."

The People Rev. Joseph Willis:

He is esteemed among both those in the "Redbone" community as well as Baptists in Louisiana. Willis' life and ministry are described by Louisiana Baptist historian, Rev. W. E. Paxton as "the Apostle of the Opelousas." 4 According to Paxton, Willis came in 1798 with Richard Curtis and William Thompson to Cole's Creek in Wilkinson County Mississippi to constitute "The Baptist Church on Buffaloe (sic)." 5 The Buffalo was- a small creek near the Homochitto River, which lies close to the Louisiana border. Willis co-labored with the newly formed Mississippi Baptists, but he ultimately had a passion to preach the gospel west of the Mississippi River. Paxton described Willis, "He was a mulatto, and came to Mississippi previous to 1798, as a licensed preacher. He was a man of some education, full of the Holy Ghost, and was a sound Gospel preacher. Some of his productions in my possession indicate that he was a simple hearted Christian, glowing with the love of Jesus, and an effective speaker." 6

Paxton claimed that Willis was the first Protestant to preach West of the Mississippi River. He stated, "He preached the first sermon ever preached in the state west of the Mississippi River by other than Catholic priests. This was at Vermillion, about forty miles southwest of Baton Rouge. At night he preached at' Plaquemine Brule. This was during his visit in which he preached but three or four times, and that at the peril of his life. Both his color and his being a Baptist exposed him to violent prejudices, and he was often threatened with violence... He selected a place to locate, returned to Mississippi, made his arrangements, and the year following located permanently in Louisiana. The place where he settled was on Bayou Chicot in St. Landry Parish "7

Paxton said that a good work was begun by Willis, but that he had a problem. He was not ordained. Thus, he could not baptize and organize people into a church. Paxton concluded, "The result was that a Methodist minister entered into his labors, and out of the persons converted under his preaching formed a society at Plaquemine, the first organization of any Protestant denomination in this part of the State."8

According to Paxton, Willis settled in Bayou Chicot in 1804. However, he was not ordained and not permitted by Mississippi Baptists to form a church in Louisiana until November 13, 1812.9 After eight years of Willis' spiritual labor, Mississippi Baptists sent Moses Hadley and Lawrence Scarborough to Louisiana to ordain Joseph Willis. Mississippi Baptist records state, "In 1812, he [Moses Hadley] wrote again on the Union of Churches. The same year, he was sent to Opelousas, Louisiana to ordain Willis and constitute the church in Louisiana."1°

When Willis settled in Bayou Chicot, he found people like himself. It was among these people that he formed the first Baptist Church west of the Mississippi River. Unfortunately, the location of the records of the first few years of the Calvary Baptist Church are unknown. However, there are some strong indicators of those people with whom he worked in the early days. Among those with whom he began working were a people of mixed racial background. The Louisiana census of 1810 in St. Landry Parish listed Joseph Willis, Gilbert Sweat, Ephriam Sweat, and John Bass as Free Persons of Color."

Randy Willis, a descendent of Joseph Willis wrote of his racial background, "It was to a part-Indian slave of Agerton's [Willis] that his only son, Joseph, was born. The relationship of Agerton and Joseph's mother can only be speculation, but under the North Carolina laws of 1741 all interracial marriages were illegal. Since Joseph's mother was a slave he was born to a slave-status. It is clear from Agerton's will that his father considered him as his only son and loved him as one. This fact did not sit well with some other members of the family: 912

Others have viewed Rev. Willis somewhat differently. They did not see him as primarily from Indian background, but rather from African descent. According to the Reformed Reader Website, httpilwww.reibrmedreader.org/history/n egrobaptistchurch.htm, an article entitled, The Evolution of the Negro Baptist Church, states, "As moderator of the Louisiana Baptist Association he was honored and respected -- indeed, beloved and spoken of as "Father Willis." That a Negro should have the honor of giving to Louisiana its first mixed Baptist church and of being the pastor of that church -- that a Negro was the first moderator of Louisiana's first white Baptist association, and rendered the denomination fifty years of service, causes us greatly to marvel in these days of race division and race antipathy."13

When my wife and I were researching the land transactions at the St. Landry Parish Courthouse, I met an African American woman who was also researching her family history. Her maiden name was Willis and she claimed to be a descendent of Joseph Willis. Yet, another descendent of Willis, Greene W. Strother, wrote a thesis for New Orleans Baptist Theological Seminary on the life of Joseph Willis in 1934. The thesis attempted to prove that Joseph Willis was Indian rather than African."

The mystery surrounding Joseph Willis is typical of the controversy surrounding the people called "Redbones." For generations, people have speculated about the racial makeup of "Redbones." One thing is certain, these mystery people made an incredible contribution to the life of Baptists in Louisiana. Joseph Willis was the tip of the arrow that was shot across the mighty Mississippi River by Protestants in the early 1800s. When Joseph Willis came to Bayou Chicot, he found people like himself, both racially and spiritually. He found men and women who would be identified by the first census takers in Louisiana as "Free Person of Color." Those people who descended from South Carolina, known as "Redbones," would donate land for the first Baptist church west of the Mississippi River and join Willis in planting new churches in Louisiana and the early formation of what is known today as the Louisiana Baptist Convention.

Land, History, and the People Called "Redbones"

Gilbert and Francis "Fanny" Sweat:

Gilbert Sweat lived in the Pee Dee River area of South Carolina before migrating to Louisiana. Major General Erbon Wise traces the roots of Gilbert Sweat in his book, The Sweat Families of the South. Wise lists Gilbert Sweat as a sixth generation descendent of Robert Sweat, an early settler in the Jamestown colony. It should be noted that Gen. Wise uses the word "probably" in tracing Gilbert's lineage to Robert Swett. He states that the names Swet, Swett, Sweat and Sweet, were all interchangeable.'5

Robert Sweat, an Englishman in the Jamestown colony, impregnated an African woman. In a recent study of Africans in the Jamestown colony, historians cited the incident, "In 1640, when Robert Sweat (a white male) and a black woman produced a child, the woman (described only as a "servant belonging unto Lieutenant Sheppard") was to be "whipt at the whipping post." Sweat, however, was to "do public penance for his offence at James city church in the time of devine service according to the laws of England in that case pvided."16If Gen. Wise is correct in his assertion that Gilbert Sweat was a descendent of Robert Sweat, then it explains why he would have been listed in the 1810 census in St. Landry Parish as a "Free Person of Color."
In a deposition on May 25, 1830, Joshua Perkins, a longtime friend of Gilbert Sweat, said that he had known Sweat since he was a little boy. He stated further that Sweat was born in South Carolina on the Pedee River. He also said that he knew John Bass and his wife, Delaney Taylor, since they were children. Perkins stated under oath that he accompanied Gilbert Sweat in 1777 to the home of Barney Taylor, Frances' husband at the time. Perkins further testified that he and Sweat "carried off Francis" from Taylor's home.17

Evidently, Frances Smith Taylor left her husband for Gilbert Sweat and traveled to Mississippi and on to Louisiana. It was what transpired in Louisiana that later became a legal battle. After Francis Sweat died, her daughter, Delaney Taylor Bass, challenged Gilbert Sweat in court, claiming a portion of the land that Gilbert and Frances Sweat owned as her legal inheritance. However, Gilbert Sweat denied that he had ever been married to Francis, thus nullifying Delaney's claim to any property. In August 1829, Sweat's lawyer filed an answer to Delaney Taylor Bass' petition. He said, "The Defendant for further answer specifically denies that he was ever married to the aforesaid Frances Smith, deceased, who he alleges was the lifetime wife of one John Barney Taylor, who is not yet dead so far as is known to this defendant, and Frances Smith in her lifetime lived with the Defendant as a concubine."18

The question then and now became, "Were Gilbert and Frances married?" It is an important question because just three years prior to the legal battle between Delaney Bass and Gilbert Sweat, both Gilbert and Francis Sweat made a legal donation of land to the first Baptist church west of the Mississippi River. If they were not married, then Frances Smith Taylor Sweat had no legal right to donate land to the church.

I believe that they were married for several reasons. First, Gilbert claimed that "Fanny" Frances was his wife in the legal document of donation of the land to the church. It states four times in the document that "Fanny" was his wife. Then both Gilbert and "Fanny" sign their mark as husband and wife.19

Secondly, Joshua Perkins was a witness for Gilbert Sweat. There were several witnesses for both sides. However, Perkins was the most detailed and appeared to be the primary witness to testify on behalf of Gilbert Sweat. In his testimony, he states if Gilbert and Frances had ever been married, he would have surely known it. He said that he had never heard of them being married. However, Delany Taylor Bass' attorney was allowed to cross examine Perkins. In the cross examination, Perkins admitted that he had heard that a preacher or the son of a preacher had married Gilbert and Frances. He also stated that he had heard that Barney Taylor, Frances former husband had been killed in the army.2° The evidence seems convincing that Perkins was covering for his friend, Gilbert Sweat.

The final reason that I believe that they were married is that the courts of that day evidently came to the same conclusion. Gilbert Sweat died before the case concluded in 1830.211n the November 1830 term of the District Court of St. Landry Parish, the court ruled that "the plaintiff [Delaney Taylor, wife of John Bass] has satisfactorily proven the material allegations in the said petition contained, and this case of evidence by the court here that the plaintiff have final judgment.. "22 Most of the property was given to Delaney

Taylor, wife of John Bass.

If they were married, then why did Gilbert Sweat claim that Frances "Fanny" was not his wife? I believe that there is one simple reason. He wanted the property - all of it. Gilbert and Frances Sweat donated one acre of land to the Calvary Baptist Church in Bayou Chicot just three years before her death. I am not sure why they came to Louisiana. But I am sure that Baptist church members under the shepherding of Joseph Willis would not have been permitted to have a concubine.

I have read through the minutes of the early years of the Calvary Baptist Church of Bayou Chicot and the Amiable Baptist Church near Glenmora - both churches started by Joseph Willis. If there were something that the churches considered sin, and there was no repentance, the members would be excluded from the fellowship. For instance, on May 13, 1848 two people were excluded from the Bayou Chicot Church. One was removed from fellowship because of "unchristian behavior," and the other removed because there was "no evidence of repentance."23 In 1831, Delaney Bass asked forgiveness of two of the church members at Amiable Baptist Church because of things she had said. One of the church members forgave her and the other did not. The one who refused to forgive was removed from the church.24 With the kind of disciplinary characteristics in the early churches begun by Joseph Willis, it doesn't seem reasonable that Rev. Willis would have permitted land to be donated by two people who were lying about their marriage on the legal document of donation.

It appears that Frances and Gilbert Sweat donated the property to the church because they had been endeared to Joseph Willis and the church. Having been in Christian ministry for over forty years, I believe that Rev. Willis probably helped them to come to know Jesus as their personal Savior or helped them in their spiritual lives. I believe that they probably felt a sense of love and loyalty to Joseph Willis and the church. Somehow, the love and amiable spirit dissipated after Francis' death. Yet, the contribution of Gilbert and Francis Sweat remains one of historic significance.

John and Delaney Bass:

John Bass was born in 1770 in Duplin County North Carolina. He probably came with his father Jeremiah to Mississippi where his father settled on land on the Homochitto River.25 It is quite possible that John Bass met Joseph Willis in Mississippi because the property where Jeremiah Bass settled was near the "Baptist Church on Bullaloe (sic) that Joseph Willis visited in 1798 with William Thompson and Richard Curtis". An early 1828 map of Louisiana and Mississippi territories shows Buffalo Creek just a few miles south of the Homochitto River and running parallel to it.26

John Bass was present in Bayou Chicot by 1806. He gave testimony in Bayou Chicot about the murder of a Choctaw Indian on June 14, 1806.27 Court documents also list Delaney

Taylor in Bayou Chicot at' the same time. James Groves was indicted on August 1, 1806 for "assault and battery on the body of Delaney-Taylor: 48 It is interesting to note that the daughter of James Groves and his wife Mary Nash Groves later married the son of John Bass and his wife, Delaney Taylor Bass, on January 26, 1826.29 Whether John Bass met Joseph Willis in Mississippi is speculation. However, it seems unreasonable to think that he would not have known Joseph Willis in the early days of the formation of the historic Baptist church in Bayou Chicot. The church met on the property of his mother-in-law and stepfather-in-law that they eventually donated for the first location of the church. Later John and Delaney Bass joined hands with Rev. Willis in a move north and westward to found the Amiable Baptist Church, which is located just outside of present day Glenmora.

John Bass was a founding member of the Amiable Baptist Church. Those listed as founding members of this historic Baptist Church were: Isaac Johnston, John Bass, Reuben Phares, Sarah Avery, Delaney Bass, Sarah Phares, Zedekiah Gibson, Sarah Batson, Nancy Neale, Elizabeth Moore, Joseph Grimball, Eli Batson, and George Keller. John Bass was elected by this small group of church planters to represent them at the newly formed Association of Baptist Churches in Louisiana. They state, "This church called Amiable and having been constituted by Elder Joseph Willis, September 6, 1828, held its first conference meeting at the home of Eli Batson. Resolved that we build a meeting house on the east side of the Darbon, appointed Brother John Bass to represent us in the next meeting of the Association, and to ask for the reception of this Church in the Association."3'

The church record of the Amiable provides us with an accurate history of the expansion of Baptists under the direction of Rev. Joseph Willis. After learning my heritage, I had the opportunity to speak at the 188th anniversary of the church. I consider it one of the special moments of my life. Martha Winegeart, historian for the church, was gracious enough to allow me to view the historical records and make digital photographs of them.

Several items were of particular interest in those records. From the very first conference meeting of the church on February 21, 1829, it is recorded, "The church met in conference and was in peace.9131 It can be noted that the church would not go into a business meeting unless it was found to be at peace. Churches would do well to follow the example of those early pioneers. But what happened when not at peace? The minutes of August 21, 1830 stated…"The church met in conference after a sermon by Elder Joseph Willis. A dissatisfaction having risen with brother Phares and his wife against Sister Bass for relating things that she ought not. Sister Bass confessed her wrong and was forgiven by all members except Bro. Phares." 32 When I read what transpired I said, "Yes, that would was definitely be my three times great grandmother. I must have her genes because I have gotten in more saying more than I should than just about anything I know.

Delaney Bass seems to have been a feisty woman, She didn't take any flak from James Groves, who is another three times great grandfather of mine, has been described as being a very large man over six feet tall and weighing nearly 300 pounds.33 When he assaulted her, she filed charges. She later found herself asking forgiveness in the Amiable Church, and then she sued her step father to receive her inheritance.

Jane McManus traced John Bass' heritage back to another John Bass who married a Nansemond Indian in the 1630s.34 The Nansemond Indians trace their history back to this Englishman who married a tribal member. The Nansemond Indian Tribal Association official website (http://www.nansemond.org/index2.html) states, "The Nansemonds were initially wary and often hostile toward the English, but by the 1630's some of them had changed their minds. A family sermon book still in the Chiefs possession records the 1638 marriage of John Bass, and a Nansemond convert to Christianity named Elizabeth. Everyone in the modern Nansemond tribe is descended from that marriage."35 As a side note, two of my aunts, Pearl Tippit Cooley and Essie Tippit Parker (both descendants of the Louisiana John Bass) were members of the Nansemond Tribal Association before they died.

The significance of the churches and work of Joseph Willis

The sign in front of today's Calvary Baptist Church in Bayou Chicot reads, "Calvary Baptist Church — Louisiana's Oldest Baptist Church — Organized November 13, 1812." It is the oldest Baptist Church in Louisiana today. However, there was another Baptist church formally organized one month prior to the Bayou Chicot church. It no longer exists today. The official website of the Louisiana Baptist Convention speaks of the two churches, "November 13, 1812 — Joseph Willis, the first Baptist preacher west of the Mississippi River, constituted Bayou Chicot (Calvary) Baptist Church in Ville Platte. The church is still active. A month earlier, Half Moon Baptist Church on the Bique (sic) Chitto River in Washington Parish was organized. At that time, the land east of the Mississippi River was part of the Florida Parishes."36

Both churches were historic in nature. The Bayou Chicot Church is a testimony to the work of Joseph Willis in that many of the churches that he planted are still thriving nearly 200 years after they were organized.

It must also be noted that Joseph Willis was the first to proclaim the gospel west of the MississippiRiver and that marked a new era for Baptists. The Half Moon Baptist Church was located in today's Washington Parish, which sits in southeast Louisiana next to the state of Mississippi. Its location was a good distance from the Mississippi River. Protestants have historically, considered the crossing of a major body of water as a moment of significance. Moses crossing the Red Sea marked the beginning of a new era of freedom from slavery. Joshua crossing the Jordan River meant that the children of Israel would be able to enter into the "Promised Land." The Apostle Paul sailing on a ship across the Mediterranean Sea to bring the gospel to the Gentile world was perhaps the greatest move forward of the church in the New Testament. I would in no way claim that Joseph Willis' crossing of the Mississippi River to start a Baptist church was in the same league with Moses, Joshua, or Paul. However, all of those Biblical events had some things in common with the small band of men and women of mixed color who brought Baptist work across the Mississippi River. For all of them, those massive bodies of water stood in the way of their dreams. In order for them to cross those bodies of water, they had to face risk and danger. They would have to embrace the unknown. However, their acts of faith would propel their people forward and become the historical catalyst for millions of people who would come to faith in Christ through Southern Baptist churches within the next two centuries.

Joseph Willis began his congregation long before the formal organization of the Half Moon Baptist Church on Bogue Chitto River. He began meeting with followers of Christ like himself when he first arrived in Louisiana. When Joseph Willis first began his work around 1804, he requested that Mississippi Baptists ordain him. Due to his racial background, he was not ordained at that time. The church in Bayou Chicot was functioning as a church, but could not become one. Paxton told what transpired in his History of Louisiana Baptists. He wrote, "Feeling that his work was greatly hindered by want of authority to administer ordinances, he returned to Mississippi, where he still held his membership, to seek ordination. He stated to the church what works the Lord had wrought by his hands in this land of total destitution and darkness. He made known his request, but the church, having no pastor at the time, considered that they had no authority to act in the matter, though expressing a willingness that he should be ordained. They, therefore, advised him to take his letter and unite with a church which had a pastor. This he did, but the church to which he gave his letter objected to his ordination, lest the cause of Christ should suffer reproach from the humble social position of his servant." Paxton concludes his comments by saying, "Such obstacles would have daunted the zeal of any man engaged in a less holy cause. But how could he give up the people among whom he lived to ungodliness."[37]

Willis faced dangers. There were no steamboats on the Mississippi River when Joseph Willis went to Bayou Chicot. And there were no bridges to cross this great river. Crossing the mighty Mississippi River on a flatboat would have been enough to test the faith of many men. But Joseph Willis was willing to face danger from nature and persecution from men. There was a small band of people like John and Delaney Bass and Gilbert and Francis Sweat who needed his ministry. They, too, were from "mixed blood." He was willing to sacrifice his life to bring the gospel across that great divide. He was willing to minister to the people as their servant, even though he would not be officially recognized as their pastor for eight years after he began his work. The church existed informally long before 1812. Because of his "humble social position" (his race), it would take another eight years before his work would be officially recognized.

Yet, this humble and patient pastor, along with others of a similar "humble social position" would fire the first shot that would be heard for two centuries among Southern Baptists. Joseph Willis would lead the way bringing the gospel to the vast wilderness west of the Mississippi River. Rev. Willis' leadership took Louisiana Baptists and ultimately Southern Baptists across the Mississippi River to reach the vast wilderness areas of the new territory of the United States. The long term effects can be understood today when one thinks of the numerical strength of Southern Baptists. The website www.adherents.com states, "The Southern Baptist Convention is the second largest religious body in the United States (Catholics are the largest)." It gives statistics for the United States largest Protestant denomination and says that two states, Louisiana and Texas have more than four million Baptists in their membership. The road to these state conventions and today's mega churches west of the Mississippi River was paved by a humble group of people who were sometimes derogatorily called "Redbones."

Location of the first church property:

When I first learned of my heritage, I immediately realized the historical significance of the movement in which my forefathers had participated. There is no way that they could have foreseen the results of those early labors. However, as I realized the historical importance of the Calvary Baptist Church in Bayou Chicot, it set a fire in my heart to learn more about what transpired and the role that my three and four times great grandparents played in the formation of this historic church.

I traveled to Bayou Chicot about two months after I learned about my three times great grandparents, John and Delaney Bass, and also the donation of the property to the Bayou Chicot church by my four times great grandmother. I wanted to see the property. I met Pastor Leon Terrell who has been pastor of the church for more than twenty years. I asked him if he knew the location of the original property donated by my four times great Grandmother Frances Sweat and her husband Gilbert Sweat. He said that the location of that first property and meeting place remains a mystery. However, he said that he had an idea where that property might be located. He took my wife and me to a location off a main highway. We turned off the main road and on to a gravel road that led into the forests. We came upon a cemetery in those woods. That was the place Rev. Terrell believed to be the location of the property that was given. I told him that I appreciated his help. However, I left with the feeling that this was only a guess on Rev. Terrell's part. He did not give me any concrete evidence to establish why he thought that might be the property.

I returned to my home in Texas with the question of the location of the property still on my mind. Several months ago, I came across General Erbon Wise's book, The Sweat Families of the South. In the book, he had a copy of an old map of the property owned by Gilbert and Frances Sweat, and it was overlaid on a present day map.38 It intrigued me. If the maps in Gen. Wise's book were accurate, then I would at least be able to pinpoint the exact location of my forefather's property, and perhaps one day discover the exact location of the original property of the first Baptist church west of the Mississippi River. Fortunately, my father in law, Jack Sirman, has worked with those kinds of maps most of his adult life. He worked at Gulf States Utilities and his job required research using the old maps from courthouses.

When I showed him the map from General Wise's book, the first thing that he noticed was a cemetery located on one of the pieces of property. I wondered if it could be the cemetery that Pastor Terrell showed me. I trusted Gen. Wise's maps. However, I wanted to see the source for those maps. That led me to the St. Landry Parish Courthouse where I was able to make a copy of them. They were as Gen. Wise had documented in his book. Gen. Wise stated that Gilbert Sweat owned about 552 acres himself and co-owned another 1354 acres with Peter McDaniel.39 I found those old land maps in the St. Landry Parish Courthouse.° I knew that the property given to the church had to have been from the 553 acres because the document of donation stated that the land given to the Bayou Chicot church was owned by Gilbert and Frances Sweat. There was no mention of Peter McDaniel in the document of donation.

When I studied the location of that land today, I found that Highway 167 runs through the middle of the property. It sits approximately one mile north of the present day community of Bayou Chicot. The community today is not an incorporated town. However, the Calvary Baptist Church is located there as well as a school and a few stores. My wife and I drove from Ville Platte to Bayou Chicot to see how that land looked today. We drove up Highway 167 and as we entered the Bayou Chicot community, you could see a sign directing you to the Calvary Baptist Church. It sits just off the highway. We drove one mile up the highway and realized that spot should have been the beginning of the property owned by Gilbert and Frances Sweat. At that point, we noticed a small gravel road leading into the forest. We turned on to that road and found ourselves at that little cemetery in the woods — the same one that Pastor Terrell brought us to.

It was with a sense of awe that I stood on that ground. The donation document read, "Gilbert Sweat and his wife Fanny hath or into or upon all and singular, a certain lot of piece of land containing one square acre which the meeting house stands on, situate lying in the settlement of Bayou Chicot and in said Parish and State, viz, being a part of a tract of land belonging to said Gilbert Sweat which he now lives on, together with all and singular, the Church, woods, waters, ways, privileges, and appurtenances that, belonging or in any wise appertaining, to have and to hold all and singular, the said Church, woods, waters, ways, and privileges thereto belonging or in any wise appertaining, for a place of worship unto the said Joseph Willis and the members of the Baptist Church of Chicot and their successors in office forever, in trust...."41 Even though I did not know if I was standing on the exact place of that meeting house, I knew that it was very close. My hope is that sometime in the near future I can acquire the assistance of an archeologist and determine the exact location of the property.

History was written on that piece of land. The history of a people called "Redbones" and the history of the Louisiana Baptist Convention and even America's largest Protestant denomination, Southern Baptists. It all began with a few humble families of a mixed racial background - Joseph Willis, Gilbert and Frances Sweat, and John and Delaney Bass. Certainly, they all had their weaknesses and faults. Yet, they wrote history with their faith and sealed it with their actions. They could never have imagined how far reaching those deeds would become. It has been an interesting journey since I received that phone call from my sister. I would never have dreamed that my life and ministry would have been so impacted by land, history and a people called "Redbones."

JAMES BASS, 1807-1850-60

FIGURE 3 PHOTO: JAMES BASS

James Franklin Bass was born February 5, 1807 in St. Landry Parish, Louisiana the son of John Bass, Sr. and Delaney Bass. He married Emily "Millie" Groves (pictured elsewhere here) He died in1855 in Calcasieu Parish, Louisiana, and he is buried Leesville, Vernon Parish, Louisiana.
Father of
Josiah Bass;
James Gilbert Bass;
Mary Ann Bunch;
John Jackson Bass;
Amelia Millie Wales and 5 others. He was the brother of John Bass, Jr.; Samuel T. Bass; Mary Delaney Bass; Moses Bass; Drury B. Bass

FIGURE 4 PHOTO: JEREMIAH M. BASS

Birth: Feb. 16, 1838, Rapides Parish, Louisiana,
Death: Sep. 3, 1891, Burial at Laurel Hill; Cemetery in Hicks Vernon Parish, Louisiana. He was the son of James F. Bass (1807 – 1855) and Emily Groves Bass (1804 - 1860). (Pictured elsewhere here)
Siblings:
  Mary Bass Bunch (1826 - 1880)
  John Jackson Bass (1834 - 1906)
  Amelia Bass Wales (1835 - 1909)
  Jeremiah Moses Bass (1838 - 1891)

He married Emmaline Smith (1844 - 1928). They were married on Feb 17, 1870. He married Emeline Smith on Feb. 12, 1870 in Rapides Parish, LA and had 8 children. He married Elizabeth Ventioner and had 3 children. Jeremiah served a private during the Civil War with Company C 27th Reg.

Children:
Pollie Ann Bass Gordy (1873 - 1934)
Eliza Jane Bass Tippit (1874 - 1942)
Marion Columbus Bass (1874 - 1945)
Margaret Elizabeth Bass Laurence (1878 - 1944)
Catherine Lucretia Bass Williams (1880 - 1948)
John M. Bass (1882 - 1882)
Moses J. Bass (1883 - 1927)

FIGURE 5 PHOTO: JAMES GILBERT BASS

Birthdate: May 6, 1836
Birthplace: Rapides Parish, LA
Death: Died March 9, 1911 in Nacogdoches, TX
Son of James Franklin Bass and Emily "Millie" Bass (pictured elsewhere here)
Husband of Margaret A. Bass
Father of Jesse Bass; Phcobe Ann "Febban" Phillips; Raulston Edward Bass; Diana Bass; James Thomas Bass and 6 others
Brother of Josiah Bass; Mary Ann Bunch; John Jackson Bass; Amelia Millie Wales; Jeremiah Moses Bass and 4 others

Endnotes:

1.   Copy of the original records and minutes and founding of the Amiable Baptist Church near Glenmora. Martha Winegeart, Amiable Baptist Church historian, permitted the author to make digital photos copies of the minutes and records, which he has in his possession.
2.   Copy of St. Landry Parish Clerk of Court Donation Book, 192, June 28, 1826. Sent to the author by Jane McManus. The Document states that Gilbert Sweat and his wife "Fanny" donated the property to Joseph Willis and the members of the Calvary Baptist Church. "Fanny" was a nickname used by Francis Smith Taylor Sweat.
3.   A Backward Glance, Jane Parker McManus, Published by Parker Enterprises, 1986, p. 45.
4.   A History of Baptists in Louisiana from Earliest Times to Present by Rev. W. E. Paxton, C. R. Barns Publishing Company, St. Louis, 1888, p.23. The book can be found in the Archives in the Louisiana Baptist Convention building in Alexandria, Louisiana.
5.   Ibid, p.31.
6.   Ibid, p.139.
7.   Ibid, p. 140.
8.   Ibid, p. 141.
9.   Ibid, p. 143.

10.   Mississippi Baptist Preachers, L. S. Foster, National Baptist Publishing Company, St. Louis, MO, 1895, p. 328. Copy of document obtained from the Hill Memorial Library at Louisiana State University in Baton Rouge, Louisiana.

11   The 1810 census lists John Bass, Joseph Willis, and Gilbert Sweat as heads of household and as Free Persons of Color. Bass is listed as having 8 "fpc" in his household; Willis 13 "fpc" in his household, and Sweat 3 "fpc" in his household. Willis and Sweat owned slaves, but Bass did not.

12.   Article written by Randy Willis and published on his website: http://www.rand_ywillis.org/joseph.html. The article is copyrighted by Randall Lee Willis 2000.

13.   Article found   at http://www.reformedreader.org/history/negrobaptistchurch.htm attributes the quote to The Negro Year Book, 1918-1919, p. 236; Benedict, History of the Baptists, p. 376.

14.   Thesis by Greene W. Strother, written May 1934, for a degree of .Master of Theology at The Baptist Bible Institute in New Orleans, Louisiana. Copy of the thesis was provided by Jane McManus. And can be found at the New Orleans Baptist Theological Seminary.

15.   The Sweat Families of the South, Maj. Gen. Erbon Wise, copyright 2002 by Erbon W. Wise, pp. 7,   25. 10 -12.   26.

16.   A Study of the Africans and African Americans on Jamestown Island and at Green Spring, 1619-1803, Martha McCartney, prepared for the   27. National Park Service, U.S. Department of the Interior, Prepared by the Colonial Williamsburg Foundation, Marley Brown - Principle Investigator, Williamsburg, Virginia 2003, p. 42.

17.   St. Landry Parish Clerk of Court's Office, District Court, Delaney Taylor, wife of John Bass versus Gilbert Swett, Filed Aug. 27, 1829, Testimony for the defendant listed as testimony "c".

18.   Ibid. Response from Gilbert

29. Sweat's attorney to the above

30. petition.

19.   Copy of St. Landry Parish Clerk of Court Donation Book, 192.   31.

20.   Clerk of Court St. Landry Parish,

32. District Court, Testimony "0".

21.   Sweat Families of the South,   34. p.15.

22.   District Court of St. Landry Parish, November term, 1830, No. 1533, Delaney Taylor, wife of John Bass versus Gilbert Sweat - Judgment.   36.

23.   Author has in his possession a copy of the early records of the Calvary Baptist Church of Bayou Chicot. This particular incident is recorded May 13, 1848. These

37. records were compiled by Jane Parker McManus and sent to

38. author.

24.   Amiable Baptist Church early

39. Records and minutes, October

40. 1830..A Backward Glance. p.43.

1806 map of Louisiana found in the Louisiana Digital Library website and can be viewed at: http://vvww.rootsweb.com/-usge nweb/maps/louisianal

Copy of "State vs. William Thomas - Shooting an Indian, Killing George, June 14, 1806. Author secured a copy of the testimony of John Bass in this case from Louisiana State Archives Building in Baton Rouge, Louisiana.

Assault and Battery Indictment against James Groves in case of Delaney Taylor on Territory Orleans, 1806. Author secured a copy from Louisiana State Archives Building, Baton Rouge, Louisiana.

A Backward Glance, p. 49.

Copy of the Amiable Baptist Church historical records in possession of the author.

Ibid., February 21, 1829.

Ibid., August 21, 1830.

A Backward Glance, p. 242. Ibid., pp. 11 - 31.

Nansemond Indian Tribal Association official website: Quote can be found at
http://www.nansemond.org/index 2.html
Quote can be found at the official website of the Louisiana Baptist Convention at
http://www.lbc.org/pages/templat e3.aspx?id=290
History of Louisiana Baptists, p.142.
Sweat Families of the South, p. Ibid.
St. Landry Parish Courthouse, Old Land Maps, Southwestern District, Map of T. 3 S. Rl.E,
41.   St. Landry Parish Courthouse, October 23, 1837. The document of donation Gilbert
Courthouse made copies of the Sweat to the Calvary Baptist map and gave to the author. Church.

Grave Houses: A Review

By Don C. Marler

[This material was presented in different format at the Second Annual Conference of the Redbone Heritage Foundation in Natchitoches, La. (September, 2006). The relevance to Redbones is that the Redbones of southwest Louisiana have a tradition of maintaining their cemeteries well, and the cemetery featured here has the most grave houses in the US, and is in their territory]

Background

In order to understand the grave house phenomena it is necessary to look at the origins of, and influences on, funerary practices in America. Nowhere are the problems of transmission of history and custom by oral methods alone more evident than in our funerary practices. The problems of oral transmission have been well documented. Oral transmission is highly dependent upon such factors as the differing perceptions of the individuals involved, the emotional nature of the subject, changes in circumstances and therefore in the customs developed to deal with these changes, and the great expanse of time involved.

In early America the weakness of the oral history method was exacerbated by the melding of customs from many countries and religions. These customs migrated to America from Africa, Europe and with the Amerindians. Many of these customs grew out of Paganism-- and passed to us through the Egyptians, Greeks and Romans.

Catholic cemeteries in America today are considered sacred and are elaborately adorned with statues, emblems, artifacts and icons.

Protestant cemeteries are not so adorned with few muted exceptions such as an emblem of a dove, lamb, bible or organizational affiliation. John Wesley said that consecration of burial grounds was a "... mere Romanish superstition." This belief is reflected in the use of secular names such as: Little Hope and Dark Corner.' My own survey of Vernon Parish, La. cemeteries reveals that of 123, only 14 are, by name, church related.2 Many burials from early times are on private grounds for various reasons, not the least of which is that many people on the frontier were little concerned with religion. And if they were concerned established cemeteries were often far away. Funeral services, if they were held, were sometimes delayed for months or years until a minister came to the area.

FIGURE 6 & 7 PHOTOS: TALBERT-PEIRSON CEMETERY GRAVE HOUSES, VERNON PARISH, LOUISIANA

FIGURE 8 PHOTO: TALBERT-PEIRSON CEMETERY GRAVE HOUSES, VERNON PARISH, LOUISIANA

Some common practices from Paganism can be seen in the following:

1.   Burials on high hills or slopes predate Christianity,
2.   Flowers and evergreen were used in the Pagan religion—including planting roses and other flowers in burial places and their use in funeral services. The rose was associated with the Mediterranean Mother Goddess, cedar trees (tree of death) was associated with the Cedars of Lebanon.3
3.   Burial east and west (feet east); in the American South outlaws are sometimes burie north and south.

4.   Wife is buried to the South of the husband.

Flowers were not used at funerals in England and America until the 1800s, and then used over the objections of Christian leaders.4 Another Pagan holdover is placing shells on graves. Pagans being concerned with fertility rites used the shell and up-right stone marker as symbolic of the female and male genitalia respectively. Grave houses have evolved over time from cave burial to pyramids, our own grave houses, sepulchers and mausoleums.

Grave Houses in America

As stated above, grave houses in America were influenced by Paigan religion and also African kind Amerindian beliefs and practices. They have been found in Africa, Scandinavia, Europe and all over North America. Most of the surviving ones are in the southeastern part of the U.S. and the upper South. The Talbert/Pie son Cemetery in Vernon Parish, La is reported to contain the largest numb r of grave houses of any cemetery in the .S. (See photos).

Considering the above background it should not be a surprise that our customs and practices have outlived our knowledge of the meaning of those customs. Not much is known about the original purpose of grave houses and the current purposes seem to have evolved to fit the conditions of society in America. Some ideas about the purposes seem to be guesses or rationalizations to cover lack of knowledge of the real or original purpose.

FIGURE 9 PHOTO: GRAVE HOUSES TALBERT-PIERSON CEMETERY VERNON PARISH, LOUISIANA

Some stated purposes are to:

A.   Keep livestock and wild animals off the graves. This is attributed to the days of open range for livestock. It ignores that the cemetery could have been fenced with less effort than erecting and maintaining grave houses.

B.   Keep rain off the grave.

C.   Provide shade and resting placer family members.

D.   Provide a memorial to loved ones--usually babies or older honored persons.

E.   Provide a status symbol.

F.   Give comfort to the spirit of the dead.

G.   Provide a home for the spirit of the dead. Provisions for the furney of the dead could be left unmolested. At the Talbert-Pierson Cemetery, it was in the past, a strong custom to build the grave h o use before nightfall on the day of the funeral. This custom suggests forgotten purposes. Some others were totally enclosed with windows, curtains, etc., but most of the ones made of wood had pickets and a gate. Most cover one or two graves, but as many as six have been observed.

Figures 10 Grave houses Talbert-Pierson Cemetery

Grave Houses: A Review

Many grave houses are neglected today and they are disappearing; some are maintained by family members. The Talbert/Pierson Cemetery is maintained by Parish (County) prisoners, but the grave houses are still maintained by family members. Two members of the Talbert family who live near the Talbert/Pierson Cemetery, Susan Talbert Bass and her mother Sarah Talbert, were interviewed for information on the grave houses. Susan recently lost a son who had a young family, and a grave house is planned for him. When asked why it was not built before sundown on the day he was buried she said that the tombstone had yet to be put in place by heavy equipment and the grave house would be built around it later. Perhaps this is another bit of evidence that times and circumstances change, and customs match the change.

Both of these ladies said they would like a grave house when they die "if the family will do it for me". This statement suggests that there is still a strong value placed on grave houses by this family even though they have lost track of the original purpose of the houses. And it suggests that they are hopeful but uncertain about the future of grave houses in the current culture.

Terry Jordan in his book, Texas Graveyards: A Cultural Legacy has a wonderful summary statement with which I will close.

> "The traditional southern cemetery, then, contains a disorderly array of European, African and Amerindan (sic) material culture. In the main, the customs and artifacts displayed are pagan, and almost without exception, the original symbolic meaning is unknown to ... the people who maintain these graveyards. They have no knowledge of the ancient fertility cults and animism that provided the individual elements of their funerary culture. They do not know they are perpetuating millennia-old practices."

The message of the folk cemetery, for those who would read it, is that there is a lot of European, a fair amount of African, and more than a trace of Indian in all southerners, regardless of their skin color. In the cultural sense the people of the South have much in common with each other. For three centuries the three groups exchanged ideas and genes, creolizing the culture to a remarkable degree. Nowhere is that blending more apparent than in places we have set aside for our dead. These traditional graveyards are not merely repositories for our dead, but museums full of reminders from our ancient past and distant, diverse ancestral homelands.

Endnotes:

1, Terry G. Jordan, Texas Graveyards:
A Cultural Legacy (Austin: University of Texas Press, 1982), p. 33.
2.   Jane Parker McManus, L'est We Forget, (Alexandria, La. Parker Enterprises, 1995), and Don C. Marler, Redbones of Louisiana, (Dogwood Press Hemphill, 2003), p. 255.
3.   Op.cit., Jordan.
4.   J. Mitford, The American Way of Death, (New York. Simon and Ne'luster. I 4-) Crissmdn, Declltiii Drifigiyt   K. (Central Appalachia, (Chicago, University of Illinois Press, 994). Op. cit..
Jordan, pp. :39-4

FIGURE 11 PHOTO: GRAVE HOUSE TALBERT-PIERSON VERNON PARISH. LOUISIANA

Book Review

By Don C. Marler

Melungeons: The Last Lost Tribe in America Paperback – March 29, 2006

By Elizabeth Caldwell Hirschman

The title of this book was especially titilating since there have been so many theories about the Lost Tribes of Israel in America in the past few decades. In the opening chapters Professor Hirschman rehashes some of the old theories of Melungeon origins, with heavy reliance on the work of Bonnie Ball, Jean Bible and Brent Kennedy. Though she adds her commentary to these accounts, one begins to suspect that the Lost Tribe theories will get the same rehash treatment.

What a pleasant surprise is in store for the reader when she gets into the evidence for a strong Jewish presence in Melungeon heritage. The evidence she presents for Jewish influence both culturally and genetically is fascinating and thought provoking. The tissue that ties members of the Melungeon community together is family surnames. Professor Hirschman identifies and discusses Jewish surnames and other evidence of Jewish influence among Melungeons to good effect.

The second surprise punch she delivers is her insight into the Masonic connections of Sephardic Jews, the dispersion of both during the Inquisition, and the affinity Melungeons held for Freemasonry. She traces Jewish Freemasons to Charleston, S.C. and proposes that they served as the communications mechanism to bring scattered people together into the Appalachian safe haven.

Those interested in Redbone origins may be reminded of their close relationship to Melungeons, their Jewish surnames and affinity for Freemasonry.

Some Jewish surnames in early America listed by Professor Hirschman are: Abraham, Allen, Andrews, Coleman, Carter, Davis, Franks, Goodman, Hart, Harris, Henry, Hunt, Jackson, Jacobs, Johnson , Jones, Joseph, King, Lawrence, Lee, Lewis, Miller, Morris, Newman, Nichols, Collins, Powers, Price, Rice, Robinson, Ross, Russell, Shaw, Simons, Smith, Solis, Taylor, Watson, Williams, Wolf, Yates, Hall, Green, Wynn, Hale, Goen, Carrico, Chaffin.

As Brent Kennedy said in the forward to this book "Whether one agrees or disagrees with Hirschman's premise, the reader will likely never look at Appalachia or our nation, or even the Diaspora in quite the same way".

(Mercer Press, 2005) $39.00 Hardcover, 186 pages, dust jacket, photos, maps, footnotes, bibliography, index.

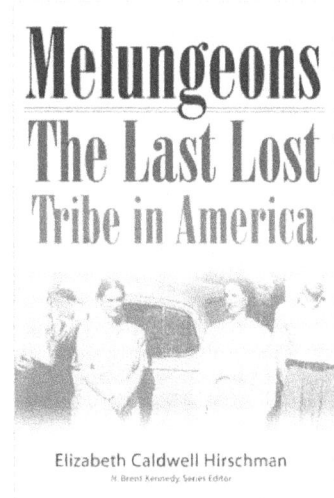

The Ethnic and Geographic Origins of the Melungeons *Part 1*

By James H. Nickens, *M.D.* Virginia Indian Historical Society

Figure 12 James Nickens with family, children playing in front of family home

Introduction

Following in the aftermath of the Revolutionary War, migrants from east of the Appalachian Mountains pushed westward into contested Indian Lands. The new United States government erected The Territory of the United States Southwest of the Ohio River. In order to more firmly establish territorial claims and to compensate Revolutionary War Patriots for their service, veterans were encouraged to settle the western frontier. Much of the Territory today lies in the state of Tennessee.

Among the pioneers were descendants of specific colonial era Indian tribes of Maryland, Virginia, and the Carolinas. Many were patriots in the American Revolutionary cause. Others had good reason to see the coast-bound colonial governments as their enemy rather than the British. Many thus supported the English Crown by default. It is significant that the names Bass, Collins, Gibson, Hart, Minor, Riddle, and Sizemore are prominent among the Tories, Loyalist, and North Carolina Regulators.

Tennessee became a multigenerational lay-over point for migrant descendants of Algonquin, Iroquois, and Sioux-speaking people of the Chesapeake Bay, Atlantic coastal plain, and the piedmont. Many crossed the Mississippi and proceeded eventually into the western Indian Nations. Others remain in Tennessee today. These citizen Indian migrants are best envisioned in the context of Blu's "English speaking Indian farmers". They came in kinship groups, acquired land, and raised families. One such migrant community from the headwaters of the New River settled a remote area of the Appalachian Mountains along Newman's Ridge. Reputed to be "the friendly Indians who came with the whites as they moved west" they were said to have "helped to build Fort Blackmore".

As their numbers mounted the denizens of Newman's Ridge became increasingly recognizable as a distinct community, a community which differed from their surrounding neighbors. Distinguished by their relatively darker skin tone and exotic facial features, the colony around Newman's Ridge drew an increasing amount of attention. Local whites took note of the unique nature of this community and gave a name to the swarthy mountain people — The Melungeons.

Figure 13 Photo: James Nickens speaks to Melungeon Heritage Association "MHA" Union Gathering, Kingsport, Tn. 2006

Melungeon Origins

The ethnic identity and geographic origins of the Melungeon people have perplexed investigators of many disciplines for more than a century. Anthropologist, geographers,

The Ethnic and Geographic Origins of the Melungeons
Part1

historians, sociologist, and genealogists have applied their considerable talents to the mystery of the Melungeons. Historically these academic investigations have lacked proper focus, relying heavily on the problematic racial conventions utilized in colonial records, and ignoring records of colonial Indians. The more fruitful approach would have been to investigate records of colonial Indians of Maryland, Virginia, the Carolinas, and those of the 17th century Virginia Gypsies.

Many varied and imaginative proposals have been set forth in the attempt to determine the origin of the Melungeons. Theories of descent from Phoenician, Carthaginian, or pre-Columbian Welsh explorers have been suggested. Others believed the Melungeons to be a lost tribe of Israel, survivors of the Roanoke Colony, or from some mountain in Angola. Still others have speculated that Melungeons are the descendants of Spanish explorers, shipwrecked Portuguese sailors, or Turkish pirates. Court cases challenged the civil rights of Melungeons by seeking to deny them the vote. The resulting court decisions established "Melungeon" as a distinct and obviously problematic racial identity - that of a relatively dark mountain people, formerly classified white, Indian, or Free People of Color, but later "of the Melungeon race". Melungeons thus became the stuff of mystery and legend.

A wide variety of physical descriptions have been given to the Melungeons. Among those recorded descriptions are "Indian", "not as dark as the Indian ", "a race of light skinned Indians", and "not the color of the mulatto". A Tennessee senator in Nashville characterized Melungeons as "dirty Indian sneaks". The legislator's comment that there are Melungeons "under this Capitol" leaves unclear whether he was referring to the Newman's Ridge Melungeons or an earlier arriving group centered in Davidson and Wilson Counties.

Nevertheless, the recurrent theme in Melungeon lore, and indeed genealogy, has been that of Indian ancestry. It is this aspect of the Melungeon legend that commands the attention of the Virginia Indian Historical Society. Cherokee ancestry has been generally presumed by the Melungeon people of today. In general genealogical data suggests otherwise. Various investigators have stated that the Melungeons of East Tennessee were Saponi Indians, or were descendants of Powhatan tribes. It is, however, the Nanticoke, Tuscarora and Catawba who supply the most reliable genealogical links to the East Tennessee Melungeons.

It is here that genealogy, specifically Indian genealogy, has brought correction to the "vanishing Indian" myth. Investigators of the Melungeons, Choctaw of Mobile and Washington Counties, Alabama (Cajan Indians), and Redbones of Louisiana will find an ancestral trail that leads to the seventeenth century Nanticoke and Pocomoke River tribes of Maryland, the eighteenth century Meherrin and Tuscarora of North Carolina, and the eighteenth century Catawba on the North Carolina-South Carolina border.

Figure 14 Photo: LtoR: Gary "Mishiho" Gabehart Chickasaw Redbone Heritage Foundation and James Nickens MHA Gathering Kingsport, Tn. 2006

The 1903 interview of Lewis Jarvis, a Sneedville, Tennessee attorney and neighbor of the Melungeons, provided a partial yet crucial oral history of Melungeon origins. Jarvis stated that "They came from the Cumberland County and New River, Va., ..." In his quote Jarvis mistook Cumberland County, North Carolina for Cumberland Co Virginia. This error has been made by Melungeon researchers for decade obscured the identity of one of the Gibson families considered to be original Melungeons.

Among the families of Cumberland County, North Carolina, and that p. of Cumberland which became A son County, were the Gibson, Jordan, and Shepard surnames. These names are familiar to all Melungeon researchers as surnames or Christian names of the first Melungeons. This area of the pepper Cape Fear River is traditionally own as a Highlander settlement. The Gibsons, however, were from a lon line of 17th century Lowland Scot mariners and traders. Among those Gibson's are Walter, James, Sylvanus, and Andrew. A Walter Gibson was among the Tuscarora signing the Indian Woods Tuscarora Reservation deeds in Bertie County, North Carolina.

FIGURE 15 PHOTO: JAMES NICKENS LEFT MHA GATHERING 2006

The Jarvis interview stands as the sole first hand documentation of Melungeon origins. Jarvis provided the link between the family of Shepard "Old Buck" Gibson and the Tuscarora Reservation in Bertie County, North Carolina. It also distinguished the Tuscarora/Scot Gibson family from the Gypsy descended Gibson's of Louisa County, Virginia. This connection had escaped Melungeon researchers for more than a hundred years. It is the letter Gibson family which was referenced in the Stony Creek Baptist Church minutes uncovered by Jack Goins. Jo k's discovery stands as the first known appearance of the word "Melungeon". Any connection to the Romani legend of Melengro is at this time no more than speculation.

The primary focus of The Virginia Indian Historical Society has been placed upon the examination of the Melungeon claim to Indian ancestry. Primary genealogical focus is placed upon four families: Collins, Gibson, Gibson, and that Goins/Gowen family descendant from "Gowin the Indian". The Sizemore and Hart families, in an examination of oral traditions of Indian people, provide proof of Catawba ancestry for the Melungeons. These trader families link to the Catawba by way of those Catawba Indians resident at the Echota Cherokee Mission. This may form the basis for some Melungeon families' claim to Cherokee ancestry, but the chain of records over time clearly relate to the Catawba.

The reader is advised that in keeping with the mission of the Virginia Indian Historical Society, emphasis here is focused upon the Indian descended component of the Melungeons. For the most part this study ends around 1800. This is not to imply a lesser role for any other ethnic contributors to this complex ethnic population. Indeed Gypsy ancestry was established in a proto¬Melungeon family a century earlier.

The Melungeon DNA study demonstrated that in the year 2000 the genetic pool of the Melungeon population under study was predominantly European. The Native American and African component each averaged about 5%. Genetic traces of the small 17th century Virginia Gypsy enclave were in evidence. While at least one of the Gypsy families was quite active in the Indian trade, only circumstantial evidence exists for such trade activity among the Louisa County, Virginia Gibson family. It is anticipated by this investigator that wider DNA testing of complex ethnic populations, coupled with more accurate interpretation and understanding of DNA results, will reveal the extent of 17th century Gypsy ancestry found in modern Complex Ethnic Populations.

Complex Ethnic Populations

The systematic investigation of the Melungeons began with the inclusion of Melungeons within a number of distinct populations of obscure ethnic origins. These long enduring populations formed distinct cultural islands and fell outside of the traditional white-black-mulatto racial construct employed by American social scientists of the day. These rogue communities' defied racial classification, which was apparently felt to be of some concern in a malignant racial environment. Some of the mystery people asserted that they were Indians.

Aloof from both whites and blacks, these self-sustaining populations were often afforded the civil rights reserved for whites. In a sense some of the rogue groups were in essence whites who were not white, and were afforded a seat on a lower social rung. Their neighbors almost uniformly often felt that there was undeclared African ancestry lurking about, and employed pejorative titles for those who they did not understand.

Researchers coined the term Tri-Racial Isolates with reference to these aloof and problematic cultural elements. The assumption was made that these populations were some ill-defined mixture of the perceived races, presumed to be Indian, white and Negro. The Gypsy and East Indian never entered into the discussion.

The conclusions of the Tri-Racial Isolate theorists are deficient in seven critical areas:

1.   Unfamiliarity with colonial Indian history,
2.   Lack of even rudimentary knowledge of Indian genealogy,
3.   Failure to identify Indian people outside of an official tribal context,
4.   A race-driven American paradigm that ignores ethnicity and favors the discredited concept of race,
5.   Failure to identify the Gypsy (Rom) and Asian Indian components of the 17th century Virginia population,
6.   A practice of building new research upon a foundation of deficient and erroneous older data,
7.   Falling victim to the siren lure of the "sexy record", an attention grabbing but misleading written record around which one builds an inaccurate historical and genealogical scheme. In short — insufficient research.

Genealogical examination of the so-called Tri-Racial Isolates of the south has demonstrated that not one single group so defined is limited to only Indian, white, and African ancestry. Most, if not all, have been shown genealogically to include the descendants of seventeenth century Gypsy (Rom) and/or East Indian (Asian) Virginians.

The more prudent course would be found in the study of early records of or pertaining to Indians. This is by far the more difficult but certain route to the revelation of Melungeon origins. The Indian researcher, and by extension the Melungeon researcher, is faced with the task of overcoming the false trails laid down by historians and anthropologist for more than a century. The "disposal" of Indians at the hands of academia looms large as a deterrent to a full and accurate history of colonial Indian people. Historical accounts of tribal migrations provided by early scholars have "disposed" of the Meherrin, Nanticoke, Piscataway, and Tuscarora in their native lands. The implication being that all of those Indian people subsequently vanished from their homelands. Such a proposed scenario strains credulity and has appeal to only the most naïve.

Given that those populations previously referred to as Tri-racial Isolates have been proven to be neither tri-racial nor isolates, it is the considered opinion of this investigator that Complex Ethnic Populations be employed as the more accurate and appropriate descriptor. It should be noted that each Complex Ethnic Population has an ancestry, composition, history and culture unique to that group. Failure to recognize the unique elements of each Complex Ethnic Population is a failure of history.

Paul Heinegg and the Distortion of American Ethno History

In recent years much of the investigation into Melungeon origins has been driven by the extensive, outstanding, yet flawed genealogical narratives provided by the genealogist Paul Heinegg. Through the spin put upon his genealogical narratives, Heinegg has provided his unique personal version of American ethno history. Heinegg frequently omits references which identify families as being of Indian, East Indian, or of Gypsy origin, and refers to anyone not-white as a "Free African American". Heinegg takes full yet dishonest advantage of the problematic racial conventions employed in early records. Those same problematic racial conventions have thwarted accurate and meaningful investigation into ethnic origins and ultimately led to the Walter Plecker phenomenon.

The peculiar personal philosophy of Paul Heinegg is revealed in the "Intro-duction" section of his volumes. The following entries are but a few examples taken from the 2005 edition of Free African Americans of North Carolina, Virginia, and South Carolina.

1.   "Free Indians blended into the free African American communities. They did not form their own separate communities".[1]
2.   "Indians who adopted English customs became part of the free African American communities".[2]
3.   "I did not find any nuclear Indian families...."[3]
4.   "Some of the lighter-skinned descendants of these (Free African American) families formed their own distinct communities which have been the subject of anthropological research". [4] This reference is to those Complex Ethnic Populations previously known as Tri Racial Isolates.
5.   In an incredible pronouncement, Heinegg states in regard to the Nansemond Indian Bass family of Norfolk County, "There is no evidence that the family ever adopted any Indian customs".[5]

Perhaps the most outrageous of Heinegg's assertions is to be found in the Introduction to Free African Americans of Maryland. Under the heading "Indians" Heinegg, in reference to "light-skinned African American" landowners, makes the assertion that "Southeastern states solved this problem by calling these communities 'Indians'."

These extraordinary and problematic statements published by Heinegg are of some concern, given the place of prominence that he has been afforded in genealogical circles. Heinegg's work begs the question as to whether the reader is subjected to the product of insufficient research, or to a discriminatory racial bias levied against the Native American and other non-African people of color.

In a "build it and they will come" phenomenon, researchers of the various complex ethnic populations have gravitated to Heinegg's works seeking the ethnic identity of their ancestors. Heinegg, however, represents American Indians, Asian Indians, Gypsies, and others as "Free African Americans", skewing history in an inaccurate and prejudicial fashion. It is well worth noting the frequency with which Heinegg and others unwittingly cite the "standout records" of Gypsy families as examples of the African American history. This spurious practice dilutes the power of the African American experience and distorts ethno history. Mr. Heinegg has demonstrated a willingness to make partial corrections, but as any lawyer will tell you, you can't un- ring a bell.

Figure 16 Photo: Gary "Mishiho" Gabehart, Stacy Webb, James Nickens, Kingsport, Tn. MHA Union Gathering

The Gypsy Factor

The surprise discovery in the quest for Melungeon origins was the revelation of a family with descent from a 17th century Gypsy enclave. A quick review of surnames found in other complex ethnic populations of the Southeast revealed the widespread dispersion of Gypsies from a small 17th century community. The early and widespread dispersal of surnames, coupled with the widespread occurrence of these surnames in Indian Tribes, suggests the possibility of participation in the Indian fur trade. At least one patriot Gypsy family left clear records of intense involvement in the Indian trade.

Descendants of the original small Gypsy community are found in every south-eastern population formerly considered to be tri racial isolates. Further, it is clear that the Rom gravitated to core Indian populations. Although misunderstood, the increasing popularity of DNA studies has exposed evidence of Gypsy DNA in the descendants of Complex Ethnic Populations of the south and southeast. The omission of the Gypsy from the American historical dialogue stands as a most egregious error.

The supporting records are not new findings. This information has been publicly available for more than three hundred years, ignored by scholars and lost in the maze of inconsistent and nonspecific racial conventions employed since 1705. One might speculate that it may have the Gypsy component which provided the exotic element to the mystery cultures of the south.

The East Indian Factor

Genealogical investigation into the multiethnic populations of the south-eastern United States has uniformly revealed a minimum of four, and often five ethnic contributors. While the role of the Gypsy in Virginia history escaped notice, the role of the Asian Indian did not. Helen Rountree brought to light an observation made by Hugh Jones in his 1724 publication The Present State of Virginia. Speaking of Virginia Indians, Jones observed that "they seem to like the East Indian". No family more clearly demonstrates the accuracy of Jones observation than the Weaver family as illustrated below.

Lancaster County, Virginia

13 Aug 1707

Will vs Pinkard

Action is brought to this Court by Will an East Indyy Indian agt Tho: Pinkard At ye prayer of Deft: Lycence of Imparleance is granted until next court Weaver vs Pinkard Action is brought to this court by Jno: Weaver an East Indy Indian agt: Thomas Pinkard at the prayer of the Deft: Lycence of Imparleance is granted until next Court and the aforesd: East Indy Indians pray leave of the Court to have time to produce evidence relating to their freedom agt: the next Court in order whereunto this Court do assign them five days time but not to depart the Coty to any remote Coty without giving security to return to their Master within the time allowed.

10 March 1707/8

Will Jack v. Pinkard The action brought to this Court by Will and Jack two East Indians against Capt. Pinkard is dismissed neither appearing

11 April 1711 Indian Weaver

Judgement is granted to Richard Weaver an East Indian agst ye Estate of Andrew Jackson decd for 400 lbs of tobac due by bill the plaintiff making oath and ordered to be forthwith Paid by James Jackson exc of Andrew Jackson agst his estate Plantif consenting to pay cost.

The Weavers, descendant from Indian Will, John Weaver, and Richard Weaver, demonstrate the integration of the Asian Indian into the culture of the American Indian. Intermarriage within the Cherokee, Choctaw, Meherrin, and Nansemond Tribes solidified American Indian status. In Norfolk County, Virginia the Weaver families occur in various records as Indians from 1833 to the 1930 census. These records include the Special Indian Census taken in 1900 and 1910. In this regard they mirror the Bass family.

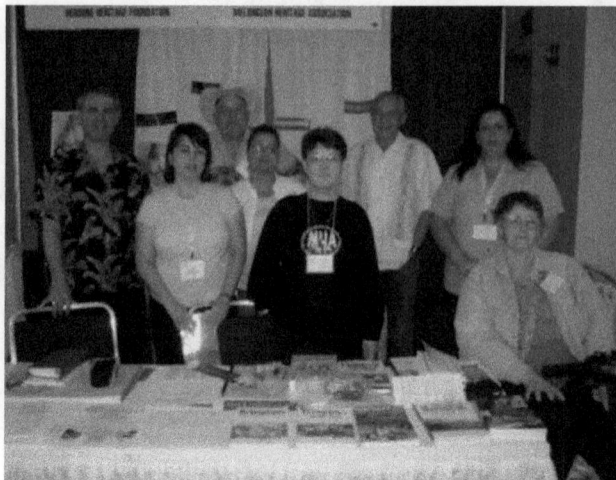

Figure 17 Photo: Jamestown "Before 1607" Melungeons In The New World. Melungeon Heritage Association & Redbone Heritage Foundation at the National Genealogical Association Conference 2008. L to R: Houston Bridges, Gary"Mishiho" Gabehart, James Nickens, Stacy Webb, Unknown (yellow shirt), Tammy Glass, S.J. Arthur, Phillis Starnes.

The Indian Trade

A handful of modern families are able to trace their genealogies to a specific Indian ancestor in the 1600s. The roots of each and every one of these families can be found in records of or pertaining to colonial fur traders. The traders Nathaniel Bass, Edward Bass, William Clawson, William Cook, and Thomas Hobson are of particular interest. Francis Yardley and Jenkin Price are possibly due consideration in this regard.

The earliest example of the trade-genealogy connection is illustrated by the Bass family. Nathaniel Bass received an early commission to conduct trade with Canada and New England. The trader Edward Bass, son of Nathaniel Bass

> "took in marriage one virtuous Indian Maydy by the Christian name of Mary Tucker and went to live amongst the Showanoes in Carolina....." Edward and Mary married in 1644. "He went to Carolinas in latter years in pursute of trade"....."Dyed in 1696 A. D."

The quotes are from "the book of John Bass", son of Nathaniel and brother of Edward. John Bass had

> "married ye dafter of ye King of ye King of ye Nansemund Nation, by name Elizabeth in Holy Baptism and in Holy Matrimonie ye 14 day of August 1638" "John Bass Dyed in 1699".

The Ethnic and Geographic Origins of the Melungeons
Part1

Nathaniel Bass and William Tucker each led expeditions against the Nansemond Indians after the 1622 Indian reprisals in which nearly 400 whites were killed. Nathaniel Bass was charged with the task of recovering English hostages held by the Nansemond. William Tucker received a land patent in Upper Norfolk County in 1642. Hostage taking has been a part of English-Indian relations as far back as the Roanoke Colonies. One must consider the possibility that Mary Tuckeit and Elizabeth may have been hosta0s or descendant from hostages taken as a result of the 1622 war which continued until 1636. John Bass himself may have been taken hostage in the initial 1622 attack. A similar 17th century scenario is under investigation with regard to the Nansemond Collins family in relation to the Shoewcraft family of Lancaster County, Virginia.

…………………*To be continued*.

Endnotes:

1.   Paul Heingg, Free African Americans of North Carolina, Virginia and South Carolina, (Baltimore: Genealogical Publishing   Co.,   2005 Introduction, p. 1

FIGURE 18 PORTRAIT: OLD BILLY BOWLEGS 1858

Yamassee/Seminole Ethnocide
By Govinda S. Sanyal

Prophet Abraham, my third great grandfather escaped from Dr. Sierra's home in Pensacola, Florida where he was enslaved.' He made it to the Suwanee River where he joined Old Bowleg's Seminole band. Abraham was originally an Atlantic Creole. The Atlantic Creoles were the descendants of Portuguese Jewish fathers referred to as lanzados, who historically wedded primarily Fulani (Berber/Moorish) women when they fled Spain and Portugal during the Inquisition.2 Prophet Abraham descended from royalty; his mother was the daughter of Futa Toto, a powerful Moorish Fulani (Berber) king.

Oral tradition has it that the Moors originated anciently in Yemen and were part of the Lost Tribe of Israel that eventually migrated to West Africa via Egypt. These unfortunate mixed blood descendants were caught in an ethnic war between the Mandingo and the Moors in the Senegambia region of West Africa that lasted about half a century. As a result of their involvement in the African slave trade they had become easy pawns for private captors for the slave industry. Prophet Abraham was victimized by this ethnic war, which ultimately claimed him as a slave in Florida. Abraham's Moorish name was Yobly (Ublai) a possible namesake of Ublai Khan one of the sons of Genghis Khan.3

Abraham (aka Tustenugee Souanoffee--various spellings) was described as eloquent, with the mannerism of a Venetian courtier. He spoke several languages. His military might and skill were proven when Old Bowlegs, chief of the Suwanee village, eventually adopted him into his band and gave him the busketa name (a Green Corn traditional ceremonial naming event) of Souanoffe Tuskenugee—meaning Shawnee or Suwanee Dog Warrior. Traditionally, Abraham (Tustenugee Souanoffee) was given all the rights and privileges given to any full blood Shawanogi or Seminole. Barbara Alice Mann wrote that, "adoptees of any race were traditionally considered 100% Native upon adoption and those mixed bloods of any race whose mothers were Native had always been recognized traditionally by Natives as Natives."4 Traditional standards would indicate that Abraham received all of the benefits, services and status of a full blood native.

When Old Bowlegs died, Tustenugee Sounoffee was advised by Micanopy to marry Old Bowleg's widow Hagar. Hagar was Micanopy's "sister", a matriarchal sibling according to Seminole Muscogee traditional social hierarchy.5

Conceivably Abraham and Hagar's children (my ancestors) inherited all of the rights and privileges of any full blood native. My ancestral Indian connections from Abraham and Hagar is based on the fact that Hagar was native and Tustenugee Souanoffee (Prophet Abraham) was adopted with all the rights and privileges of a full blood Shawanogee (Suwanee) Seminole. Micanopy's mother's people were Yamassee and therefore Hagar would be also considered Yamassee . Micanopy's Yamassee blood was accounted for by his exceptionally dark skin.6

Micanopy was not the only Seminole Creek of Yamassee heritage. Jumper and Alligator, two of the Seminole traditional war chiefs that were captured and imprisoned along with Osceola whom the United States army considered hostiles, claimed descent from the Yamassee Indians. Jumper was originally living among the Upper Creeks according to Swanson's Bulletin-The Early Creeks, but was driven along with his tribe to an island where only a few survived.7 The Upper Creeks were governed by the Tuckabatchee, whom Thomas F. Meagher reported as Shawanogee. The Tuckabatchee were governed by Efau Harjo, who also descended from the Yamassee.8 Gallatin suggested in, Indian Antiquities, that the Shawnee were Yamassee.

Figure 19 Portrait: Osceola aka "Wm. Billy Powell
see Y-DNA matches to various surname Redbone families.

Observers reported that the Yamassee had dark skin, wooly hair, thick lips and flat feet.9 W.H. Gilbert reported to the Bureau of American Ethnology that among the Cherokee was a small group of people who did not exhibit the standard Cherokee characteristics of aquiline features and olive skin.10 Their complexions were as dark as burnt coffee with hairy foreheads (that became recessive as they got older) and they had short thick hair. This population was possibly the old Yamassee who predated the Cherokees in the Blue Mountains. Oral Tradition dictates that the Yamassee came out of the Cherokees." It is probably more accurate to say that it was more of a geographic location in regards to the Blue Hills than to a tribal affinity. According to the late tribal

Eastern Cherokee Chief, Hicks, the Cherokees of Northern Iroquoian descent, upon arrival at the Southern Appalachian Blue Mountains erected their council houses on the already established sacred sites of the preexisting aboriginal population.

Giovanni da Verrazano, traveling along the North Carolina coast in 1524, came across the Cape Fear Indians, alias Sampee/Sampit Indians. According to Horatio Hale and his Tutelo writings, the Sampit were a Cusabo tribe related to the Yamassee. He described their complexion as "not being unlike the Ethiopian" (an early connotation for African),I2 Many of the dark skinned or black skinned Seminoles were frequently mistaken for "Negroes" and or slaves. This is not to diminish the fact that there were "Negro" towns of newly escaped slaves whose inhabitants were Seminole military allies with whom intermarriage was not uncommon.

Hagar, my third great grandmother, (Bowleg's widow, Micanopy's sister and Prophet Abraham's wife) was the daughter of Peggy and the granddaughter of Fia, who was captured by Cow Keeper ca. 1750, when the Yamassee were defeated by the Oconee Creeks. As a result of this war, the Oconee Creeks under Brims slaughtered the Yamassee warriors and married their women at St. Augustine.13 The detached Oconee Creeks defected from the Creek Nation and were regarded by the Spanish and Creeks as Cimarrones or wild and unruly men. However, the term was applied to runaway slaves, indicating that the Yamassee were regarded as slaves according to the statutes of the Colonial government of South Carolina." They had been so considered since 1715 when they were defeated by South Carolina and their Creek allies.

Cassells Spanish-English Dictionary defines Cimarron as a lazy black sailor, and indeed, the Yamassee were seafaring people who introduced the prominent Yamassee stroke as a paddling technique along the Atlantic seaboard extending from South Carolina southwards to Florida. The Yamassee stroke is still used today in coastal South Carolina among the local Gullah folk as well as the fragmented Seminole Yamassee families found from coastal Georgia and northward to Sandy Island (known by the Indians historically as Yourhenny), South Carolina included among the local "Geechee" communities. Newton D. Mereness in Travels, speaks of the Yamassee as the Comantles or "Tamathlis the wooleyed haired ones."

Yammassee/Seminole Ethnocide

Fia had two daughters—Dolly and Flora. Dolly married Old Mikasuki's son, Pompey, and had several children: Prince, Peggy (the mother of Hagar), Scilla (Cow Tom's grandmother. Cow Tom was chief of the Refugee Creeks, alias Eufalas/Hogologees and Tuskigis.) Either Fanny or Eliza was the mother of Micanopy, according to Seminole matriarchal tradition, since he (Micanopy) was Hagar's sister. Scilla's daughter, Maggie Cow Tom, married. Holata Miko, alias Silas Jefferson, the Yuskegee/Talisi Chief of the Wind Clan and the interpreter for the Creek Nation in Indian Territory. Hagar had several children: Philip Washington, Phillis (my great great grandmother) and Ned who married Flora Reed. Ned and Sarah/Flora were my great great grandparents. Istifani (Stephany/Steep) was the son of Phillis and July. Jr. Issabelle (Tee) married Isitifani. She was the daughter of Ned and Flora Reed

As a result of Seminole War II, my great great grandfather, Ned, was captured with his family and brought to Charleston with Osceola as a child and enslaved by Alfred Huger, the Postmaster General of Charleston, South Carolina. Alfred Huger documented Ned as a mulatto slave, who was incidentally treated as a nominal slave.15 He would leave home for months at a time to be with his wife Flora Reed. It greatly displeased the other slavers that Ned was given so much freedom. Ned and Phillis were the children of Tustenugee Souanofee (Prophet Abraham) and Hagar, the widow of Old Bowlegs.16

The Seminole emigration rolls also enumerated Tustenugee Souanoffee as Abraham and his wife, Hagar, as the daughter of Peggy, the granddaughter of Polly and Pompey. Pompey was the son of Old Mikasuky and Dolly who was the daughter of Fia, a Yamassee captured by Cow Keeper ca. 1750 at St. Augustine when the Oconee Creeks fought and destroyed the Yamassee. In the 1750 Yamassee War, when the Oconee slaughtered the Yamassee warriors and took their maidens as wives, they were asked to return to the Oconee town but refused. They also rejected their nation's request by not fulfilling purification rites that had to be performed within one year as a result of their intimacy with women considered outside of their clan system. These detached segmented bands eventually became confederated as Seminoles, but were called runaways, separatist and strayed beast by their Creek suppressors, according to the transliteration of the Creek word Seminole."

The Oconee had set up a satellite town called Peliklikaha, where both of my grandfathers, Abraham and July (Tcu Lee) became town chiefs under Micanopy.18 However, Abraham became the Seminole Nation's ambassador and Micanopy's advisor and speaker. Eventually my July and Reed ancestors would become enslaved under the orchestration of Major. Benjamin D. Heriot, Hernandez and General Jesup.

Flora, my great great grandmother was a daughter of Ben (the names are enumerated as Ben not Benjamin) and Jane. The family was enumerated in the Seminole Emigration rolls of Florida. The names on the given rolls appear as Ben, male age 40, Jane female age 35; and their children were listed as Flora, female age 13, Patty, female age 12, Charles, male age 11, Polly, female age 9, Joe, male age 7, Betty, female age 4, Elsey, female age3, and Robert, male infant. The family was listed under Micanopy as a tribal town and owner. All of their ages were estimated on the rolls and the family claimed to be free.

When captured by Colonel William Reed in the Wahoo Swamp ca, 1838, Ben exclaimed to his European captors that he was not a slave, but one of Micanopi's people and was never owned by a white man. Regardless of his assertions he and his family were enslaved because they were considered hostile Indians, and because of their dark skin or blackish skin, were conceived by these slavers as black or Negro.19 Ben was one of Micanopy's leading military men who had led hundreds of Yamassee Seminoles and their families against European slavers and their Creek allies. The Heriots owned the plantation, Mt. Arena, the neighboring plantation to Pipe Down where three generations of my Seminole family were living in slavery since their captivity along with Osceola and imprisoned on Sullivan's Island in Charleston. Porter reported that my ancestors were shipped up to Charleston for "safe keeping"2° but were diverted as slaves of the Pettygrews, whose origins were among the Eastern Chickasaw at Breed Camp and the Savanna River area of South Carolina and Georgia.21

Among the Alston Papers, at the Carolina Library, at Columbia, South Carolina there is a slave bill of sale that falsely enumerated my Seminole family as slaves and Negroes. The appellation "Negro" was used in this hemisphere to apply to descendants of slaves of African origin and any other people of color considered as chattel or slaves. These groups included: Indians, Malays, East Indians, among others and even, infrequently, whites.

To be a Seminole was not a tribal ethnicity but a multi-tribal/multi-ethnic designation, bound by a common thread of revolutionary separatism, and militarism. Ethnocide was a tactic used to detribalize my family and to fulfill the void created by a lack of slaves to work on the expanding U.S. territories gained since importation of foreign slaves became illegal ca. 1808. By 1870 and 1880 Joe Reed and Sarah alias Flora Reed (e) Huger (pronounced Eugee) were enumerated on the Federal Census for Georgetown, South Carolina, as black and mulatto. Ethnic inconsistencies within the same family groups are significant to families of native origin. The ethnicity of Phyllis in the 1870 and 1880 Federal Census for Georgetown, South Carolina was inconsistent, reporting her as black and at other times as Mulatto.

It is significant that the Yamassee were legally considered slaves in South Carolina. It was written into South Carolina law following the Yamassee War of 1715 that if any native nation was in enmity with the colonial government they would be considered potentially slaves and ultimately and statistically would lose their Seminole or Indian status and be reported demographically as Negro in order to legitimize enslavement.22

It is a good thing that those descendants of African slaves are self-identifying themselves as African American and ridding themselves of all slave connotations. Likewise many mixed blood Native communities are attempting to undo the centuries old dilemma of ethnocide by asserting their Nativeness by self-identification and not allowing outside sources dictate their ethnicity or cultural orientation.

Endnotes

1.   Kenneth W. Porter. Papers, Schomberg Center for Research in Black Culture, New York.
2.   Ira Berlin, "From Creole to African: Atlantic Creoles and the Origins of African American Society in Mainland North America" The William and Mary Quarterly, 3rd Ser., Vol. 53, No. 2 (Apr., 1996), pp. 251-288. See Atlantic Creole Theory at Melungeon Family Genealogy Forum at Geneology.com
3.   Phylon, (1940-1956), Vol. 2 No. 2 (2nd Qtr., 1941, pp. 102+105-116. doi: 10.2307/271778. Volume XXX July, 1951-April, 1952 Florida Historical Society, p. 12.
4.   Barbara Alive Mann, Native Americans, Archeologists, and the Mounds, pp288; 441/2003. Any African Native mixed blood who is Native by culture, memory and self-identification is Native American; however, on the other hand, Native mixed Blacks who are African American by culture, memory and self-identification are African American. The same thing could be applied to any Native mixed blood such as Mestizos (Natives mixed with European), Red Bones, Brass Ankles, Cajuns, Creoles etc.
5.   Susan A Miller, Coacoochee's Bones, p. 66, 2003; Sattler, Richard A., Seminole Italwa: Socio-Political Change among the Oklahoma Seminoles between Removal and Allotment, 1836-1905. Ph.D. diss. Univ. of Oklahoma, 1987

6.   Charles H. Coe, Red Patriots; the Story of the Seminoles, pp. 25-26. Also spelled as Mikanopah-- aliases Top King and Pond King. Mokonopy's Busketa (Green Corn name) name was Sint Chakee. George Catlin the celebrated Indian portraitist had visited the Seminoles and described Mikanopy as a very lusty dignified man of very dark or black complexion indicating the presence of Yamassee or Negro (African) blood but it is more than certain that his mother was a Yamassee as validated by historical accounts. R.J. Cotteril, The Southern Indians, pp. 232, 429,430. The journal of the commissioners makes the interesting suggestion that the predecessors of the Seminoles were Yamassees.

7.   John R Swanton, Early History of the Creek Indians and Their Neighbors, p. 106, 1998. Jumper was Micanopy's sense bearer but after his death he was replaced by my ancestor Abraham (Tustenugee Souanoffee).

8.   George Stiggins. Creek Indian History: A Historical Narrative of the Genealogy, Traditions and Downfall of the Ispocoga or Creek Indian Tribe of Indians by One of the Tribe, (1788-1845.) Marler, Don C. , General Thomas S. Woodward and Woodward's Reminiscences, Dogwood Press, p.113. The Indians that originally inhabited from the middle of the parts of the Carolinas (South Carolina) and Georgia to the seaboard were known as Yamacraws or Yamassees, Oconees, Ogeechees, and Sawanokees or People of the Glades. The Sowanokees known as the Shawnee - the other Indians know them by no other name than to this day but Sowanokee, and the Savannah River was known as Sowanokee Hatchee Thlocka, which signifies the Big River of the Glades or what we call Savannah....The other little tribes with the Uchees, they being the same "fireside" Indians with the Shawnee, all dwindled away among the Creeks and lost their language except the Uchee Reed Win, Alexander & McMillan James B., Indian Place Names In Alabama, p. 143/84 — In 1751 the Chief of "Shalapheaggee had signed a deed along with other Creek Chiefs granting the coastal Sea Islands off Georgia and South Carolina including its barrier islands to the English with the exception of those islands deeded to Coosaponokesa alias Mary Musgrove, also known as the Queen of the Creeks and maternal niece of Emperor Brimms (Royal Chief of the Creeks). In 1758 Jerome Courtonne, a trading partner to the mixed blood Chickasaw John Pettygrew, included "Shalapheaggee" in his lists of Creek towns. The Pettygrews will ultimately capture and own part of my Seminole family as indicated in the above text.

9.   Don C. Marler, General Thomas S. Woodward and Woodward's Reminiscences, Dogwood Press, 2001.

10.   W.H. Gilbert, American Ethnology Bull. 135; Anthropological Paper No. 23 p. 1939.

11.   John R. Swanton, Indian Tribes of North America, Bull. 145, p. 106. Tom Hatley, The Dividing Paths, Cherokees and South Carolinians through the Revolutionary Era, pp6, 18, 27, 28, 34..

12.   Pat Spurlock Elder, Melungeons: Examining An Appalachian Legend, Continuity Press, 1999, p. 39.

13.   Thomas Woodward, Woodward's Reminiscences of the Creek, or Muscogee Indians, contained in letters to friends in Georgia and Alabama: Montgomery, Ala.: Barrett and Wimbish, Book and General Job Printers, 1859, pp. 129-139. A war of extermination took place at Tallahassee when the Creeks slaughtered about a thousand of the remaining Yamassee warriors and saved the Yamasse females from a death by intermarrying with them. According to tradition the ceded band of Oconee Creeks were required to remain separated from their original Oconee hometown for a year in observance of tribal purification rites. However before the year concluded the Oconee braves had married their captured concubines and became a Nation of separatists, expatriates and runaways. Col Woodward speaks of the Seminoles as a mixed race and gives their name as meaning wild or runaway or outlaw.

14.   Cotterril, Judicial Cases Concerning Slavery, p324 (See Reed vs. Price).

15.   Michael P. Johnson and James L.Roark, Black Masters, p. 193.

16.   Daniel F. Littlefield, Africans and Seminoles: from Removal to Emancipation: Westport: Greenwood Press, 1977. (See Littlefield's Appendix). See internet source: http://freepages.genealogy.rootsweb.com/—texlan ceiseminoles/index.htm

17.   From the private collection of Dr. Heriberto Dixon. PhD.--Native American historian.

18.   John, R. Swanton, Early History of the Creek Indians, p. 404, 407-408 spelled also as Pelaclekaha in item no. 23 reported that this town was the residence of Micanopy, Chief or Miko of the Seminole Nation.

19.   Frederick Webb Hodge, Handbook of American Indians, Part 2 , Bull. 30, 1910, p. 987. Leitch J. Wright, Jr. Creeks and Seminoles, pp. 303-304. — Mixed blood African--Indians and dark skinned Indians were frequently illegally enslaved by such people as the Heriot and Tucker firm and the U.S. Army i.e. Gen. Wellbourn — as reported by Grant Foreman in Indian Removal p.368.

20.   Porter, Kenneth W. Papers, Schomberg Center for Research in Black Culture, New York 21.

      See Pettygrew "Who Was Who Among the Southern Indians a Genealogical Notebook, 1698-1907", by Don Martini; Richard A. Colbert and James Logan Colbert of the Chic saws: The Man and the Myth. The North Carolina Genealogical Society Journal, Vol XX, No. 2, May 1994, pp. 82-95, in file #HR-986. James R. Atkinson, Splendid Land Splendid People, pp. 22, 205, 211, 225.

22.   R.A. Lafferty, Okla Hannali, p. 28. —During the years 1832, 1833 and 1834 about 50,000 Indians were removed from the old South to Indian Territory. Indian stragglers were murdered and stubborn or so-called hostile Indians were declared black and enslaved such as in the case of the Seminoles, Ogeechee (Hodge pt.1) and the Yuchi (see the Extra Census Bulletin of the Five Civilized Tribes) U.S. Government Printing Office, 1898. In 1832 Flora, a Mulatto slave and her children inclusive of Sarah possible ancestors were sold by Robert Childs of Charleston, South Carolina to Charles Brown Moses also of Charleston, South Carolina. Up to 1861 the Moses family were neighbors to Alfred Huger, the Post Master General of Charleston, South Carolina which possibly resulted in the marital alliance between Ned his Seminole nominal (so-called Mulatto) slave and Sarah/Flora the enslaved Native girl next door which took place about ca. 1856 when my great grandmother Ka-Tee alias Grand Ma Tee and Isabella (Bella) Reed Huger Heriot was born. The Heriot surname was my great Grandmother's married name which she had assumed when she married Istifani alias Stephaney Heriot, the grandson of the Old Man July, the Tallahassee Seminole. The Heriot surname was the namesake of General Benjamin Heriot who had captured and enslaved my family during the Seminole War.

Biography

Govinda S.Sanyal M.Ed. M.S. Ph.D.

[Editor's note: We plan to have one biography in each issue of the Redbone Chronicles, featuring writers whose articles appear here. I have corresponded for several years with Govinda who lives in New York. He has a unique perspective of the history of mixed-blood peoples. Welcome to the Redbone Chronicles, Govinda.]

Greetings to the members of the Redbone Heritage Foundation, Inc. I welcome the opportunity to contribute to this, the inaugural issue of the Redbone Chronicles.

I am a member of the Natchez Tribe of Oklahoma, a Treaty Tribe of the Creek Muskogi Nation. For the past several years I served on the Council for the Texas and Mexican Seminoles. The Natchez Nation of Oklahoma had chosen me to be their ambassador to all the tribes of the Eastern Woodlands extending from New England to Florida.

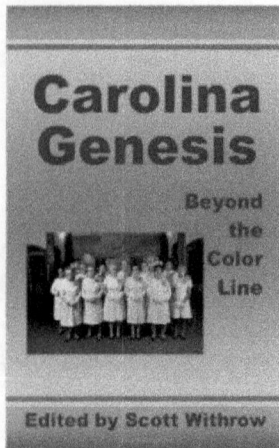

My mother is a direct descendant from the Yamassee/Cusabo/Natchez tribes of South Carolina, collectively referred to in colonial times as settlement Indians or parched corn Indians (they use to carry dry corn in their pouches for long journeys) and the Old Seminole Nation of Florida under Micanopy and Chittis Yahola (Snake Crier), alias Bow Legs 11, who led the so-called hostiles or freedom fighters along with Osceola. My ancestors were the last of the Seminoles to never surrender to the United States Army.

Amar Sanyal my father came to the United States from Calcutta, India in 1916 as part of the British Merchant Marines. My paternal lineage descends from the ancient Brahmins or Indo Aryans of the ancient Indus Valley civilization. My paternal Clan or Gotram is Kashyappa that originated from the ancient Aryan Sage, Kashyappa. (It is mind boggling that there are t w o moieties, which divided all Choctaw and were known as Hattak I Holihtah (Their Men Fortify) and Kashapa Okla (Divided People), the same name as my ancient Indo Aryan predecessors. Whether or not there was an ancient connection needs to be furthered researched). During Indian British rule many of my father's people were known as Benegalese by the Native American and British traders. These Benegalese traders provided the Native tribes on the East coast with Madras cotton and silk fabric for their colorful turbans and shawls. Many of the Benegalese traders took up with Native women and settled in early United States, but were always enumerated statistically as Native or Indian meaning aboriginal. My father was one of the last of this type of outside influence that became part of Native American society extending from the colonial period to the early part of the twentieth century

Sanyal contributed a chapter in 2009 to *Carolina Genesis*, edited by Scott Withrow

Govinda Sanyal's astonishing research uses mtDNA markers to trace a single female lineage that winds its way through prehistoric Yemen, North Africa, Moorish Spain, the Sephardic diaspora, colonial Mexico, and finally escapes the Inquisition by assimilating into a Native American tribe, ending up in South Carolina. He fleshes out the DNA thread with documented genealogy, so we get to know their names, their lives, their struggles.

Carolina Genesis: Beyond the Color Line Paperback – July 10, 2013

Biography: Govinda Sanyal

Some Americans pretend that a watertight line separates the "races." But most know that millions of mixed-heritage families crossed from one "race" to another over the past four centuries. Every essay in this collection tells such a tale. Each speaks with a different style and to different interests. But taken together, the seven articles paint a portrait, unsurpassed in the literature, of migrations, challenges, and triumphs over "racial" obstacles.

Stacy Webb tells of families of mixed ancestry who pioneered westward paths from the Carolinas into the colonial wilderness, paths now known as Cumberland Road, Natchez Trace, Three-Chopped Way, and others. They migrated, not in search of wealth or exploration, but to escape the injustice of America's hardening "racial" barrier.

Cyndie Goins Hoelscher focuses on a specific family that scattered from the Carolinas. One branch fled to Texas, becoming friends with Sam Houston and participating in the founding of that state. Other bands fought in the war of 1812, or migrated to Florida or the Gulf coast. Nowadays, Goins descendants can be found in nearly every state and are of nearly every "race."

Scott Withrow (the collection's editor) concentrates on the saga of one individual of mixed ancestry. Joseph Willis was born into a community of color in South Carolina. He migrated to Louisiana, was accepted as a White man, founded one of the first churches in the area, and became one of the region's best-loved and most fondly remembered Christian ministers.

S. Pony Hill recounts the historic struggles of South Carolina's Cheraw tribe, in a reprint of Chapter 5 of his book, *Strangers in Their Own Land*.
Marvin Jones tells the history of the "Winton Triangle," a section of North Carolina populated by successful families of mixed ancestry from colonial times until the mid-20th century. They fought for the Union, founded schools, built businesses, and thrived through adversity until the civil rights movement of 1955-65 ended legal segregation.

K. Paul Johnson traces the history of North Carolina's antebellum Quakers. The once-strong community dissolved as it grew morally opposed to slavery. Those who stayed true to their faith migrated north. Those who remained slaveowners left the church. The worst stress was the Nat Turner event. Its aftermath helped turn the previously permeable color line into the harsh endogamous barrier that exists today

Carolina Tribes & Pre Contact

By Joanne Pezzulo

Lucas Vázquez de Ayllón

Lucas Vázquez de Ayllón landed near Winyah Bay in South Carolina in 1526 with 500 settlers and 100 slaves from Spain and Santa Domingo, Hernando DeSoto followed in 1539-1540 with 600 men, Spanish and Portuguese soldiers. When they landed they found Juan Ortiz, a Spaniard left behind on an earlier expedition who had been living with the Indians. For three years DeSoto with his Portuguese and Spanish soldiers explored the American south. In 1566 Juan Pardo with another 125 Spanish soldiers for two years explored basically the same area as DeSoto.

By the early 1600s when the settlers at Jamestown began trading with these southern tribes a hundred years had passed, four or five generations of Native Americans who carried Haplogroups R, E, and likely others as well.

Researchers over the past hundred or so years have wondered how the mixed families dubbed Melungeons, Redbones, Croatans/Lumbee, Brass Ankles etc., might have descended from Portuguese people. Modern day researchers have declared them to be of Sub Saharan men and European "White" women because a portion of them have Sub Saharan haplo assignment groups, among the Y-DNA results. Apparently none of these researchers from the late 1800s to the present have studied the history of this country prior to Jamestown.

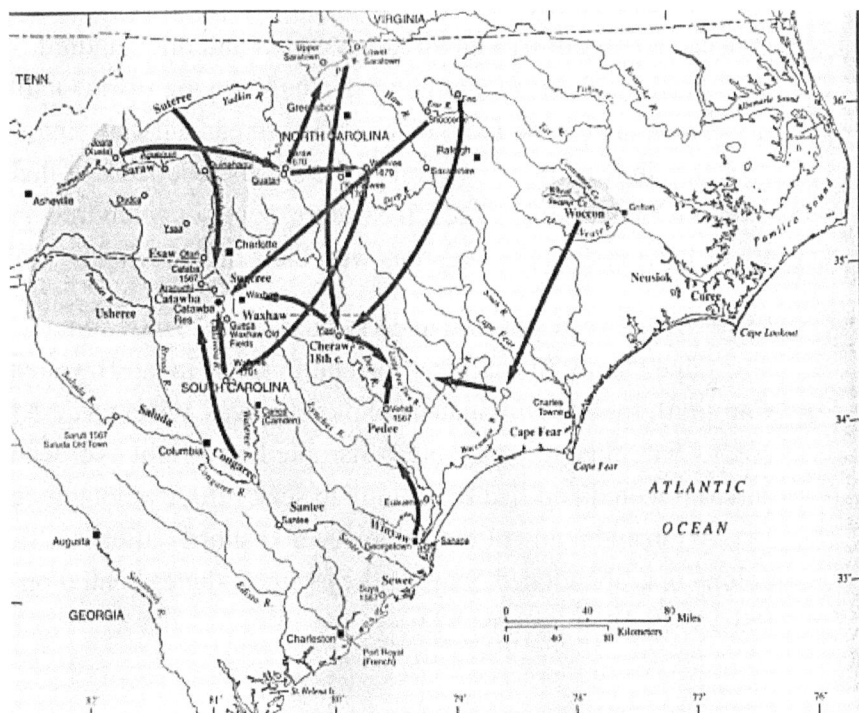

Figure 20 Map: Exploration Parties Movements

De Ayllon arrived at the Winyah Bay with his settlement of 500 colonist, men women, children and 100 slaves in 1526 which preceded Jamestown by 81 years. Later the Melungeons would tell of their ancestors "a society of Portuguese Adventurers, men and women, to a journalist which was published in 1848.

History records the first slave revolt at de Ayllon's settlement, San Miguel de Guadalupe somewhere in the vicinity of Winyah Bay and the Pee Dee River. While the extent of the revolt has not been recorded it is known that of the colonist and slaves with de Ayllon only 150 returned, and there indeed was a slave revolt. Few records from that time period have survived but I have found most historians, authors and researchers believe that at least some of these slaves and colonists that came with de Ayllon were left behind. It seems likely that some remained behind to mix with native tribes, perhaps being captured, or perhaps by choice, leaving behind their European and African Haplogroups in the Native communities as proof that they were there.

A few of these mentioned;

"The first settlement within the present borders of the United States to contain Negro slaves was the locale of the first slave revolt. A Spanish colonizer Lucas Vasquez de Ayllon, founded, in the summer of 1526, a community whose probable location was at or near the mouth of the Pee Dee River in what is now South Carolina. The settlement consisted of about five hundred Spaniards and one hundred Negro slaves. Trouble soon beset it. Illness caused numerous deaths, carrying off in October, Ayllon himself. Internal dissension arose, and the Indians grew increasingly suspicious and hostile. Finally, probably in November, several of the slaves rebelled and fled to the Indians. The next month what was left of the adventurers, some one hundred and fifty souls, returned to Haiti, leaving the rebel Negroes with their Indian friends. (Aptheker, 1993)"

"The first African slaves arrived in present day United States as part of the San Miguel de Gualdape colony (most likely located in the Winyah Bay area of present-day South Carolina), founded by Spanish explorer Lucas Vásquez de Ayllón in 1526. The ill-fated colony was almost immediately disrupted by a fight over leadership, during which the slaves revolted and fled the colony to seek refuge among local Native Americans. De'Ayllón and many of the colonists died shortly afterwards of an epidemic, and the colony was abandoned, leaving the escaped slaves behind on North American soil" (Historical-Melungeons, ND).

"Just as with De Soto's expedition, African slaves had accompanied de Ayllon's settlement colony on the Peedee River in 1526. When there was a crisis over leadership, the colony fell into disarray. In the midst of this crisis, a slave revolt further ripped the settlement apart. With the colony in shambles, many of the African slaves fled to live among the nearby native people. According to De Soto, these refugees must have lived among the Cofitachiqui and taught them the craftwork of the Europeans"(Minges, 2003).

In 1540 just a few years after the deAyllon's landing we find another Spanish explorer, Hernandez De Soto, with the Spanish, Portuguese, and slaves, visiting the same area as DeAyllon and later Pardo. From "The DeSoto's Journal" by Elvas we learn that among the men who came with DeSoto was a ship that contained the Portuguese as well as a number of slaves.

Hernandez De Soto & Andre de Vasconcelos

According to the journals one ship of Portuguese accompanied De Soto; in the month of April, of the year 1538, the adelantado delivered the ships over to the captains who were to go in them. He took a new and good sailing ship for himself and gave one to Andre de Vasconcelos, in which the Portuguese went.

Alimamos, a horseman of De Soto who "got lost," somehow wandered upon the refugee slaves. He "labored with the slaves to make leave of their evil designs" but only two of the refugees returned to De Soto. When Alimamos arrived back at the camp with the refugees who had decided to return, "the Governor wished to hang them" (Jameson, p. 177). [paragraph 6] However, the horseman also made another report. He stated that "The Cacica remained in Xualla, with a slave of Andre de oncelas,(the Portuguese jp) who would not come with him (Alimamos), and that it was very sure that they lived together as man and wife, and were to go together to Cutafichiqui." (Jameson, p. 177)

The Cutafichiqui were on the Pee Dee River - deAyllon's settlement was on Winyah Bay - Pee Dee River -- deSoto was on the Pee Dee River -- these Native Americans were mixed long before anyone got to Jamestown. And the Melungeons said they came from the Pee Dee River and were Portuguese who mixed with the Indians?

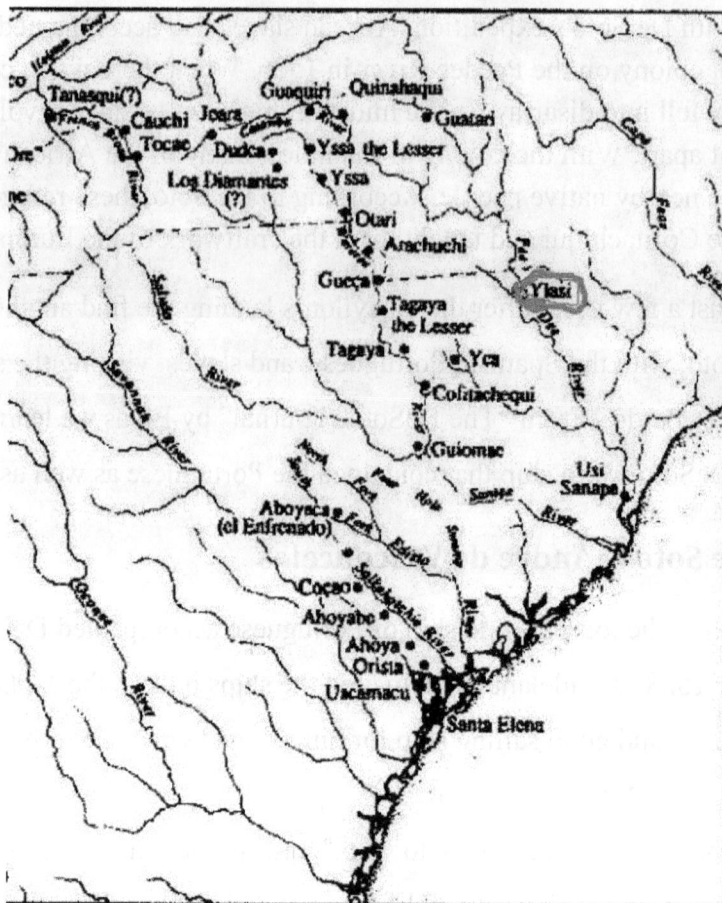

Figure 21 Map: Portuguese Settlements and Exploration Party Camps

TRUE RELATION OF THE HARDSHIPS SUFFERED BY GOVERNOR HERNANDO DE SOTO & CERTAIN PORTUGUESE GENTLEMEN DURING THE DISCOVERY OF THE PROVINCE OF FLORIDA.

NOW NEWLY SET FORTH BY A GENTLEMAN OF ELVAS. 1557

As Luis de Moscoso passed through Elvas, Andre de Vasconcelos spoke with him, and requested him to speak to Don Hernando de Soto in his behalf, and gave him patents issued by the marques de Vilareal, conferring on him the captaincy of Ceuta, so that he might exhibit them. The adelantado saw these and found out who he [Vasconcelos] was and wrote him promising that he would favor him in every way and would give him men to command in Florida.

HOW THE PORTUGUESE WENT TO SEVILLE AND THENCE TO SAN LUCAR; AND HOW THE CAPTAINS WERE APPOINTED OVER THE SHIPS, AND THE MEN WHO WERE TO GO IN THEM DISTRIBUTED. (The DeSoto Chronicles)

"The Portuguese left Elvas on the 15th of January. They reached Seville on St. Sebastian's eve and went to the governor's lodging. They entered the patio upon which looked some balconies where he was. He looked down and went to meet them at the stairs where they went up to the balconies. When they were up, he ordered chairs to be given them so that they might be seated. Andre de Vasconcelos told him who he and the other Portuguese were and how they had all come to accompany him and to serve him on his voyage. He [i.e. Soto] thanked him and appeared well pleased with their coming and proffer. The table being already laid, he invited them to eat; and while they were eating, he directed his majordomo to find lodgings for them near his inn. From Seville, the adelantado went to San Liicar with all the men that were to go with him. He ordered a muster to be held, to which the Portuguese went armed with very splendid arms, and the Castilians very elegantly, in silk over silk, and many plaits and slashes. As such finery was not pleasing to the governor on such an occasion, he ordered a muster to be held on the next day and for every man to appear with his armor. "

"To this the Portuguese came as at first, armed with very excellent armor, and the governor set them in order near the standard borne by his alferez. Most of the Castilians wore poor and rusty coats of mail, and all [wore] helmets and carried worthless and poor lances. Some of them managed to get a place among the Portuguese. Thus they passed in review, and those who were to the liking of Soto and whom he wished were counted and enrolled and went with him to Florida. Those who went numbered in all six hundred men. He had already bought seven ships and had placed in them the provisions necessary, appointed captains, and assigned his ship to each captain, giving each one a list of the men he was to take."

HOW THE ADELANTADO AND HIS MEN LEFT SPAIN AND ARRIVED AT THE CANARY ISLANDS, AND AFTERWARD AT THE ANTILLES.

In the month of April, of the year 1538, the adelantado delivered the ships over to the captains who were to go in them. He took a new and good sailing ship for himself and gave one to Andre de Vasconcelos, in which the Portuguese went.

The Lady of Cofitachiqui and Her Husband the 'Slave'

As they were on their journey, the Lady of Cofitachiqui "left the road, with the excuse of going in the thicket, where, deceiving them, she so concealed herself that for their entire search she could not be found." De Soto, frustrated in his quest to find her, moved on to Guaxule (Jameson, 1907, p. 176).

Alimamos, a horseman of De Soto who "got lost," somehow wandered upon the refugee slaves. He "labored with the slaves to make leave of their evil designs" but only two of the refugees returned to De Soto. When Alimamos arrived back at the camp with the refugees who had decided to return, "the Governor wished to hang them" (Jameson, p. 177). [paragraph 6] However, the horseman also made another report. He stated that "The Cacica remained in Xualla, with a slave of Andre de Vasconcelas,(the Portuguese jp) who would not come with him (Alimamos), and that it was very sure that they lived together as man and wife, and were to go together to Cutafichiqui"

Biedma's version: RELATION OF THE ISLAND OF FLORIDA by Luys Hernandez de Biedma with the Hernando de Soto Expedition

DESOTO's FLORIDA LANDING

"We departed from here for the town of Cofitachique, which was two days' journey from this little village. It was on the bank of a river that we believe was the river of Santa Elena, where the licenciado Ayllon was. Having arrived at this river, the lady of the town sent us a niece of hers, and some Indians brought her on a litter with much prestige. And she sent a message to us that she was delighted that we had come to her land and that she would give us whatever she could and had, and she sent a string of pearls of five or six strands to the Governor. She gave us canoes in which we crossed that river and divided with us half of the town. She was with us three or four days and then went away to the woods.

The Governor sent people to look for her, and when she could not be found, he opened a temple that was there, where the important people of that land were buried, and we gathered from there a quantity of pearls; there must have been up to six and a half or seven arrobas of them, although they were not good because they were damaged through being below the ground and placed amidst the adipose tissue of the Indians. Here we found buried two Castilian axes for cutting wood, and a rosary of beads of jet and some margaritas of the kind that they carry from here [Spain] to barter with the Indians. All this we believed they had obtained from barter with those who went with the licgnciado Ayllon."

Indian women - deSoto & DNA

Recorded by the Gentleman Elvas

"They went over a swampy land where the horsemen could not go. A half league [1] from camp they came upon some Indian huts near the river; [but] the people who were inside them plunged into the river. They captured four Indian women. Juan Rodriguez Lobillo

---

[1] Spanish customary units. There are a number of Spanish units of measurement of length or area that are now virtually obsolete (due to metrication). They include the vara, the cordel, the league and the labor. The units of area used to express the area of land are still encountered in some transactions in land today. For example, the 'vara' is still used in Costa Rica when ordering lumber.

reached the camp with six men wounded, one of whom died. He brought the four Indian women whom he had captured in the quarters or huts. From there the governor sent two captains, each one in a different direction, in search of the Indians. They captured a hundred head, among Indian men and women. Of the latter, there, as well as in any other part where forays were made, the captain selected one or two for the governor and the others were divided among themselves and those who went with them.

The governor left Toalli on March 24. At supper time on Thursday he came to a little stream where a footbridge was made on which the men crossed. Benito Fernandez, a Portuguese, fell off it and was drowned. As soon as the governor had crossed the stream, he found a village called Achese a short distance on. Although the Indians had never heard of Christians they plunged into a river. A few Indians, men and women, were seized.

At the time of his departure, because of the importunity of some who wished more than was proper, he asked the cacique for thirty Indian women as slaves. The cacique answered that he would talk with his principal men; but one night, before returning an answer, all the Indians left the town. The governor ordered him to be summoned and he came immediately. After exchanging some verbal promises with the governor, he gave him the necessary tamemes and thirty Indian women as slaves."

JUAN PARDO 1566

"At Aracuchi, Pardo decided to divide his force, sending half on to Cofitachequi, while the other half traveled to Ylasi. Ylasi is clearly the same town as deSoto's Ilapi." p203 (The Forgotten Centuries - Charles Hudson)

In 1566 Juan Pardo and about 250 Spanish soldiers spent two years [two separate expeditions] exploring much of the same area as DeSoto building forts across the Southeast. One such town near Morganton, North Carolina [where many of the 'mixed race' families called home] has been under excavation since the early 2000s. These Forts; Guatari (Trading Ford), Joara (Morganton), two in the Appalachian Mountains and two in South Carolina were manned by Spanish soldiers, at least two were reported to have married into the Indian tribes.

Father Juan Rogel, a Jesuit, wrote from Havana in July 1568 that five of the Southeastern forts had fallen. He placed the blame on the Spanish soldiers' lust for Indian women. Spanish harassment of Indian women would complicate the Spanish conquest of North America for two more centuries. Spanish empire failed to conquer southeast - By Geitner Simmons. Originally published in the Salisbury Post, Salisbury, N.C. 1999

Trading Girls - John Lawson 1707

As for the Indian Women, which now happen in my Way; when young, and at Maturity, they are as fine-shap'd Creatures (take them generally) as any in the Universe. They are of a tawny Complexion; their Eyes very brisk and amorous; their Smiles afford the finest Composure a Face can possess; their Hands are of the finest Make, with small long Fingers, and as soft as their Cheeks; and their whole Bodies of a smooth Nature. They are not so uncouth or unlikely, as we suppose them; nor are they Strangers or not Proficients (Sic) in the soft Passion. They are most of them mercenary, except the married Women, who sometimes bestow their Favours also to some or other, in their Husbands Absence. For which they never ask any Reward. As for the Report, that they are never found inconstant, like the Europeans, it is wholly false; for were the old World and the new one put into a Pair of Scales (in point of Constancy) it would be a hard Matter to discern which was the heavier.

As for the Trading Girls, which are those design'd to get Money by their Natural Parts, these are discernable, by the Cut of their Hair; their Tonsure differing from all others, of that Nation, who are not of their Profession; which Method is intended to prevent Mistakes; for the Savages of America are desirous (if possible) to keep their Wives to themselves, as well as those in other Parts of the World. When any Addresses are made to one of these Girls, she immediately acquaints her Parents therewith, and they tell the King of it, (provided he that courts her be a Stranger) his Majesty commonly being the principal Bawd of the Nation he rules over, and there seldom being any of these Winchester-Weddings agreed on, without his Royal Consent. He likewise advises her what Bargain to make, and if it happens to be an Indian Trader that wants a Bed-fellow, and has got Rum to sell, be sure, the King must have a large Dram for a Fee, to confirm the Match.

These Indians, that are of the elder sort, when any such Question is put to them, will debate the Matter amongst themselves with all the Sobriety and Seriousness imaginable, every one of the Girl's Relations arguing the Advantage or Detriment that may ensue such a Night's Encounter; all which is done with as much Steadiness and Reality, as if it was the greatest Concern in the World, and not so much as one Person shall be seen to smile, so long as the Debate holds, making no Difference betwixt an Agreement of this Nature, and a Bargain of any other. If they comply with the Men's Desire, then a particular Bed is provided for them, either in a Cabin by themselves, or else all the young people turn out, to another Lodging, that they may not spoil Sport; and if the old People are in the same Cabia along with them all Night, they lie as unconcern'd, as if they were so many Logs of Wood. If it be an Indian of their own Town or Neighbourhood, that wants a Mistress, he comes to none but the Girl, who receives what she thinks fit to ask him, and so lies all Night with him, without the Consent of her Parents (5).

A New Voyage to Carolina; Containing the Exact Description and Natural History of That Country: Together with the Present State Thereof. And A Journal of a Thousand Miles, Travel'd Thro' Several Nations of Indians. Giving a Particular Account of Their Customs, Manners, &c. (spine) Voyage to Carolina. John Lawson LONDON: 1709.

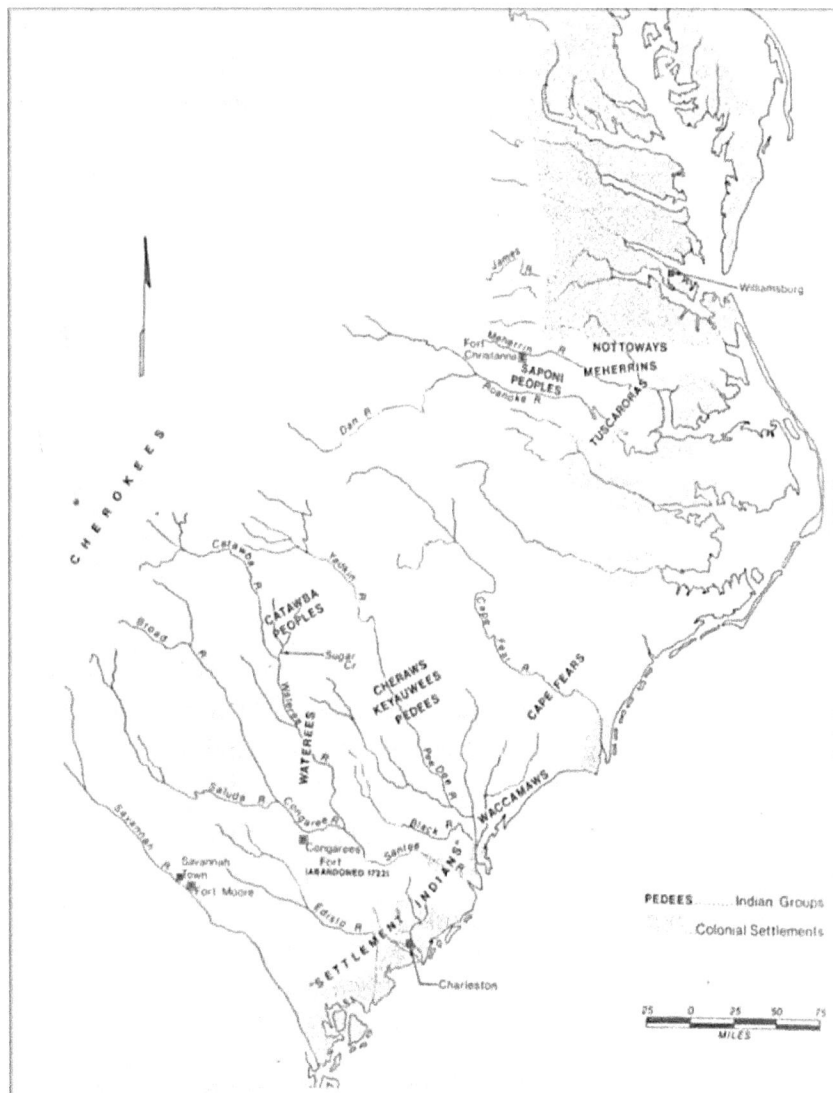

Figure 22 Map: Colonial Settlements Pee Dee Indian Groups

The Traders - Their 'Mixed Families' - DNA - & their Spanish, Portuguese and African Ancestors: CHIPPOAKES CREEK TO BLADEN COUNTY

As early as the mid 1600's in Virginia on Chippoakes Creek we find the Ivy, Chavis, Gibson, Sweat, Collins, Ivy etc., these families later found in Bladen/Robeson County all of whom claimed Portuguese descent and called Croatan/Lumbee, Redbone, Melungeons, etc. In 1754 Governor Dobbs requested reports from the militia commanders of North Carolina's counties. The Bladen militia submitted the following:

"The Colonel and Captain William Davis, who had a troop of light horse, both said "no Indians" in that county. Colonel Rutherford of that county, who was also the receiver-general, added this memorandum; "Drowning Creek, on the head of Little Peedee, fifty families, a mixed crew, a lawless people possess the lands without patent or paying quit rents; shot a surveyor for coming to view vacant lands, being enclosed in great swamps."

A number of ethnologists, archaeologists, historians, etc., have identified these 50 mixt families living on Drowning Creek as the ancestors of the Lumbee Indians. So who was living in Bladen County in 1754? The records show that these families who would later be called Lumbee, Melungeons, etc., were, in fact, living on Drowning Creek - Pee Dee River area in 1754.

While the report calls these people 'a mixed crew' without patent or paying rent we know that at least some of the families owned their land, their extended families and kinfolk living nearby 'without patents.'

12th December 1746: "Read the Petition of Gideon Gibson, shewing That the Pet'r has been a residenter in this Province ab't 15 years and never having taken up any Lands in this Province, and now willing to Cultivate some of his Majesty's vacant land thereon, humbly prays that a Warrant do Issue for laying out to him 50 acres in a place called the Duck pond on the south side of the Pee Dee River. Decem'r 12th 1746. The prayer was thereof was granted.

Read the Petiton of Gideon Gibson Jun'r shewing That the Pet'r has four Persons in Family viz Himself, his wife and two children for whom as yet not any Land has been assigned him and being willing to Cultivate and improve some of his Majesty's vacant land humbly prays that by virtue of Family right that 200 acres of vacant land be laid out to him at a place called the Duck pond on the south side of Pee Dee River where the Pet'r at pres't resides.... The prayer thereof was granted."

12 November 1747: "Gideon Gibson petitioned the South Carolina Council stating that he had been granted a warrant for 650 acres in the Welch Tract where he had settled fifteen years previous and had kept it as a cow pen with a servant on it for about two years. He had since settled in Persimmon Grove and had nine persons in his household: a wife, seven children and a slave."

12 Nov 1747: "Gideon Gibson had a Warrant for abt 650ac in the Welsh tract and settled it abt 15 years ago and kept it as a cowpen with a servant on it for about two years & paid tax for same, being the Plantation now of Colonel Pawley's and delivered up being in the Welch tract. And has since settled at a place called Persimon Grove and has nine persons in family to wit - wife, 7 children and one negro for which your Pet'r never had any land but as above expressed, your pet'r prays to order a warrant to run out the land for himself and family and that he may have grants for same. Sig: Gideon (his mark) Gibson. Prayer granted. Ordered that the Deputy Secretary prepare a Warrant for 450ac. [Page 54: Petitions for Land from SC Council Journals, Vol I 1734/5-1748, Brent H. Holcomb, SCMAR, Columbia, SC, 1996, p 297]"

27 August 1753: "John Johnson Jr. entered 100 acres in Bladen County, North Carolina on the north side of Pugh's marsh whereon John Oxendine was then living. (Bladen County Land Entries #805). In 1759, he and two of his sons, John and Benjamin, lived in the Drowning Creek area of Bladen County, North Carolina which is the upper part of the Lumbee River area.

1754: Moses Bass was living near "the drains of Drowning Creek" on 1 February 1754 when Robert Carver entered 100 acres there [Philbeck, Bladen County Land Entries, nos. 677, 934]

1755: Thomas Ivey 300 acres on Drowning Creek where James Roberts formerly lived on 26 September 1755 [Philbeck, Bladen County Land Entries, nos. 974, 1048].

1754: Robert Sweat was granted 100 acres on Wilkerson Swamp near the Little Pee Dee River on 23 Dec 1754. This land adjoined the land of Joshua Perkins and was sold to Phillip Chavis.

Gilbert Sweat Case 21 Aug. 1829…St. Landry's Parish LA… Testimony of Joshua Perkins – Gilbert Sweat was born about 1756 in what was then Marion Co. SC on the Pee Dee River. About the year 1777, Perkins helped Sweat run away with Francis Smith, the wife of J.B. Taylor. Sweat moved from South Carolina to Tenn., to North Carolina to Big Black River, Mississippi and arrived in LA in 1804.

31 Mar 1753 Grant: To Daniel Willis, 300 acres in Bladen County on Saddletree Swamp adjacent Thomas Ivey [Colony of NC 1735-1764 Abstracts of Land Patents, Margaret M. Hofman, Vol. 1, p10, grant #111]

17 November 1753 Bladen County land which had been surveyed for Gideon Gibson in North Carolina on the north side of the Little Pee Dee River was mentioned in a Bladen County land entry [Philbeck, Land Entries: Bladen County, no. 904].

20 Feb 1754 Land Entry: Thomas Ivey enters 150 acres including his own improvements, on the 5 Mile Branch in Bladen County. [North Carolina Land Entries 1753-1756, A. B. Pruitt, Vol. 2, p127] "

"Fayetteville, North Carolina --- Dec. 2, 1845 -- Extreme Old Age -- A writer in the Highland Messenger says he had just visited Spencer Bolton, a resident of Buncombe County, who is now almost one hundred and ten years of age! He was born (1735) on Big Pee Dee River, in South Carolina, and is still sound in mind and body. He was in several skirmishes under Marion in the Revolutionary war. Has been for 65 years a member of the Methodist Church. Health generally good. In early life, principal diet bread, rice, potatoes, and milk; slept on straw beds; generally up before day-light; and much accustomed to bathe in cold water. To the influence of these habits he ascribes his long life. (Spencer Bolton is father of Solomon Bolton who was identified as a Portuguese/Melungeon in 1874 court case in Hamilton County, Tennessee."

These are but a few of the families who were known by Melungeon, Redbone, Croatans/Lumbee, Brass Ankles etc., they lived on the Pee Dee River, went to court and proved by the testimony of their neighbors, tax collectors, the sheriff, etc., that they descended from the Portuguese people.

"Whole Indian nations have melted away like snowballs in the sun before the white man's advance. They leave scarcely a name of our people except those wrongly recorded by their destroyers. Dragging Canoe ~ Treaty of Sycamore Shoals – 1775

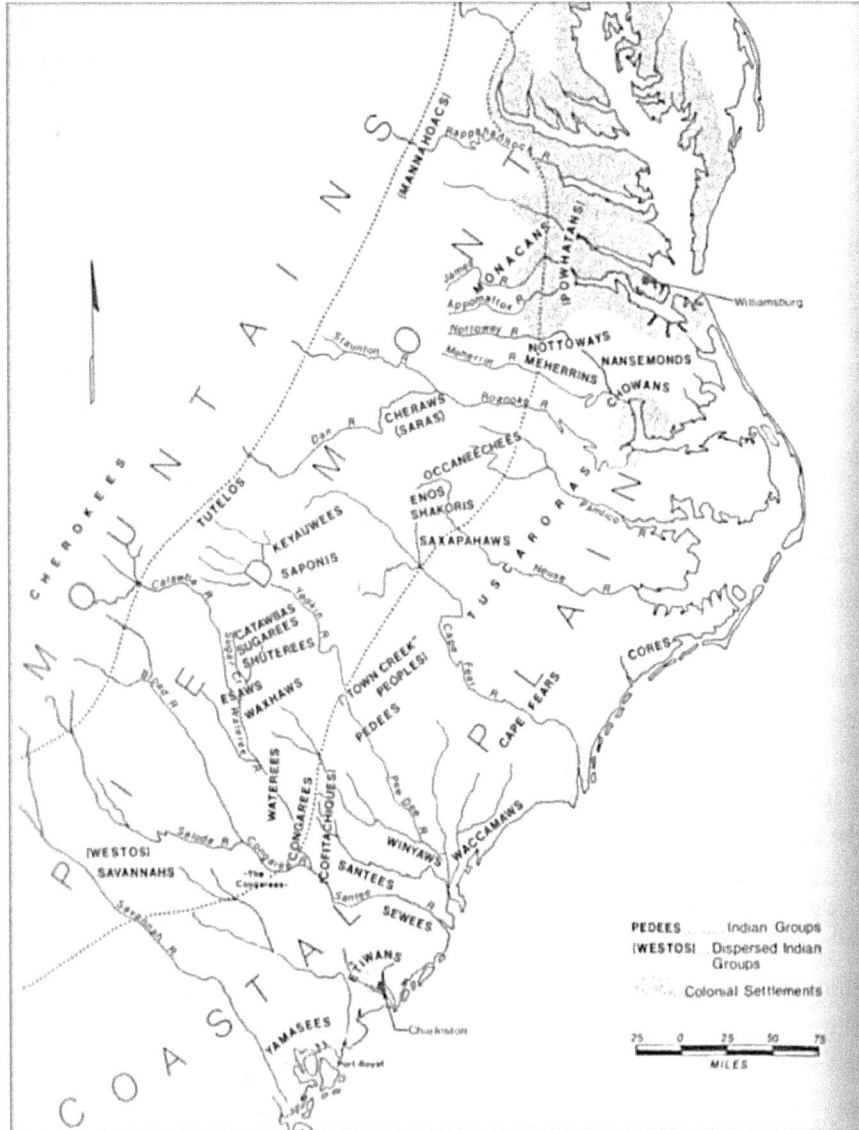

Figure 23 Map: Pee Dees Indian Groups

End Notes

Adventurer John Lawson sailed from Cowes, England on May 1, 1700. An acquaintance who had been to America assured Lawson "that Carolina was the best country I could go to," and the young traveler was eager to see Britain's colony in the New World.

After a harried ocean voyage lasting nearly three months, Lawson's ship put in at New York Harbor. In late August, following a brief stay in New York, Lawson sailed for the bustling colonial port of Charleston. By December, the young adventurer had been given a daunting task. The Lords Proprietors — wealthy Englishmen appointed by the Crown to govern the settlement of Carolina — assigned John Lawson to conduct a reconnaissance survey of the interior of the province.

The Carolina backcountry at that time was an unknown and forbidding place. There were no adequate maps, and little was known about the Native American inhabitants of the region — including their attitude toward English settlers.

The Lawson Expedition

On December 28, 1700, Lawson — with a party of five Englishmen and various Indian guides picked up along the way — set out on a brave journey through the wastes of Carolina. Following the Santee and Wateree Rivers through southern Carolina, Lawson's party met with members of several Native American tribes in the region, including the Santee, Congaree, Wateree, and Waxhaw Indians.

In late January 1701, the Lawson expedition crossed into what is now North Carolina in the neighborhood of present-day Charlotte. More tribes were encountered — including the "Esaws," Sugaree, and Catawba Indians — and the explorers resumed their journey along the famous Trading Path. This trade route stretched north and eastward through the interior of the province.

The group crossed the Uwharrie River on February 5, and came to the village of Keyauwee Town. Three days later most of Lawson's party decided to travel straight to Virginia from Keyauwee Town. Lawson and a companion, however, resolved to continue their trek through Carolina. The route eastward from Keyauwee Town led Lawson across a tangle of creeks and rivers to Occaneechi Town, near present-day Hillsborough. At Occaneechi, Lawson picked up a trusted Indian named Enoe Will, who agreed to guide the explorer to the English settlements along the coast.

With Enoe Will and several other Indians, Lawson's group left the Trading Path, crossed the Eno River at Ocanneechi Town, proceeded to the village of Adshusheer (near present-day Durham), and crossed the falls of the Neuse River on February 18. Two days later they reached the "hunting quarter" of 500 Tuscarora Indians.

Aided by several of these Indians, the party made its way through the densely settled Tuscarora country. They passed near the present site of Goldsboro, crossed Contentnea Creek near present-day Grifton, and crossed the Tar River at what is now Greenville. Finally, on February 23, 1700, the explorers reached the English settlements on the "Pampticough" River, in the vicinity of what is now Washington, North Carolina. Lawson's excursion came to an end at the Pamlico River, at the plantation of a man named Richard Smith.

In the dead of winter, guided solely by Native Americans, the expedition had lasted 59 days and covered some 550 miles through the forbidding Carolina backcountry. And the curious Lawson, with a keen eye for detail, recorded a wealth of information along the way.

Soon after settling in the Pamlico region, Lawson built himself a house near the Indian town of Chatooka — future site of the town of New Bern. The adventurer noted that his home "stood on a pretty high Land and by a creek-side," a stream that is now known as Lawson's Creek.

John Lawson's Journey through Carolina

The Co-Founder of Bath Town

Within a few years of arriving in Carolina, John Lawson acquired a tract of land in the Pamlico region along the banks of Old Town Creek (now known as Bath Creek).

Bath County had been established in 1696, and its large landowners included Joel Martin, Simon Alderson, Nicholas Daw, and David Perkins. Sometime around 1704 or 1705, Perkins transferred about 60 acres of his property to Lawson, Martin, and Alderson.

The Town of Bath was established by an act of the General Assembly on March 8, 1705 — thus becoming North Carolina's first incorporated town. Lawson, Martin, and Nicholas Daw were the village's first commissioners.

The first recorded sale of lots in Bath was on September 26, 1706 — and John Lawson was one of the purchasers. Lawson's layout of the town called for 71 lots, each of which contained one acre and four poles. Lawson bought two lots at the tip of the peninsula, and made his home in Bath.

Lawson was active in Bath's political and economic life and that of the county. From January 1706/7 to August 1708, he served as clerk of court and public register of "Pampticough Precinct."

In 1707, Lawson, Chief Justice Christopher Gale, and Dr. Maurice Luellyn erected a "horse-mill" in Bath. The agreement between these men — three of Bath's most prominent citizens — stipulated that "no owner would grind any grain but what was properly for his own family's use nor grant permission for anyone else to grind their grain at the mill without the consent of the owners."

A Writer and Historian

A gentleman by birth, John Lawson was a well-educated man. During his long journey through Carolina, Lawson had kept an extensive journal. In addition to recording detailed notes on the varied and abundant flora and fauna of the region, he also started a small vocabulary of Native American language.

Though Lawson claimed that his reason for coming to America involved a desire to travel, there is good reason to believe that he may have been urged or hired to make the trip by James Petiver. Petiver was a London apothecary and the greatest collector of botanical specimens of his era. The two corresponded frequently, and Petiver claimed that Lawson was "the most knowledgeable" of the apothecary's correspondents in America. And the volume of data collected by Lawson was thorough, indeed.

Lawson also engaged in surveying work, and soon became the deputy of Edward Moseley, the province's surveyor-general. He would eventually succeed Moseley in the post.

Early in 1709, Lawson sailed back to England to oversee the publication of his book, A New Voyage to Carolina. The provincial historian had assembled his notes and observations into a comprehensive narrative. The massive work contained an introduction, Lawson's journal entries, a general description of North Carolina, notes on the present state of the colony, the natural history of Carolina, and detailed observations on North Carolina's Native American population. This monumental "history" was the only book to come out of proprietary North Carolina. It is one of the most valuable early volumes on North Carolina, and is one of the best travel accounts of the early eighteenth-century American colonies.

In July 1709, the Lords Proprietors appointed Lawson and Edward Moseley as commissioners for North Carolina's interests in the long-running border dispute with the colony of Virginia. (When the final line was run in 1728, it was very close to Lawson's observations).

For most of the decade that Lawson lived in North Carolina, the colony was in political turmoil and confusion. Efforts to establish the Church of England and legal discriminations against Quakers and other "dissenters" caused tension that soon reached a boiling point. The conflict spawned "Cary's Rebellion" in 1710, but Lawson managed to steer clear of political controversy during this time.

An Untimely End

With Christopher Von Graffenried, Lawson also co-founded the town that became known as New Bern. He persuaded Graffenried, leader of the Swiss and Palatine colonists at New Bern, and Christopher Gale, receiver-general of the colony (his friend and neighbor at Bath), to accompany him on an exploring trip up the Neuse River. Gale, however, did not accompany the party because his wife and brother were sick with yellow fever.

While Graffenried eventually returned from this expedition, John Lawson did not. The party fell into trouble with the powerful Tuscarora Indians, and Lawson was savagely executed. Thus the famous explorer became the first casualty in a terrible war, as the disgruntled Native Americans sought revenge against injustices brought by white settlers.

Elvas, The Gentleman of. "The DeSoto Chronicles; TRUE RELATION OF THE HARDSHIPS SUFFERED BY GOVERNOR HERNANDO DE SOTO &." By Translated James Alexander Robertson. Florida State Historical Society, 1933.

Hofman, Margaret M. "Colony of NC 1735-1764 Abstracts of Land Patents." Vol. Vol. 1. n.d. 10, grant #111.

Holcomb, Brent H. "Petitions for Land from South Carolina Council Journals." *VOL I 1734-35-1748*. Columbia, South Carolina: SCMAR, 1996.

J.G.M. Ramsey, A.M., M.D. *Extracted from "The First American Frontier, The Annals of Tennessee to the End of The Eighteenth Century.".* Philadelphia: Lippincott, Grambo & Co., 1853.

Aptheker, Hebert. *American Negro Slave Records.* New York: International Publishers, 1943-1993.

Biedma, Luys Hernandez de. "Bieda with the Hernando DeSoto Expedition: RELATION OF THE ISLAND OF FLORIDA by Luys Hernandez de Biedma with the Hernando de Soto xpedition." In *The Conquest of Florida.* 1544.

"Bladen County Land Entries." no. #805. n.d.

Charles Hudson, Carmen Chaves Tesser. *The Forgotten Centuries: Indians and Europeans in the American South, 1521-1704.* University of Georgia Press, 1994.

Congress, Library of. *History in Photos.* Washington, 1915.

Williamson, Hugh. *The History of North Carolina, 1735-1819.* Vol. 1. n.d.

Lawson, John. "A New Voyage to Carolina; Containing the Exact Description and Natural History of That Country: Together with the Present State Thereof. And A Journal of a Thousand Miles, Travel'd Thro' Several Nations of Indians." London: Manners, & c., 1709.

Pruitt, A. B. "North Carolina Land Entries 1753-1756." Vol. Vol. 2. n.d. 127.

Simmons, Geitner. *Spanish Empire Failed to conquer Southeast.* North Carolina: Salisbury Post, 1999.

McPherson, O.M. *Indians of North Carolina:Letter from the Secretary of the Interior.* Vol. 2. Washington, D.C.: U.S. Government Printing Office, n.d.

Redbones and Redbone Communities

By Stacy R Webb

Figure 24 Ramsey Sumter Co., SCOct. 17th 1891

Clerk of the Court

Dear Sir: During the past summer an account of a "Redbone" riot in your parish was published in the newspaper in South Carolina we have a rather peculiar people called "Redbones"-a people in which I am interested. I would like to know what kind of people are the "Redbone" of your State. Any information about them which you send me will be appreciated.

I wrote to the Sheriff of your parish about the Redbones, but my letter has never been answered.

I hope that you will excuse a stranger troubling you. I write because I really desire to hear from you.

Sincerely yours

McDonald Furman

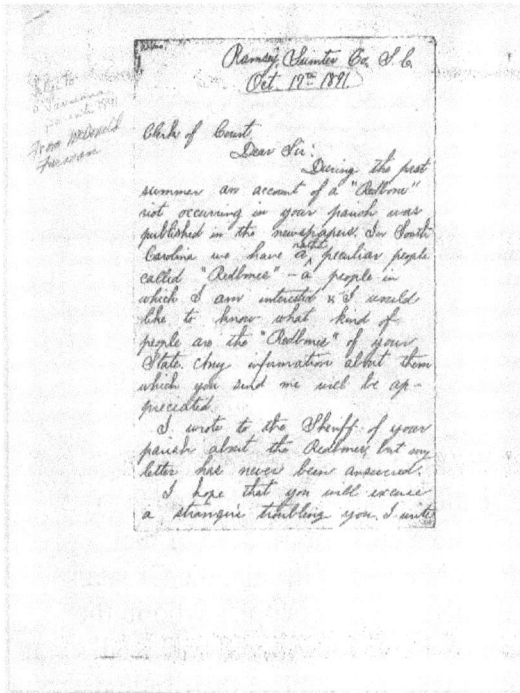

Figure 25 "The Redbones are a mixture of blacks, whites and Indians with the laziness of the negro, and the savage vindictiveness of the Indian " Thad Hays, Clerk

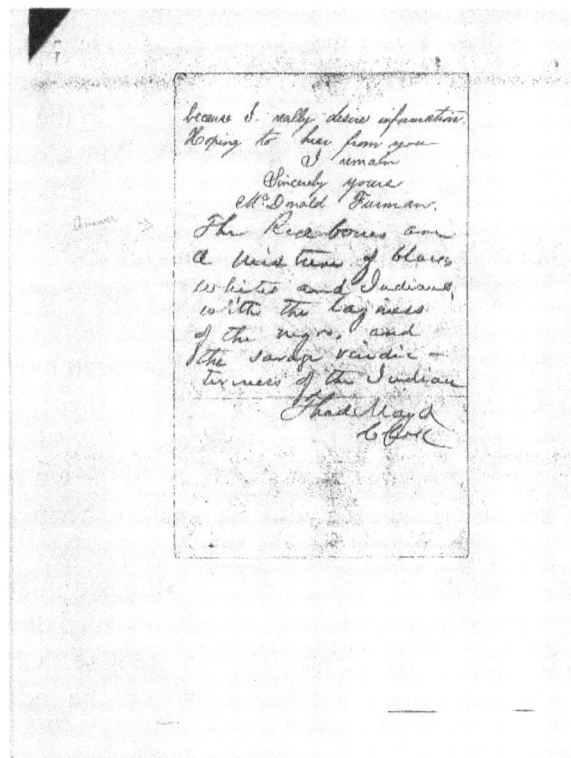

Figure 26 James Mooney article "Phase in Ethnology"

Washington Post
1902
PHASE IN ETHNOLOGY
Mr. James Mooney Investigates Early Portuguese Settlements.

Mr. James Mooney, who has just returned from Indian Territory, where he has been making a study of the Kiowa tribe for the Bureau of Ethnology, has also during his career as an anthropologist done considerable work in the way of investigating the Portuguese settlements along the Atlantic coast of the United States, a subject about which less is known than most any other phase of the modern ethnology of America. All along the southern coast there are scattered here and there bands of curious people, whose appearance, color, and hair seem to indicate a cross or mixture of the Indian, the white, and the negro. Such, for example, are the Pamunkeys of Virginia, the Croatan Indians of the Carolinas, the Malungeons of Tennessee, and numerous other peoples who in the days of slavery were regarded as free negroes and were frequently hunted down and enslaved. Since the war they have tried hard by act of legislature and other wise to establish their Indian ancestry. Wherever these people are found there also will the traveler or investigator passing through their region encounter the tradition of Portuguese blood or descent, and many have often wondered how these people came to have such a tradition or, in view of their ignorance, how they came to even know of the name of Portugal or the Portuguese. The explanation is, however, far simpler than one might imagine. In the first place, the Portuguese have always been a seagoing people, and according to Mr. Mooney, who has looked up the subject, the early records of Virginia and the Carolinas contain notices of Portuguese ships having gone to wreck on the coasts of these States and of the crews settling down and marrying in with Indians and mulattoes.

Moreover, there are records of Portuguese ships having sailed into Jamestown Bay as early as 1655, and since then there has been more or less settlement of Portuguese fishermen and sailors from Maine to Florida. Now it has been the history of the Portuguese race that wherever they settled they mixed in with the darker peoples forming the aboriginal populations of the countries occupied by Portuguese settlers, and this is the reason and cause of the Portuguese admixture among the tribes along the coast of the United States. In further proof of this he calls attention to the case of a colony of Portuguese fishermen who settled on the coast of Massachusetts a few years ago. These settlers have nothing whatever to do with the white or Yankee population around them, but are intermarrying and intermixing among and with the small remnant of the Narragansett Indians who have survived down to the present day. In short, it has been the history of the Portuguese that wherever they settled along the Atlantic coast they have intermixed and intermarried among the remnants of the Indian tribes that were once the sole proprietors of that region.

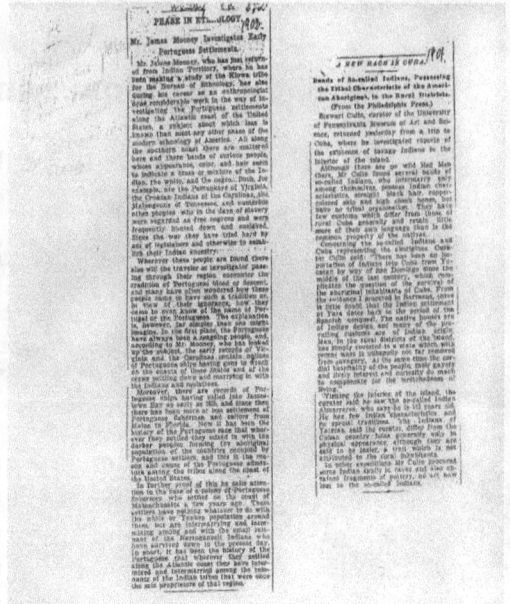

Figure 27 Document: The Name of Goins

Ramsey, Privateer Township,
April 29, 1897

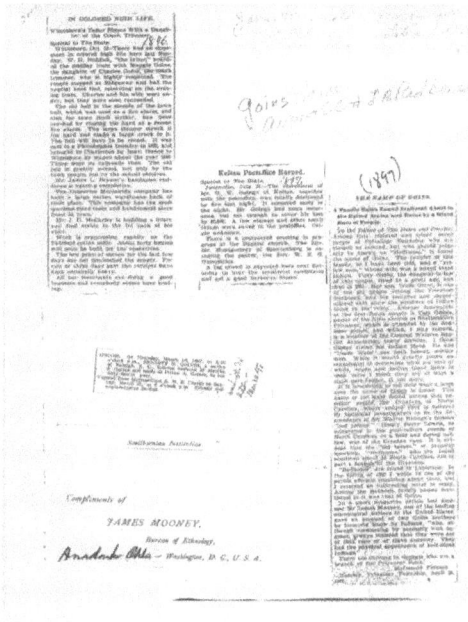

A Family Name Found about in the United States and Borne by Mixed Race People. To the editor of the News and Courier: among that isolated and mixed breed people of Privateer Township who are classed as colored but who should properly be known as "Redbones" is found the name Goins. The founder of this family, so I have been told, was a "yellow man" whose wife was a mixed breed Indian. Vicey goins, the daughter-in-law of this couple lived to a great age, and died in 1887. Her son, Wade Goins is one of the people among the Privateer Redbones, and his features are copper-colored skin show the presence of Indian blood in his veins. Another Privateer, which is attended by the Redbone people, and and which, I might remark, is a member of the Colored Wateree Baptist Association. lower division. I think Gibbes, shows his Indian blood. He and "Uncle Wade" are both honest, and worthy men. While it would greatly puzzle an ethnologist to determine what per cent of white, negro and Indian blood flows through in their veins I think they are at least a sixth part Indian, if not more.

It is interesting to see over what a large area the name Goins is found. This name is (or was) found among that peculiar people, the Croatans of North Carolina, which unique race is believed by historical investigators to be the descendants of Sir Walter Raleigh's famous "lost colony." Henry Berry Lowrie, so celebrated in the post bellum annals of North Carolina as a bold and daring outlaw, was of the Croatan race. It is evident the the "old issues" or, properly speaking, "Redbones" who are found in South Carolina, are in part a branch of the Croatans.

"Redbones" are found in Louisiana. In the spring of 1893 I wrote to one of the parish officials inquiring about them, and I received an interesting letter in reply. Among the Redbone family names mentioned it was that of Goins.

In a short magazine article last summer Mr James Mooney, one of the leading ethnological writers in the United States, gave an account of two Goins brothers he formerly knew in Indiana, "who, although associating by necessity with negroes, always insisted that they were not of that race or of slave ancestry. They had the physical appearance of half-blood Indians." There are Goins in Georgia, who are a branch of the Privateer Stock.

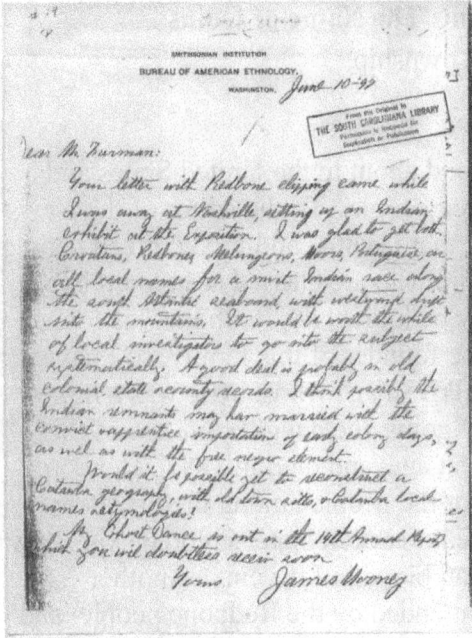

Figure 28 Document: Smithsonian Institution Bureau of American Ethnology June 10, 1897

Dear Mr. Furman,

Your letter with Redbone clipping came while I was away at Nashville, setting up an Indian exhibit in the expedition. I was glad to get the Croatans, Redbones, Melungeons, Moors, Portuguese are all local names for a mixt Indian race along the South Atlantic Seaboard with westward drift to the mountains. It would be worth the while of local investigators to go into the subject systematically. A good deal of is probably in old colonial state or county records. I think possibly that Indian remnants may have married with the old convict & apprentice of the early colonial days as well as with the free negro element. Would it be possible get to reconstruct a Catawba geography with old town sites and Catawba local names ethnologies?

My Ghost Dance is not in the 14th reply which you will doubtless receive soon. Yours, James Mooney

Figure 29 Document: Page 1 Treasurer's Office A. Rigmaiden, Treasurer Calcasieu Parish Lake Charles, La. May 6, 1893

Mr. McDonald Furman

    Ramsey, S.C.

Dear Sir in reply to yours of April 22nd I will state that I an not able to tell you how the name Redbone originated for the people who are called Red-bones, but I think the negros are the first to give them that name as they (the negros) have no use nor love for them and they do not like the negros any better. I suppose you know the kind of people who are called red bones they are neither white, nor black and as well as I can find out the oldest ones came from SC many years ago there is a great many of them in this parish & in Rapides and Vernon Parish some in other Parishes in this state & a good many in Texas too. Some of these

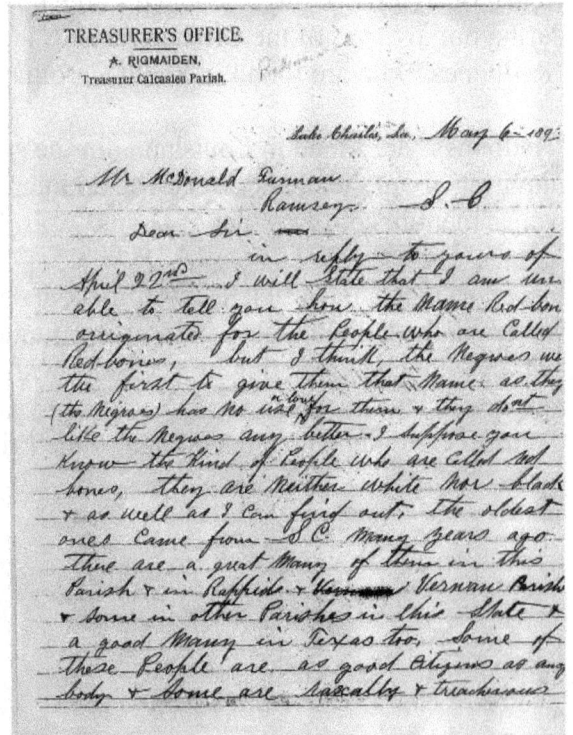

people are as good citizens as anybody & some are rascally and treacherous but

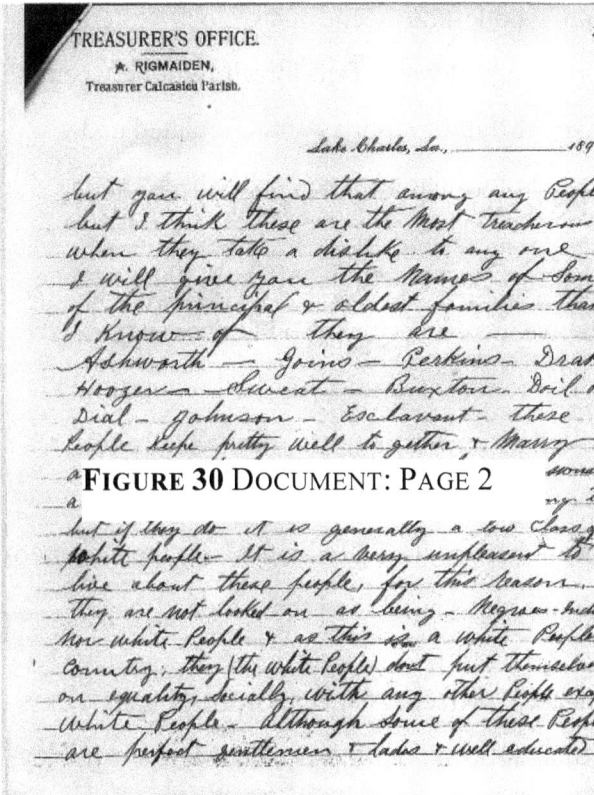

FIGURE 30 DOCUMENT: PAGE 2

Page 2 you will find that of any People but I think these are the most treacherous when they take a dislike to anyone I will give you the names of some of the principle & oldest families I know of they are----Ashworth—Goins---Perkins---Drake---Hooser—Sweat---Buxton---Doil or Dial—Johnson—Escalavant—these people keep pretty well together and marry among themselves mostly but occasionally a white man or woman marries among them but if they do it is generally a low class of white people. It is a very unpleasant to live about these people for the reason they are not looked on as negro-indian-or as white people and this is a white people country. They (white people) don't put themselves on the same equality socially or any other people except white people. Although some of these people are perfect gentlemen and ladies and well educated.

Page 3 I think they get along exceedingly well & peaceably , considering all of these drawbacks. I have given you as near the facts as I am able to trusty it will provide the desired information. Yours Truly, A. Rigmaiden

Fight Between Cattlemen and a Gang of Thieves and Roughs.

St Louis, August 4-A dispatch from Orange, Texas Says: Belder Sanders, who has just returned from Lake Charles, La. confirms the report of a riot at Lockmore & Co's ranch.

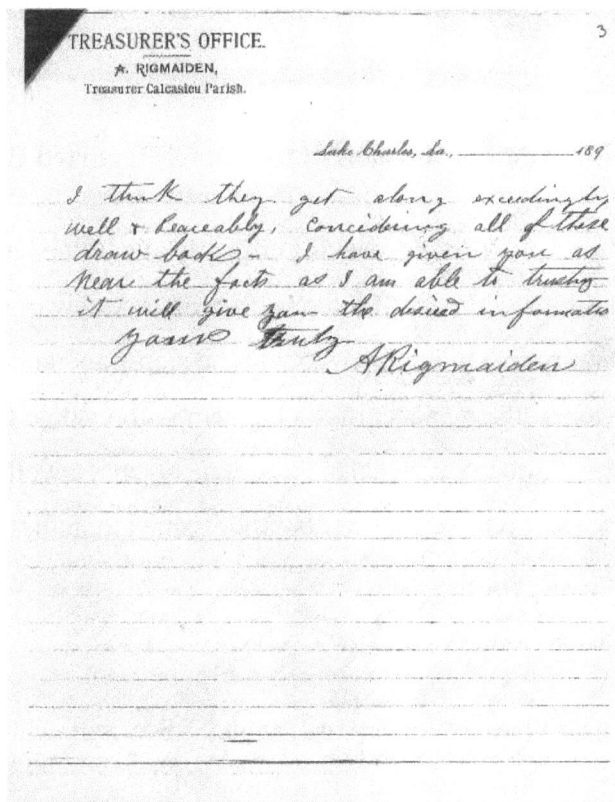

FIGURE 31 DOCUMENT: PAGE 3

The last account he heard was from a wounded man, who left the scene at 4 o'clock yesterday, who stated that fourteen men were killed and two missing. It was a free-for-all fight between the "Redbones" and the whites. Sanders stated that many different reports were circulated and nothing more authentic could be learned. Officers and physicians have gone to the scene.

Another account of the riot coming from West Lake, Louisiana, is to the effect that the emeute was caused by the breaking out of of an old feud between a band of robbers known as the Ashworth gang and the cattlemen of that section. The former it is said, had been committing depredations upon the community, and they had killed a number of cattle. They had been notified by the ranchmen to desist and leave the county, but the gang continued their proceedings, and at last they were caught and the fight began. The "Redbones" are the leaders of the cattlemen. A man named Webster led the gang of toughs and killed three men.

- A late report increases the number of wounded to sixteen. A special from Orange, Texas gives a partial list of the killed and wounded as follows: Killed-Dyson, Marion Markley, Lee Perkins and Owen Ashworth, all of the Redbone Gang, and Jesse Ward, one of the cattlemen. The wounded are: Willette Dupre and Lecomb. The latest reports are to the effect that everything is quiet. The coroner has gone to the scene and investigation is now going on.

Still Another Account of the Much Reported Bloody Affair in Calcasieu Parish, Louisiana.

Houston, Tex. August 5- Further details of the battle on Lockmoor & Co's tramway on Sunday says that a party of Redbones, a mongrel crew of mixed whites, Indians and negroes, about twenty five in number, went to the stores and announced that they would drive away Hooker Morris, the manager of the log camp, in revenge for an insult offered to two of the party. They were well armed and lead by Jessie Dyson, a well-known and desperate character. The white men, who had gathered about the same strength, were led by Jesse Ward. In the battle which ensued Ward killed Jesse Dyson, and was at once killed from behind, when the fight became general.

List of killed: Jesse Ward, white, T.S. Swap, white, Jesse Dyson, L.E. Perkins, Andrew Chariz, Owen Ashworth and Marion Markel.

Wounded: Dupre, Larcombo, keeper of the store and saloon, and his son was shot in the leg. Larcomb's wife ran into the woods with her children and escaped injury.

The complete list of wounded cannot be obtained, but about twenty are known to have been hurt. Sunday afternoon thirty Redbones came to camp after the bodies of the dead and dispersed the officers who were at the scene, and who, under threats, are organizing a strong force to storm the strongholds of the desperadoes. More trouble is feared. The above is the report of the morning fight.

In the afternoon it was reported at a store down the road that the Redbones were massacring the women and children and every one that came across the camp. Hearing this reinforcement went up from along the line of Calcasieu, Vernon and Shreveport road. In going up Mr T.T. Swan, an old and respected citizen of Calcasieu, was murdered from ambush. Excitement is running high, and more trouble maybe expected at any time. The log camps are situated about sixteen miles from Lockmoor & Co's mills, and about five hundred men are employed.

Senator Wade Hampton tells about a race of people in South Carolina called Redbones. Says he,

> "Their origin is unknown. They resemble in appearance the gypsies, but in complexion they are red. They have accumulated considerable property, and are industrious and peaceable. They live in small settlements at the foot of the mountains and associate with non but their own people. They are a proud and high spirited people. Caste is very strong among them. They enjoy life, visit the watering places and mountain resorts, but eat by themselves and keep by themselves. When the war broke out several of them enlisted in Hampton Legion, and when the legion reached Virginia there was a great outcry among the Virginians and the troops from other States against enlisting negroes. They did not resemble the African in the least, except in the cases where Africans had amalgamated with Indians. This intermixture, which is common in the Carolinas, produced marvelous results. It takes the kink out of the hair of the African, straightens his features and improves him in every way except temper. These Afro Indo people are devils when aroused and as slaves were hard to manage. In the first Bull Run battle they proved how well they could fight and all prejudices against them disappeared".

Who are the Redbones?

"They did not resemble the African in the least, except in the cases where Africans had amalgamated with Indians. This intermixture, which is common in the Carolinas, produced marvelous results. It takes the kink out of the hair of the African, straightens his features and improves him in every way except temper." **Dr. James Mooney**, Ethnologist Smithsonian Institute, Indian Affairs.

Redbone Communities

By Stacy R. Webb

The Redbone people can trace familial relationships to many Mixed blood Indian clans and tribes, including the Saponi, Oceenechi, Moors of Delaware (Nanticoke), Vann Dunk "Chief Red Bone" the Ramapough Indians of New York and New Jersey, the Cheroenhaka (Nottoway), Meherrin, Tuscarora, Ypsilanti Georgia, Chief Red Bone, Smiling Indians, Brass Ankles of Sumter South Carolina, The Melungeons, Lumbee, Choctaw and Choctoos (spoke Mobilian, and were mentioned in Dr. Sibley Indian agent notes at Opelousas District along the Calcasieu River, Louisiana), Cheraw of Pee Dee Region South Carolina, Smiling Indians, Ramsey's Privateer "Old Issue", Chickasaw, Creek, Seminole[2] Cherokee, (Lenape, Old Settlers, Chickamauga) , Shawnee, Kiowa and Coushatta, Apalachee (Apalachicola to Alabama to Rapides Parish), Adaesanos at Fort/Mission Los Adaes No Man's Land, Pakana Muscogee, Thompson Choctaw of Louisiana and East Texas, Saponi Settlements in Texas; Baratarian's of the Gulf Coast. This is not a complete list, more research is needed. Some families also were slave owners, and large ones at that. Some of the early Mississippi Territorial archives, Spanish records the movements of large amounts of slave into the colonies, from the No Man's Land, Natchez, and Port Gibson areas. Many brought them from the South Carolina Pee Dee region and Wateree District in the early 1800s to Louisiana and further into Texas and are listed among the Free Negro Slave Owner of South Carolina. Several of these men leaving slaves to their heirs in their estate. Don Marler wrote about these activities in his book, No Man's Land, *Backdoor to the Unites States.*

Redbone DNA results prove the most prevalent admixtures, White (European), Native American (varying degrees),South Asian matches with the Rom "Gypsy" Hindu Kush of North India and the Punjab region, Middle Eastern/Muslim Conquest

---

[2] The word *Seminole* is a corruption of *cimarrón*, a Spanish term for "runaway" or "wild one".

Palestinian/Egyptian/Turk/Tunisia (varying degrees), Spanish/Iberian (varying degrees), Mediterranean North African Rim (varying degrees) France and Italy, Pacific Islander Canary Islander (varying degrees), Aboriginal Australian, Papua New Guinea.

But, somewhere along the not so distant genetic tree, Redbones mixed heavily with the Rom Gypsy People, likely of the Old Colonial families brought to this country as religious and undesirable exiles from Europe during Spanish/French/Portugal/Italy & other European and North African and Mediterranean Rim countries to the new world as slaves, settlers, and soldiers to protect the Spanish and Portuguese forts and missions system. Weaver, Cooper, Banks, Mitchell, Nash/Ash surname to name the few we suspect. The Thompson returned with a Middle Eastern origin and some of our families illustrate a Moorish or Berber ancestral background. The Ashworth's heavily Armenian and Turkish admixture, with a European origin haplogroup assignment. Others show very high amounts of Native American, Greek and Guinea and Goa African both part of the Portuguese Empire. The Goynes returned with an Egyptian in haplogroup assignment. But, we feel every family should be researched and studied independently to get a more accurate picture of each family's origins, and admixtures. The Redbones are a colorful group whose history and ethnic origins are only now being studied and documented. Very little has been established about this small ethnic clan who appear in early Virginia records as Free African Americans, Free People of Color, Mestizo, Mulatto, Free Other and many other "classifications" applied to many people of other than White ancestry.

Moreover, the ever migrating Redbones were never enslaved and later in the lower colonies, and were a noted prosperous clan but for many obvious reasons were not always the White settlers nor the US Government allies. American and European power struggles in the colonial south were a force in and of themselves. Powerful struggles for premise, racial restriction and commitment to slavery, dominion over land and trade thrusting the Redbone into a nearly constant nomadic like migration spanning 1600-1900's.

Known Migrations and Settlement

Feud like ethnic wars burst out across the territories as White settlers encroached on Indian lands, causing the Redbone to keep on the move in waves of small bands and migrating familial clans. Lingering legend of pirate treasures and looted bounties of silver, and gold moving through the generations, but the earliest known legend is about the Redbone Cave full of Gold. The legend goes something like this, in about 1720, somewhere along the north bank of the Tennessee River close to Muscle Shoals, now in Colbert County and when Indians ruled the land of Alabama. A group of Chickasaw Indians took a trapper prisoner. The white trapper was placed in a cave for a short period of time, and while the trapper was held in the cave, as he reported later, the cave was full of gold and silver bars that went from the floor of the cave to the ceiling, along with chests overloaded and filled with golden figurines, jewels, silver and gold coins. A couple of finds have been discovered throughout the region and the quest for this treasure increased with each of these discoveries. "Close by the Natchez Trace Bridge in Colbert County, in 1971, two men discovered a gold ingot about the size of a brick; a farmer working a field south of Smithsonian in Lauderdale County found a gold bar that had either Indian or Spanish markings. Many people believe that both of these discoveries were from the treasure in Redbone Cave; however, there are many others that believe they came from different sources. If there have been any other finds no one is talking about them. As far, as anyone can tell, the treasure the trapper saw back in 1720 is still hidden away in Redbone Cave."

Ypsilanti, Georgia and in the Gulf of Mexico assisting the sly but debonair Lafitte Brothers, Jean and Pierre to rape the Spanish Crown of all her riches which dared to enter the Gulf of Mexico. The Barratrians, who smuggled slaves purchased by the pound and all the pirate loot they could load in their Pequions (small boat navigable through bayous and marshy lands). Purchasing the pirates plunders at the Lafitte's auction near Booty Island, just below New Orleans and later at Campeche on the Trinity River and at Galveston Island. The Redbones associated with such rebel characters as Jim and Resin Bowie who controlled most of the slave trade through No Man's Land. Later, William "Bill" E/Inglish who entered Texas from Arkansas with the Goyens, Williams and John Aaron Cherry Chary would replace these men as a land pirates and slave trader.

Figure 32 Portrait:Aaron Cherry/Chary "Leader of Jean Lafitt's Baratarians" Father-in-law of Roxaline Buxton, she married John Aaron Cherry/Chary the daughter of Alexander Buxton and Arminta Goins (Thomas and Nancy Johnson Goyens of South Carolina) all early Republic of Texas settlers via Louisiana and large slave owners. His descendants became Chief and principle men of the Coushatta Indian tribe in Texas, pictured below at an unveiling ceremony to honor ancestor Aaron Cherry and his service to the republic of Texas during the Texas Revolution. Aaron was named for a great uncle which has been a confusing issue for descendants. Aaron Cherry was born in Virginia (great uncle born in Ohio and associated with Cherokee traditionalists and Tories, Corn Silk's people) in 1746 and died in Liberty Co., Texas in 1856. He is buried at the Plantation Ranch located on the east side of the Trinity River near Romayor, Texas in north Liberty County. He served in the Revolutionary War out of Pennsylvania but little else is known of his service record. Many of his descendants are named along with Thomas and Nancy Johnson Goyens laid claim to Wm. "Bill" Goyens of Nacogdoches estate when legal notice appeared in 1937 Texas newspapers asking relative heirs to appear and settle land divisions in preparation of the flooding of Toledo Bend Reservoir.

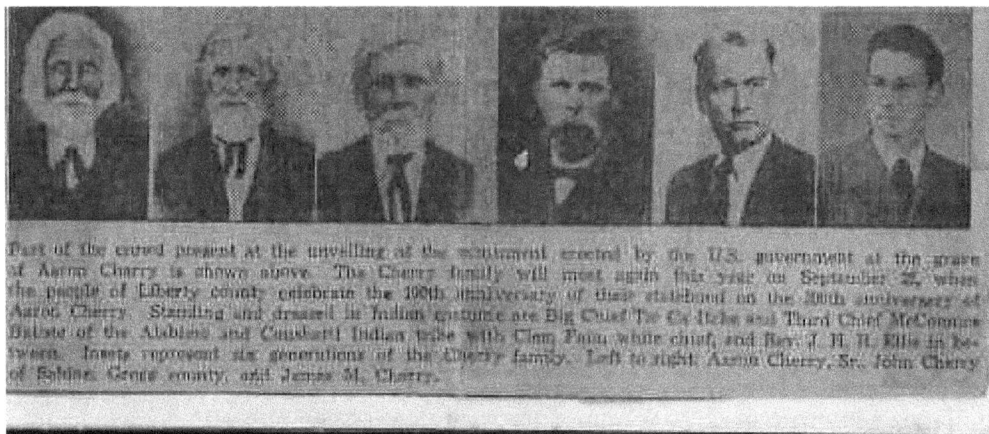

Figure 33 Newspaper Article: Unveiling Ceremony for Aaron Cherry's memorial Headstone 100th anniversary "descendant headmen Chiefs of the Alabama and Coushatta Indians tribe" heirs of Aaron Cherry. Liberty County, Texas

Stand Owners Along The Natchez Trace

By Stacy R. Webb 2007
Presentation and Handout Copies
Redbone Heritage Foundation
Melungeon Heritage Association presentation 2007

Origins of the Natchez Trace

The Old Natchez Trace, one of the oldest roadways in the world, saw its beginnings as a trail cut through the wilderness by herds of buffalo and other animals. It was later used by America's First People, the native tribes of Mississippi, who connected these series of trails to use as hunting and trade routes. The Natchez Trace was a 440-mile-long path extending from Natchez, Mississippi to Nashville, Tennessee, linking the Cumberland, the Tennessee and Mississippi rivers. It was used extensively by Native Americans and early Caucasian explorers as both a trade and transit route in the late 1700s and early 1800s. Today, the trail has been commemorated with the 444-mile-long Natchez Trace Parkway which follows the trail's approximate path. The three major tribes that the Natchez Trace was once home to were the Choctaw, Natchez and the Chickasaw. The Choctaws lived in central Mississippi. The Chickasaws lived in Northern Mississippi, close to Tupelo, MS. Their village consisted of huts (not tepees). The Natchez is an extinct tribe today, but in the 1600's, they lived in southern Mississippi. After Native Americans first began to settle the land, they began to blaze the trail further, until it became a relatively (for the time) well-worn path traversable by horse in single-file, though it may have been traveled in part before, particularly by famed Spanish explorer Hernando de Soto. These tribes continued to use the trail up until the time that the white European settlers of the new United States began forging west to claim the lands. Between 1699, when the French first arrived on the Mississippi gulf coast, to 1733, they had explored the area well enough to draw a map. The map showed an Indian trail running from Natchez to the Choctaw villages near present day Jackson, Mississippi, and then on to the Chickasaw villages in the northeastern part of the state. At this time the southern portion of the Natchez Trace was known as the "Path to the Choctaw Nation", while the northern part of the Trace was called "Chickasaw Trace". The first recorded Caucasian to travel the Trace in its entirety was an unnamed Frenchman in 1742, who wrote of the trail and its "miserable conditions." To Caucasians, who were not conditioned to the rigors of the journey, the assistance of Native Americans—specifically, the Cherokee, Choctaw and Chickasaw—was vital. The earliest formal usage of the trail, in fact, was for trade between those three Native American nations through which the trail passed. But these 3 Indian tribes were not the first humans to settle in this region. Archeological evidence has found in the many ceremonial mounds and village sites on the Trace, human habitation and remains which date back as long ago as 8000 years. Indian burial grounds called mounds still exist along the Trace. Indians were buried in these hill shaped graves, often a whole tribe together. Pottery, beads, and weapons were also buried in the graves.

The word "trace" is an old French word which meant a line of footprints or animal tracks. This is the first known use of the word "trace" being used to describe the trail. French traders, missionaries, and soldiers traveled over the old Indian trade route during this time. By the time the French arrived only a remnant of the Mississippian nations survived, and the Chickasaws claimed the Tennessee region along the river. In birch-bark canoes Pere Jacques Marquette and Louis Joliet passed by the future state in 1673. Robert Cavelier de La Salle and his men landed near the mouth of the Hatchie in 1682, where they constructed Fort Prudhomme. Following these early explorations, the French settled the middle Mississippi Valley in the early 1700s, trading down river to the French port of New Orleans. Bold and without racial arrogance, the French found the Indians sympathetic and their women attractive. Wherever they journeyed they established liaisons which ripened into marriages, and so was created a type of men who were bred by the fur trade and belonged to the trade and the company. As the trade moved westward, so did the men, and now the brides were no longer Huron but Cree and Chippewa (Salteaux). The hybrid offspring were sometimes known as Bois-Brulés (the people whose skin was like scorched wood) and sometimes as Métis (Mixedblood). Their patois was a French dialect out of Normandy and Picardy to which was added much Algonkian (Cree); the language grew more French as they dealt with outsiders and more Indian around the domestic fire. By the mid-eighteenth century they numbered about 30,000 and were neither Indian nor White, but exhibited the qualities of the hybrid. Not yet a people, a tribe, or a nationality, they shared a common status and an attachment to the fur trade. In the East and on the rivers, they used the canoe and traded in beaver; in the West and on the Great Plains, they hunted bison and developed the Red River Cart, on which they could haul hundreds of pounds of meat and hides. Many followed the Indian custom of having gardens along the river beds, and the European custom of running some livestock in a commons.

In the mid-1700's, the Ohio River, the Mississippi River and the Natchez Trace were important trade routes. Explorers, shopkeepers, and pioneers transported their goods down the Ohio and Mississippi Rivers to Natchez, Mississippi. They then used the Natchez Trace to travel back home. This allowed trade to increase because people in the central United States could sell their goods to people in the lower Mississippi region. In 1716, the French established Fort Rosalie at present-day Natchez, Mississippi. This fort was the first European settlement near the Natchez Trace. The Natchez Indians lived near the fort in the Grand Village of the Natchez. By 1743, the French wiped out the Natchez. A settlement near Fort Rosalie took the tribe's name. Today, this town is called Natchez, Mississippi. Natchez was an important town because it was located on the Mississippi River. First France ruled the town, then Spain, and then Britain. In 1783, the United States gained control after defeating Britain in the American Revolution. On April 7, 1798, the U.S. Congress established the Mississippi Territory, and Natchez became the territory's capital.

Once Europeans learned of the river, it became the target of diplomatic and territorial battles between the French, Spanish, and English, who viewed the river system as the key to an inland North American empire. In 1763 the Spanish gained control of New Orleans and attempted to assert their rights in the Tennessee region, which was also claimed by England and later the United States. In 1785, in an effort to establish land warrant claims, North Carolina sent Henry Rutherford to survey the "Western District." Beginning at Key Corner, he laid out land grants on Coal Creek Bluff. In 1795 the Spanish became concerned about American activities in the territory along the Mississippi and sent Don Miguel Gayoso de Lemos to erect Fort San Fernando de las Barrancas near the Chickasaw Bluffs at the mouth of the Wolf River. The struggle for control of the east bank ended with the Treaty of San Lorenzo (1795), and the Spanish dismantled Fort San Fernando in 1797. The United States took control of the Mississippi Valley in 1803 with the Louisiana Purchase. A brisk traffic in flatboats and keelboats carried Middle Tennessee pork, corn, whiskey, and hides down the Mississippi to New Orleans, where goods and boats were sold; crews returned home by way of the Natchez Trace. The first steamboat on the Mississippi, the New Orleans, passed by Tennessee in December 1811, and the crew witnessed the destructive force of the New Madrid earthquake. By 1816, the continued development of both Memphis and Jackson's Military Road, a direct line to New Orleans, Louisiana from Nashville, began shifting trade both east and west. A rich history, filled with brave explorers, dastardly outlaws and daring settlers.

Importance of stands along the Natchez Trace.

Stands gave people a place to eat and rest. Between 1800 and 1820, more than twenty stands were built along the trail. Although the stands were mostly shacks, they gave people a place to eat and rest. Smaller stands served greasy food and provided soggy cots. Travelers preferred to stay in these stands rather than eating nothing and sleeping on the ground.

The best known stands were Doak's Stand, French Camp, Mount Locust, and Red Bluff. Doak's Stand later became a stagecoach stop. French Camp was opened by Frenchman Louis Le Fleur in 1810. Mount Locust and Red Bluff were large enough to be called inns. Today, Mount Locust is the only restored stand remaining along the Natchez Trace.

The stands were still a dangerous place because of robbers. Travelers tried to protect themselves by burying their valuables before entering the stands or taking turns sleeping.

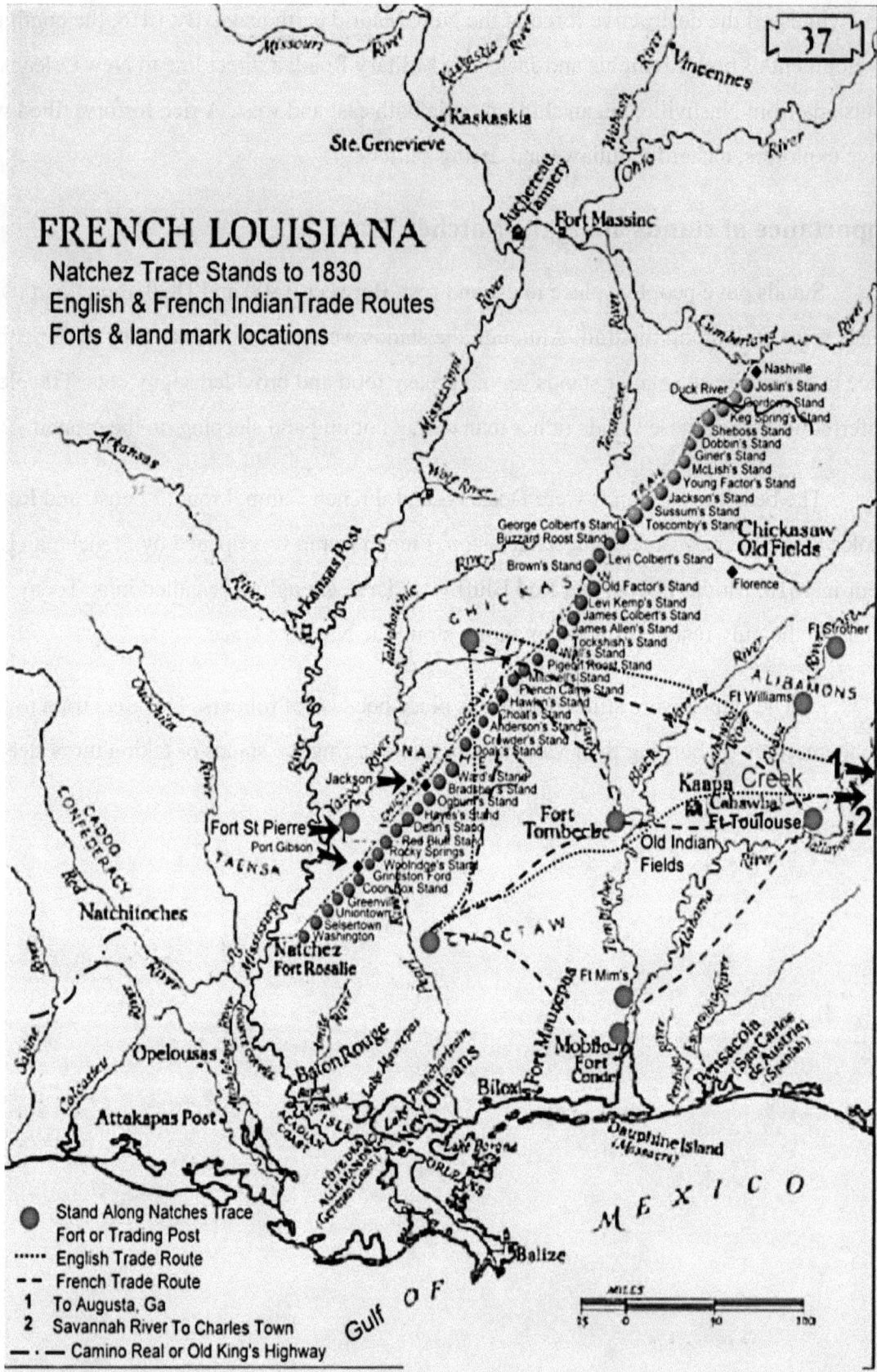

FRENCH LOUISIANA
Natchez Trace Stands to 1830
English & French IndianTrade Routes
Forts & land mark locations

37

Missouri River

Kaskaskia River

Ste.Genevieve

Kaskaskia

Wabash River

Vincennes

Juchereau Tannery

Fort Massinc

Ohio River

Cumberland River

Nashville

Duck River · Joslin's Stand
Gordon's Stand
Keg Spring's Stand
Sheboss Stand
Dobbin's Stand
Giner's Stand
McLish's Stand
Young Factor's Stand
Jackson's Stand
Sussum's Stand
Toscomby's Stand

Arkansas River

Mississippi River

Wolf River

Tennessee River

Chickasaw
Old Fields

George Colbert's Stand
Buzzard Roost Stand
Levi Colbert's Stand

Brown's Stand
Old Factor's Stand
Levi Kemp's Stand
James Colbert's Stand
James Allen's Stand
Tockshish's Stand
Wall's Stand
Pigeon Roost Stand
Mitchell's Stand
French Camp Stand
Hawn's Stand
Choat's Stand
Anderson's Stand
Crowder's Stand
Doak's Stand

Florence

Ft Strother

ALIBAMONS

Ft Williams

Arkansas Post

Arkansas River

Ouachita River

CADDO
CONFEDERACY

Natchitoches

Red River

TAENSA

Tallahatchie River

CHICKASAW

NATCHEZ

Jackson

Fort St Pierre
Port Gibson

Ward's Stand
Bradbury's Stand
Ogburn's Stand
Hayes's Stand
Dean's Stand
Red Bluff Stand
Rocky Springs
Woolridge's Stand
Grindston Ford
Coon Box Stand
Greenville
Uniontown
Selsertown
Washington
Natchez
Fort Rosalie

Fort Tombecbe

Old Indian
Fields

Kaapa Creek
Cahawba
Ft Toulouse

1
2

Sipsey River

Black River

Tombigbee River

Alabama River

CHOCTAW

Ft Mim's

Mobile
Fort
Conde

Pascagoula River

Pensacola
San Carlos
de Austria
(Spanish)

Opelousas

Baton Rouge

Biloxi

New Orleans

Lake Pontchartrain

Lake Borgne

Attakapas Post

Calcasieu River

Sabine River

COTE DES
ALLEMANDS
(GERMAN COAST)

Dauphine Island

MEXICO

Balize

Gulf OF

Stand Along Natches Trace
Fort or Trading Post
········ English Trade Route
– – French Trade Route
1 To Augusta, Ga
2 Savannah River To Charles Town
–·– Camino Real or Old King's Highway

MILES
25 0   50   100

Nashville to Natchez

Nashville

 Joshlin's Stand (TN) 1797

 Gordon's Stand (TN) 1802

  John Gordon

  Gordon's Ferry across the Duck River.

 Keg Springs Stand (TN) 1812

 Sheboss Place (TN)

 Dobbin's Stand (TN) 1808

  David Dobbins, Swan Creek

 Griner's Stand (TN) 1808

 McLish's Stand (TN) 1806

  William McLish, N/S Buffalo Creek

 Young Factor's Stand (TN) 1805

McGillavary's Stand (TN) A modern populated place, on the Natchez Trace just below Collinwood in Wayne County TN. We have not yet seen an early date for McGillavary Stand.

 Toscomby's Stand (TN) 1810

  Toscomby, an Indian's name

George Colbert's Stand (AL) pre 1806

  George Colbert, 1/2 Chickasaw

  Colbert's Ferry across the Tennessee River.

 Buzzard Roost Stand (AL) 1812

 Levi Colbert's Stand (AL)

 Brown's Stand (MS) 1815

Old Factor's Stand (MS) 1812

Levi Kemp's Stand (MS) 1825

James Colbert's Stand (MS) 1812

James Allen

Tockshish's Stand, McIntosh's Stand, Chickasaw Old Town (MS) 1797

This became the junction with "the Notchey" or so called

West Prong of the Natchez Trace.

Wall's Stand (MS) 1811

Pigeon Roost Stand (MS) 1800

Mitchell's Stand (MS) 1806

French Camp, LeFleur's Stand (MS) 1810 Duke Family

Hawkins's Stand, Harkin's Stand (MS) 1811

Choat's Stand, Choteau's Stand (MS) 1811

Anderson's Stand (MS) 1811

Crowders Stand (MS) 1813 Owned by Eli and Martha Patsy Going Crowder. Forced removal top Oklahoma with James and Gip Goins both killed in Indian uprising at Mayhew Mission near Boggy Mountain. Martha and Eli raised a large family in Oklahoma.

Doak's Stand (MS) 1810 The Treaty of Doak's Stand: Signed on October 20, 1820, in Madison County, Mississippi, between Canton and Farmhaven, the treaty gave the Mississippi Choctaw a large western territory in exchange for land sales to settlers. The terms of the treaty became a sore point in latter relations between the tribes and the government. General Andrew Jackson supervised the treaty's signing.

Ward's Stand (MS) 1811

Brashear's Stand (MS) 1806 Turner Brashear The Treaty of Dancing Rabbit Creek: Signed on September 27, 1830, in Noxubee County, Mississippi, near Macon, the treaty gave the Choctaws the option of moving to the western territories in Oklahoma and Arkansas. The government made it clear, however, that the tribe really needed to move and not remain in Mississippi. A few

Choctaws stayed in Mississippi (in fact, some stayed on with the Gaines family at Peachwood), but the majority went west over a period of several years.

Jackson (MS)

Ogburn's Stand (MS) 1810

Hayes's Stand (MS) 1815

Dean's Stand aka "Dillon's Stand" (MS) 1821, Dr. Thomas Goings owner.

"DEAN'S STAND" near the old Capital of the Mississippi Territory, Raymond just out of Jamckson, Mississippi. There is a historical library and archives of Natchez Trace's early history.

Natchez Trace: A Road Through the Wilderness.

Along the old Natchez Trace there grew up places to rest and possibly buy provisions. The common term for these hostelries came to be stands. Prior to 1820 there had been as many as 50 of these stands established along the route of this national road between Nashville and Natchez.

In October of 1820 the Choctaw Indians signed a treaty with the United States, in which the Choctaws gave up a large portion of land on the south and west of their territory. This land was quickly claimed by pioneer families. One such family was William Dean and Margaret his wife. They settled in 1823, and in addition to farming the land, they allowed the travelers and mail riders and boatmen and preachers who came along the old road, to lodge in their house. This stop along the Natchez Trace came to be known as DEAN'S STAND.

SMU Natchez Trace Collection - Hattiesburg, Mississippi

Choctaw Treaty, eliminating the boundary between the British Colony of West Florida British, and the Choctaws.

March 26 1765

Rowland, Miss Territory Archives I 476

Mississippi Herald/Natchez Gazette, 21 October 1807

Letters-J. Moore, Postmaster at Port Gibson, has the following letters in his office as of 01 October 1807: William Scott; Vance Scott; Rev. Thomas Sacley; Joshua Clark; Miss Sally Griffin; John Murdock; Stephen Bullock; James Milligan; William Pope; Mrs. Mary Elliot; Miss Rebecca Milborun; Hon. Peter Byan Bruin; Archibald Griffing; David M Farlane; Jesse Benton; Henry Trent; Rev MolesFloyd; Thomas Norris; Soloman Walker; William R Richey; Dr. Thomas Going; Berryman Watkins; Abner Wilfenson; Major John Barkley; Caleb Roberts; Caleb Roberts; Francis M'Cleland; Samuel Beach; Ignatus Flowers; William Dickson; James Thompson; Walter Slaughter; Colonel THomas White; James Knewlard; John

Boothe; Mrs. Harriet Turnbull; John Saxon; Joseph D Lewis; Roger Gypson; Joshua Rundle; Joshua Rundie; David Spurlock; Solomon Walker.

JOURNEY OF THOMAS NIXON TO **ATTAKAPAS**

Thomas Nixon writes of his journey to Attakapas where he was appointed to serve. He and Mr. Menefee rode to Mr. Overaker's where they were hospitably entertained. The next morning they rode to Washington and dined with Dr. Rollins, then spent the night in the country with one of the Tooley's (probably James) before turning toward Midway where they had an appointment to preach, preceding the Bishop who would preach on Sunday. Then they spent the night with Mr. Sojourner, dined with Brother Hodges and spent the night with

Mr. Richardson near Midway. People flocked to hear them preach the next day. On Monday the Bishop presided at McCalley's Church. On Tuesday he preached in Liberty, the county town of Amite. He took quite ill while in Liberty, but rode eleven miles on his way to Franklin County. Wednesday he appeared better and he and his companions rode 28 miles to Mr. Pickett's.

The Pickett settlement was then one of the strongholds of Methodism in Franklin County. The Bishop intended to preach there the next morning, but a chill kept him in bed all day. Having other engagements to keep, he rode six miles that night to Mr. King's where he spent a rainy night. They left early the next morning and rode 30 miles in the rain to Randall Gibson's. The Bishop was confined to bed the next day and missed his appointment for that day. He was so ill that day that Randall sent to Port Gibson for Dr. Thomas Going. By evening he was much better and came downstairs for a cheerful conversation with the family. Also convalescing at the Gibson home was James Dixon who had missed the Conference due to illness. He asked the Bishop's permission to leave the country as soon as he could travel and was granted a transfer back to Tennessee. Nixon and Menefee rode ten miles that night, and stayed with Mrs. Evans to preach to the blacks at Old Hebron, and had a gracious time.

An ACT for Thomas Going, a free man of color Thomas Going is authorized to give testimony in court. December 1, 1814.

Dillon Stand to Dean's Stand

William Dean patented 80.09 acres W1/2 NW1/4 Section 32 T5N R3W March 26, 1823.

Hinds County Tract Book

See Mrs. Ratliff, Raymond also, Phil Armintage, grandson of Wm Dean who operated stand at present site of Dillons.

55. pg 191

Dean's Stand. Site marked by family graveyard of Col. W.S. Dillon, who in 1839 acquired "a tract of land known as Dean's stand."

Dillon's Stand formally Dean's Stand

Francise B Lee, administrator of estate of Thomas Goeng..hath given, bargained and sold to Wilson F Dillon ass that tract of land W 1/2 of NE 1/4 of sec 33 T9R4E, also a tract of land N 1/2 of W 1/2 of the SE 1/4 of sec 33 T9 R4E also a tract of land known as Dean's Stand lying and being in the situated in the county of Hinds and state aforesaid on the road leading from Port Gibson to Raymond Containing 850 acres.

Feb 20, 1839

Hinds Co Deed Book, Vol 2. p227-78

Mrs. Margaret Dillon acquired the property from F. B. Lee adm. 1939

Thom. Going.

Dillon's Stand

Interrog "State whether or not Mrs. Margaret Dillon dec'd under the purchase as stated in the bill of complaint, had possession of all land which were originally conveyed to you[her] by Francis B Lee as adm of Thomas Going which were then known as Dean's Stand"

Ans "She had possession of all said land from the time of her purchase up to the time of her death"

Interrog. WF Dillion, Hinds Co chancery Records. Nov 27, 1874 No 1141

Colonel Wilson F Dillon- Obituary, May 17, 1876.

Hinds County Gazzette, Raymond, Miss., Wednesday, May 17 1876m No. 36, Page 1.

"Death of Col. WF Dillon-We greatly regret to announce the death of Col. Wilson Dillon, which event occurred at his residence near this place on 13th inst. Col. Dillon was one of the most substantial citizens of the county of Hinds, one of our most valued friends, and a prompt paying subscriber to the Gazette from its first issue. He was born in Prize Edward County, Va, 1797, and, consequently died in the 79th year of his age. He removed to Mississippi in 1827, forty-nine years ago, and settled on the place where he died, 6 miles from Raymond when this country was a wilderness. Maby years ago he connected himself with the Methodist Church, of which he continued a highly useful and devoted member, and died with true christian fortitude and resignation. Col. Dillon was an upright and positive man; was a public spirited and well informed citizen; and in early times was a power and ever delighted in speaking of their characteristics and peculiarities. For many years he was president of the board of Police of the county, and managed our public affairs most honestly, intelligently and satisfactorily. We mourn the death of our friend, but woe for the bright land 'beyond the sunset," and where he may be joined by his many kindred, friends and acquaintances."

Dillons Stand (formally Dean's Stand)

Abner & Sarah Wise to John Cook,

"all those lots or parcels of land being lots No One and two of fractional section & two acres & twenty nine hundreths of an acre"

Dec 45, 1834.

Claiborne County Deed Book, O, 3607.

Note: This document was acknowledged before Wilson F Dillon, an acting justice of the peace for Claiborne County.

"The following described property, their entire interest in the lands known a Margret Dillon estate. All of S31 exet 16 a. in NE corner also W1/2 of NW1/4 and E1/2 of SW1/4 of set 32, Except 25 acres in NE Part of NW1/4 of sec. 32 T5 R3W."

Deed of Trust given by John B Herrod & Julia A Herrod March 26, 1877.

Hinds County Deed Book, Vol 48, p.401.

In the Name of God I Samuel Going in Claiborne County in the State of Mififippi being in feble health

Edmund P Goines

The Natchez Trace assignment marked the first public task of any significance committed to the young lieutenant....In 1801 there commissioners, headed by General James Wilkinson, negotiated with the Chickasaws and Choctaws for the right to improve the old trace through their lands, and succeeded in obtaining the right to construct a military road. Thereupon Lieutenant Goines, with ten companies of soldiers accompanied by Indian guides, pushd the work so rapidly that by the summer of 1802 the United States opened that section from Nashville to Duck River Ridge of the officially named Columbian Highway.

Rise and Fall of the Choctaw Republic

Angie Debo

Library of Congress CC No 61-7973

Second printing of the second edition 1967

pg 34

As soon as the Choctaws established their homes in the new country, they began to build their school system. The initiative was taken by the missionaries of the American Board, who in 1836 reported 11 schools with an enrollment of 228 Choctaw children. Agent FW Armstrong encouraged the Choctaws to construct log buildings and organize the schools provided by the treaty annuities.

Pg 41

Only three years after the Battle of New Orleans, the Choctaws made another decision that consolidated the interests of the two races, when they invited missionaries to establish stations in their country. This request seems to have been due to the influence of the younger generations of Folsoms, LeFlores, and Ptchlynn's, whose fathers had given them some schooling, and who felt that the only hope for their people lay in education and the adoption of civilized institutions; but there is no doubt that the Choctaw people as a whole were ready for this further aquisition of the white man's customs.

Gaines

Draper Collection, Tecumseh Manuscripts pg 46-48

Pushmataha then returned to his home which was in the vicinity of St Stephens, and told Gaines he was ready to join the United States in the War against the Creeks.

Cushman, History of the Choctaw "*Indian Trails of the Southeast*" Myer, pg. 824

Another source of white influence was the increasing activities of traders, and the construction of roads in the Choctaw Country. The most important trading post was St Stephens, established by the United States in 1802. It was located on the Tombigee close to its junction with the Alabama, on the old east-west Indian trail from the Natchez to the lower Creeks; it thus tapped the trade of the old Spanish Camino Real, and could compete for all the trade coming the Alabama and Tombigee rivers, and all the trails converging towards towards Mobile. George S Gaines, a native of Virginia, who came to this place in 1805 and served first as assistant, and later as principle factor, was greatly loved and trusted by the Choctaws. Gaines was assisted by a clerk, a skinsman, and an interpreter, all of whom received substantial salaries from the United States. The Choctaws brought bear's oil, kegs of honey, beeswax, bacon, groundnuts, kegs of tobacco, and ammunition, and plows kept in stock by the Federal Government.

At first the Choctaw products were shipped from Mobile, but the United States soon secured permission from the Chickasaw tribe to carry them on packhorses to Colbert's Ferry on the Tennessee, in the extreme northwestern part of Alabama. This route, known as Gaines Trace, followed the Tombigee to the mouth of the Okibbeha; it was probably identical with a primitive trail from the Chickasaw settlements in the north, through Choctaw country, to the lower Creek towns. The road constructed under the Treaty of 1801 crossed the Choctaw country from southwest to northwest from Natchez to Nashville.

The white people who traveled these trails found the Choctaws hospitable and friendly, willing to welcome them in their homes or accept employments as guides. Public Inns were established in some places, but apparently these enterprises were usually conducted by the mixed bloods or white citizens. The most famous was Pitchlynn's Place on Gaines Trace, where the goods brought up the Tombigee were unloaded for the overland part of the journey. John Pitchlynn and his sons, Peter and John, owned most of the land in that region, and their home was a favorite stopping place for travelers. Pitchlynn was employed by the United States as interpreter and was a good friend of both Indians and whites.

Hodgeson, Letters from North America, Morse report to the Secretary of War, pg 183

The white citizen, Nathaniel Folsom, also entertained numerous travelers; he told Adam Hodgson, who visited him in 1820, that there were scarcely five days in the year when he failed to have guests, and that seventy or eighty often stopped in one day.

Continued from Dean's Stand

Red Bluff Stand, McRover's Stand and Smith's Stand (MS) 1806

Rocky Springs

Wooldridge's Stand (MS) 1806

Grindstone Ford (MS) 1797

Port Gibson (MS) (settled by Samuel Gibson)

Coon Box Stand (MS)

Greenville (MS)

Uniontown (MS)

Selserville (MS)

Washington (MS)

Natchez (MS)

In 1818 the Chickasaws relinquished their claims to the Western District, and settlement began in the Mississippi Valley. Towns quickly sprang up on the Tennessee bank of the river, and the steamboat trade flourished. By 1834 some 230 steamboats plied the Mississippi. Memphis emerged as an inland port city and a destination for immigrants arriving in the United States through New Orleans. Towns along the Mississippi tributaries benefited as well. The Forked Deer was navigable for steamboats to Dyersburg, although a few managed to reach Jackson. The Hatchie was navigable for several miles, and some boats went as far as Bolivar, though this area could not as easily engage in shipping despite its rich agricultural land.

One branch went southeast through the Cumberland Gap and was known as the Wilderness Road or Boone's Trail, while another division swung southwest through Nashville and was called the Natchez Trace, or Boatman's Trail. The main branch of the Old Miami Trace traveled due north up from the Indian town of Chattanooga on the Tennessee and then connected with the other Indian trails branching off toward the Gulf of Mexico.

As was mentioned, the trail started at Chattanooga, bounded along the west bank of the Tennessee River, branched off at Harriman, Ky., moved up the valley of the Emory River over to the Valley of the Cumberland River. Thence to the Indian settlement at the junction of the north and south forks of the river at Burnside, Ky. It then proceeded to the Indian settlements of

Central Kentucky at Danville, Lexington and Paris, where it followed the ridge of the Licking to its mouth; it then it crossed the Ohio to what is now Cincinnati. (The Wyandotte name for Cincinnati was Tu-ent-a-hab-whag-ta, "the place where the road leaves the river."). At this point numerous important trails met. From the Ohio northward the trail is called the Old Miami Trail, obviously the name being taken from the powerful Indian tribe, the Miamis, who occupied this region. The old trail was sometimes called the Fort Miami Trail, simply because it led to old Fort Miami, the oldest fortification in the State of Ohio. This fort was built under the direction of Fontenac, Governor of Canada, in 1680, as a military trading post. Its location was about fifteen miles up the Maumee from Lake Erie. The French later moved it farther up the river; the English, in 1785, rebuilt it. The Native Americans followed certain routes for both trade and warfare. The water courses and the ridges along the watersheds were used as their earthworks now show. Both the Indians and the whites followed these same trails and used the same sites for their towns.

In the decades prior to the American Civil War, market places where enslaved Africans were bought and sold could be found in every town of any size in Mississippi. Natchez was unquestionably the state's most active slave trading city, although substantial slave markets existed at Aberdeen, Crystal Springs, Vicksburg, Woodville, and Jackson. Natchez played a significant role in the southward movement of the existing slave population to the waiting cotton plantations of the Deep South. Slave sales at Natchez were held in a number of locations, but one market place soon eclipsed the others in the number of sales. This was the market known as "The Forks of the Road," located at the busy intersection of Liberty Road and Washington Road about one mile east of downtown Natchez. (Today, Washington Road is named "D'Evereux Drive," which changes to "St. Catherine Street" at the Liberty Road intersection.) The market site occupied a prominent knoll, straddling what was then the city's eastern corporation line.

Washington Road connected Natchez with the nearby town of Washington and with the Natchez Trace, a vital interstate route extending northeast into northern Alabama and Tennessee. Liberty Road, also known as "Old Courthouse Road" or "Second Creek Road," linked Natchez with points to the east and southeast, and ultimately with the southern reaches of Alabama and Georgia. Although the Forks of the Road became best known as a slave market, livestock and other items were also sold there.

The Forks of the Road intersection appears in maps of the Natchez area as early as 1808. The earliest known map illustrating slave markets at that location is a plat of St. Catherine Street drawn in 1853 (see map). In the 1853 map, two "Negro Marts" are shown at the Forks of the Road intersection: one inside the angle of the fork and another across Old Courthouse Road (Liberty Road) to the southwest. The map also shows the City of Natchez "Corporation Line," which intersected both slave markets and provides a way to accurately locate the market sites today.

The Traders

The importance of the Forks of the Road as a slave market increased dramatically when Isaac Franklin of Tennessee rented property there in 1833. Franklin and his business partner, John Armfield of Virginia, were soon to become the most active slave traders in the United States. Franklin and Armfield were among the first professional slave traders to take advantage of the relatively low prices for slaves in the Virginia–Maryland area, and the profit potential offered by the growing market for slaves in the Deep South.

Armfield managed the firm's slave pen in Alexandria, Virginia, while Franklin established and ran the firm's markets at Natchez and New Orleans. By the 1830s, they were sending more than 1,000 slaves annually from Alexandria to their Natchez and New Orleans markets to help meet the demand for slaves in Mississippi and surrounding states.

When our country was formed by treaty in 1783, the western boundary was the Mississippi River and the southern boundary was the 31st Parallel. By then, Fort Natchez, located on the Mississippi River as a well-established trading post in the Great Wild South West of this young country. Some old Indian trading trails were the only way by land to get from what became Nashville, Tennessee to Fort Natchez. As the new farmers west of the

Allegheny Mountains grew their crops of cotton, tobacco, corn, wheat; they needed a place to sell it. Fort Natchez became the place to trade. In the fall, farmers would load their crops on flat boats, float down the Ohio, Tennessee, Cumberland to the Mississippi and then to Fort Natchez, later to just Natchez. Here the farmers sold their crops and even the flat boat they came on for gold or various forms of paper money. Then, they walked more than 400 miles back to their homes by using the Indian foot path to what is now Nashville, Tennessee and then on to their home. This foot path became known as the Natchez Trace. Some called it The Devil's Backbone because of the crime committed on it, robbing and killing the farmers/traders for their money. In spite of this, it became a trail of commerce, the main mail route to the southwest, and a vital trail in development of the great southwest of the young USA between 1790 and about 1830.

The Hudson's Bay Company differed in certain important particulars in both organization and operations from its American rivals. The fortified trading post was common to both systems; the rendezvous was peculiarly an American institution; the company's trapping brigade contained several important elements that were foreign to the typical American trapping party. The usual American fur-trading expedition, for example, consisted almost exclusively of men; a Hudson's Bay Company brigade contained fifteen or twenty whites, fifty or more French-Canadian, Indian, or half-breed trappers, and a multitude of women and children.

These large and heterogeneous personnel necessitated the use of much larger supply trains and many more horses than the American system required; so that a fur brigade, bound for a distant hunt of eighteen months' or two years' duration, resembled a small-scale tribal migration. The women of the brigade did the work of the camp, dressed the pelts, tanned the skins for shirts and moccasins, and relieved the men of innumerable other essential details. They and the children became a liability only when the brigade suffered major disaster, such as epidemic, serious shortage of food, or defeat at the hands of hostile Indians.

Over the past century, considerable attention has been paid to the political history of the aspiring Metis nation but the processes by which Metis identity was formed, the content of Metis culture, and the mechanisms by which it was transmitted intergenerational still remain obscure. Perhaps this is because, despite Louis Riel's impassioned declaration of Metis consciousness "that we honor our mothers as well as our fathers," 3 the native women who mothered and nourished the growth of a Metis society have been overshadowed by their white male partners and fathers.

This essay does not hope to answer the larger questions of Metis identity and culture formation but instead explores the motivations prompting native females to marry whites in the early stages of fur trade expansion south and west of the Great Lakes, and seeks to resolve an apparent anomaly with regard to the role of women in subsequent Metis cultural development. On the one hand, as Jennifer S. H. Brown has noted in a path-breaking article, native women were both center and symbol in the emergence of Metis communities. 4 Since Metis daughters of Indian-white marriages were more likely than Metis sons to remain in the West and to maintain close ties with native mothers and kin, they were the primary contributors via their own marriages to incoming whites and Metis males to the rapid growth of a Metis population in the fur trading zone. It is not surprising; therefore, that Metis life appears to have been characterized by matrilineal organization, with the female and native side exercising the predominant influences over residence and community, behavioral roles, and ethnic filiation. Ultimately, to be Metis was to claim descent from, and the rights of, a native mother, rather than of a white father.

On the other hand, a core denominator of persistent Metis identity has been a strong attachment to Christianity. Especially among French-speaking Metis, Catholic belief and practice did, and often still does, act as the demarcator between themselves and their Indian relatives. Simply put, Metis attend Mass, not the Sun Dance. But if Metis life was matricentered and native women and their female descendants were the transmitters and translators of Metis culture and identity, what are we to make of the prominence of an intrusive European belief system? How are we to reconcile the apparently mutual influences of strong-minded, perhaps exceptional native women and the religious ideology of the colonizer? What role did Christianity play, if any, in propelling native women toward white males and why did certain women chose, or so it would seem, to abandon the traditions and lifeways of their own people?

The term certain women are deliberate. It may be fairly assumed that the majority, or even the preponderance, of tribal women did not take white husbands or succumb to the appeals of Christian missionaries at any time during the early contact phase in North America. Carol Devens has argued that among the "domiciled" Indian groups of New France, women led the resistance against missionary efforts at conversion. 5 It may also be assumed, thanks to the remarkable portrait of "women in between" painted by Sylvia Van Kirk and to Jennifer S. H. Brown's seminal ethno historical analysis of fur trade families, that the native wives of fur traders and their Metis daughters were neither degraded drudges, commodities to be bought or sold, or the casual purveyors of sexual favors, stereotypes best buried with the likes of Walter O'Meara's Daughters of the Country.

Van Kirk, in particular, has ably illustrated the intelligence and forceful personalities of a number of wives of fur traders, women capable of exerting considerable influence within both native and fur trade circles. Although her sources tend to favor the native wives and daughters of men of rank, or women who aroused comment, the women she describes had their counterparts throughout fur trade country, on both sides of the international boundary. In the western Great Lakes region alone, women such as Madame Cadotte, Susan Johnston, Sally Ainse, Madame LaFramboise, Therese Schindler, Marinette Chevalier, Domitille Langlade, and Sophia Mitchell achieved prominence as traders, church founders and patrons, and leaders of fur trade communities, while their Metis daughters and granddaughters perpetuated many of these traditions, adding the roles of teacher, translator, and interpreter.

Van Kirk and Brown have pointed to a number of factors that may have persuaded native women to marry white traders, among them heightened material comfort and physical security, access to trade goods, and personal role expansion. Other factors -- the demographic pressure caused by a possible female surplus among hunting tribes, the benefits to kin of an alliance with whites, the appeal of a more permissive sexual code, a preference for monogamous marriage, and the influence of Christianization

Such a process of expansion was general in the nation during the 1750s and 1760s, but in the late 1760s the outbreak of the Creek wars checked it in the east and south. Romans, on entering the nation from the east in 1771, had to pass through the deserted towns of Osapa issa and Itokchako before he reached the first inhabited settlement, East Abeka, and he later mentioned deserted towns along the Tombigbee. The end of the Creek wars, in turn, opened the way for renewed expansion particularly in the south and east. The Spanish census of 1784, the first detailed enumeration of towns since Romans's list of 1771, revealed four new settlements in the south, two in the east, and two in the west.

According to John Stuart, the Creeks possessed "the most extensive hunting-ground of any nation to the southward." 8 Large ranges were necessary, for one deer requires approximately one hundred acres for sustenance. Muscogulge hunters could travel freely anywhere under Creek jurisdiction in search of game. Still, it seems that most hunters tended to range in fairly well-defined areas over which their town or tribe had some claim through long occupation, assimilation, or conquest. Hunters from Coweta and neighboring towns tended to stalk game to the east and north, where Creek lands adjoined Cherokee and Georgia lands, and especially along the Oconee and Ogeechee rivers. According to Alexander McGillivray, this area was among the most valuable Creek hunting grounds and produced over three thousand deerskins annually. Hunters from the southernmost Lower Creek Towns moved south and west into the Florida peninsula. The Tallapooses and Abeikas ranged in what is today northern Alabama and central Tennessee, even crossing into non-Creek territory beyond the Tennessee River. Alabama tribesmen pressed westward toward the Tombigbee River, which was the boundary with Choctaw lands, and southward along the Alabama River and toward Pensacola in their search for deer. The fertile forests along the Tensaw and Escambia rivers were highly prized hunting grounds for all Creeks. 13 Creek hunters from Chehaw and Tallassee ventured into the Okefenokee Swamp in search of deer, bear, and alligator. The Latchoways and other East Florida villagers hunted all along the Florida peninsula, even as far south as the cape. During the long winter hunting season, Creek hunting parties could be found from Tampa Bay to the Cumberland River valley, and they trekked as far west as the Trinity River in Texas.

The Choctaws continued to settle new towns in the 1790s and the early nineteenth century, but at that time the direction of settlement shifted considerably. Of the towns appearing for the first time in the censuses and treaty conferences between 1794 and 1804, fourteen were in the northeast, five were in the west, and only one was in the south. The creation of new towns in the south during the late 1770s and early 1780s probably represented the dispersal of people previously confined by the Creek wars. The south, bordered by pinelands and with less arable land than any other district, reached its environmental limits relatively quickly, however. In the 1790s and early 1800s its people would not take up new lands within the district except within the established towns; instead, they migrated across the Mississippi to settle new villages where game was still abundant and the old economy could be reestablished in toto.

In the northeastern and western districts, however, no such environmental constraints existed. Their borderlands were not pinelands but rich loessal and prairie soils. Still, the mere existence of these lands explains nothing. Northeastern and western Choctaws faced the same crippling of the subsistence cycle as the southern Choctaws; more fertile farmland could not stop droughts and could not bring the deer back. They needed more than rich land if they were to escape continued dependence. People still devoted to the traditional hunting and farming economy did not move into the borderlands in great numbers; they moved west of the river.

Bushwhackers, Bibles and Boats

Despite its brief lifespan, the Trace served an essential function in the years it was in existence. It was the only reliable and most expedient link between the goods of the North and the trading ports of Louisiana. This brought all sorts of people down the Trace: itinerant preachers, highwaymen and traders were just a few.

The circuit preachers were some of the most notable of the lot. Unlike its physical development, the "spiritual development" of the Trace started from the Natchez end up: several Methodist preachers began working a circuit along the Trace as early as 1800, and claimed a membership of 1,067 Caucasians and 267 African-Americans in 1812. The Methodists were soon joined in Natchez by other Protestant religions, including the Baptists and Presbyterians. The Presbyterians and their offshoot, the Cumberland Presbyterians, were more active than the Methodists or Baptists in procuring converts along the Trace itself, including the Native American population—the Presbyterians starting from the south, the Cumberland Presbyterians from the north. As with much of the unsettled West, the Trace was also a hotbed for banditry. Much of it centered around Natchez Under-The-Hill, as compared with its more tame sister city at Natchez On-The-Hill. Under-the-Hill, where the port to the Mississippi was located, was a hotbed for gamblers, prostitutes and drunkenness. The rowdiest of them all were the Kaintucks, the wild frontiersmen from upriver who came in on the steamboats and flatboats loaded with goods, left them in Natchez in exchange for pockets full of cash, and summarily treated Natchez Under-the-Hill as what could be generously called an early 1800s Las Vegas, Nevada or Amsterdam. Still worse dangers lurked in the wilderness outside the city boundaries on the Trace itself. Highwaymen such as John Murrell and Samuel Mason terrorized travelers along the road, and operated large gangs of organized brigands in one of the first examples of land-based American organized crime.

The following claims were originally derived from Stewart's "History of the Detection, Conviction, Life, and Designs of John A. Murel...." ....He was known as a 'land-pirate,' using the Mississippi River as a base for his operations. He used a network of anywhere from 300 (Stewart estimate) to 1,000 (as quoted in Mark Twain's Life on the Mississippi) to 2,500 (as some newspaper reports claimed) fellow bandits collectively known as the Mystic Clan to pull off his escapades. Many of these were members of cultural/ethnic groups such as the Melungeons and the Redbones. He was also known as a bushwhacker along the Natchez Trace. To cover up his misdeeds, he played the persona of a traveling preacher. Twain's work and others say he would preach to a congregation while his gang stole the horses outside. However, the accounts are unanimous that Murrell's horse was always left behind.

Just before he was apprehended, he was about to spearhead a slave revolt in New Orleans in an attempt to take over the city and install himself as a sort of potentate of Louisiana.

The disputed details about Murrell are more numerous and controversial than the known facts. Even today, his place of birth is in question: Some sources claim Williamson County, Tennessee, others say Jackson, Tennessee. In any case, it is clear that he grew up in Williamson County, Tennessee, just south of Franklin.

Even more in debate is the location of his hideout and operations base. Once again, Jackson or Madison County are bandied about, but other places include Natchez, Mississippi in an odd depression on a bluff called Devil's Punch Bowl, Tunica County, Mississippi, the Neutral Ground in Louisiana, and even the tiny Island 37, part of Tipton County, Tennessee. One record, a genealogical note,[1] even places him as far east as Georgia; in fact Atlanta historian Franklin Garrett makes it clear there was a lawless district in that town named for him, "Murrell's Row" in the 1840s. Because Murrell has come to symbolize Natchez Trace lawlessness in the antebellum period, it's understandable that his "hideouts" (whether there were any hideouts or not) have been said to have been located at most of the well-known areas of particular lawlessness along the Natchez Trace.

Some say he began to plot his takeover of New Orleans in 1841, although he was in the sixth year of a ten year sentence in the prison at Nashville at the time, and Stewart had already published his account of Murrell's plot in 1835. Others say he was in operation from 1835 to

1857; he was in prison for ten of those years, and died of tuberculosis in 1845 shortly after leaving prison and taking up a quiet life as a Christian and blacksmith.

A river feature in Chicot County, Arkansas called Whiskey Chute is named for his raid on a whiskey-carrying steamboat that was sunk after it was pillaged. It was named such in 1855. However, he is also claimed to have been born in 1791 [2]. We know from Record Group 25, "Prison Records for the Main Prison at Nashville, Tennessee, 1831-1922," that Murrell was born in 1806, most likely in Williamson County, Tennessee.

The traders also introduced the Indians of North America to distilled liquor. Very early they discovered that the Indians had no cultural resistance to the pleasures of rum or whiskey, and that these constituted the ideal means for lubricating the trade of furs or the sale of land. All that the Whites required, beyond the liquor, was caution (or a stout fort), for the drunken Indian men usually went on a wild emotional spree, fighting, shooting, and even killing. President Jefferson secured from Congress authority to prevent the sale of liquor to Indians, and 30 years later Congress passed further legislation to restrain this traffic. But, as with the later attempt at general Prohibition, the law was difficult to enforce; the Indian desire for liquor was too strong and the profit from conveying it to them was fantastic. The American Fur Company, the creature of John Jacob Astor, was repeatedly accused of violating liquor regulations, and smuggling into Indian Territory great quantities of whiskey and rum, which its agents then exchanged for furs at the most outrageous rates. The Indian agent at Camp Leavenworth estimated that from 1815 to 1830 the fur trade on the Missouri had totaled over $3 million, and that half of this was clear profit. About the same time, William B. Astor was acknowledging that the operation of the fur company was yielding even larger returns, namely $500,000 per year (Myers, 1909, Vol. I, p. 124). Livestock became important only in the context of this larger economic and social breakdown. Those people who first moved into the borderlands were not traditionalists. The pioneers of this new settlement were the intermarried whites and the mixed-bloods, and they came not to reestablish the old economy but to raise cattle as Franchimastabe predicted the whole nation must do. Many full-blood Choctaws settled with them in the borderlands, and gradually the way of life and the interests of these people would diverge from their kinsman in the old towns. White men had first settled extensively among the Choctaws and intermarried with them in the years preceding the Revolution. These men, who were French, American, and

English, largely traders and ex-traders, recognized in the borderlands surrounding them an excellent cattle range. The prairies, the open forests with their grassy floors, and the canebrakes all promised abundant forage. Intermarried whites first introduced cattle among the Choctaws sometime around 1770, but initially the animals seem to have reThe Choctaw herds fueled this expansion and then symbiotically grew because of it. By 1805 John Pitchlynn's property consisted mainly of livestock. His children and other mixed-bloods grew to adulthood not as hunters but herdsmen; their earliest duty was watching their parents' cattle and horse herds. The full-bloods' herds, stocked in part with animals stolen from the Americans who had settled along the Mobile and lower Tombigbee rivers, and in part with animals acquired from the herds of intermarried traders, grew at a considerably slower rate.

Greenwood Leflore born of a French father, Louis LeFleur, and Choctaw mother, Rebecca Cravat, niece of Chief Pushmataha, he had adopted the language and culture of both. At the age of twelve his father, by then a successful tavern keeper in the Choctaw Nation, had allowed him to go to Nashville with Major James Donly, who had a government contract to carry the mails between Nashville and Natchez on the Natchez Trace, a road made possible by the Treaty of Fort Adams in 1801. Leflore was educated in Nashville, at seventeen married the fifteen-year-old daughter of his benefactor, returned to the Choctaw Nation, and at twenty-two was elected chief of the Western District. Though never popular with many of the full-blood tribesmen, he became aIn a later conversation with Samuel James Wells, a historian whose Ph.D. dissertation at the University of Southern Mississippi had been "Choctaw Mixed Bloods and the Advent of Removal," I learned that the Brashears family was well known in the Creek, Chickasaw, and Choctaw tribes. They were widely scattered, and the given name "Turner" was common. One Turner Brashears furnished liquor to the Chickasaws at Muscle Shoals, Alabama, in the early 1790s. Another Turner Brashears, or the same one, had a trading stand northeast of what is now Jackson, Mississippi. Another, or the same one, helped the Spanish with maps and treaties, and a Turner Brashears went to Washington with the Choctaw chiefs as interpreter in 1804. Any one of these things might have been enough to entitle him to the land which was to become Providence. Still, the treaty stated that a Turner Brashears lived on Section Thirteen in 1830. It is not likely that a mixed or full-blooded Choctaw of such accomplishments would have been living on the edge of these remote bluffs in 1830 when he had access to land along the Tennessee River in Alabama, a trading post on the Natchez Trace, or even a spread in northern

Florida. So what am I to conclude about the Turner Brashears who was given Section Thirteen under the terms of the Treaty of Dancing Rabbit Creek? Did he join his brother Bolokta in Oklahoma? Did he become William McKendree Gwin. Then I discovered such lettering did not become fashionable until around the turn of the century. I located many examples of the same pattern in front of fashionable Jackson homes built about that time. It was during that search that I first came across the name "Providence" referring to Section Thirteen and the surrounding area. It had to do with a famous outlaw band of the 1820s–40s known as the Murrell Gang. Operating out of a cave near Tchula, they carried on a slave and horse-stealing traffic and were notorious for their violence. Often victims were robbed and then murdered along the Natchez Trace. Slaves and horses were stolen under cover of darkness and hidden in the swamps of the Big Black River until they could be taken to a distant market, where they were sold. I had heard the stories of how Murrell was captured by a farm woman and her husband named Nevels. In a bicentennial edition of the Durant, Mississippi, Plaindealer, published in 1976, I found a story that described the capture of John Murrell, leader of the gang. Having assigned his highwaymen and thieves to other chores, Murrell was in the Delta region alone. In early morning he stopped at the Nevels's home and demanded that Mrs. Nevels fix him breakfast. Pretending to go to the smokehouse for meat, she alerted her husband of Murrell's presence. The husband waited until Murrell sat down to eat, then, seeing the outlaw's gun carelessly leaned against an outside door, Nevels grabbed the gun, captured Murrell with no resistance, and took him to Vicksburg for trial. The article stated, "Tradition holds that Murrell was captured at Providence Plantation near Tchula at the home of the Nevels family." Although there was a sizeable reward offered for Murrell's capture, Nevels declined to accept it, insisting he had only done his civic duty.

The trail led up the river to Natchez, and this far, through the Spanish territory, it was tolerably policed. Leaving Natchez, however, the road plunged straight through the wilderness, swampridden, Indian-infested. "The road from Nashville to Natchez was estimated to be five hundred and fifty miles. The road was a mere trace or bridle-way through the woods and cane-brake." This road was the Natchez Trace. "Kentuckians and Tennessean's took boats laden with produce down the river, which they sold at Natchez or New Orleans, and then returned to their homes by this route, carrying their money, which was sewn in raw hides. . . ." For years, the Natchez Trace had a bloody history--of robbery, of ambush, of murder--as the bandits prowled there. Toward the close of the century, a Government mail route had been established, linking the American settlements and the Spanish province: from 1796 until about 1810 he was one of its messengers. His memoirs give a graphic picture of the conditions at the time. The mail consisted of "a few letters and government dispatches, with a few newspapers": beside his mail-pouch, he carried "one-half bushel of corn for his horse, provender for himself, an overcoat or a blanket, and a tin trumpet." It took him ten days for the trip to Natchez.

"He would leave Nashville on Saturday night at eight o'clock"; he would go clattering down Market Street from William Tab's store where the post office was located, and so out through the cabins of the town, already darkened for the night. Toward midnight, he would reach the Big Branch of the Harpeth River: here lay Tom Davis' cabin and clearing. Davis' dogs would bark at his galloping passing; Swaney would answer with a hailing cry. This was the last white man's dwelling: beyond lay the wilderness. "Sunday morning he would get to Gordon's Ferry on the Duck River, 51 miles from Nashville, which was then the line between Tennessee and the Choc taw Nation. There he fed his horse and ate breakfast. "He had then to ride 80 miles to Colbert's Ferry, on the Tennessee River, before night set in, where the Indians would set him across." This was a hard day's riding, after a night in the saddle, but he had to make it. "The Indians were contrary, and would not come across the river for him if he failed to get to the landing before bed-time."

This ferry was operated under the auspices of old James Colbert, chief of the Chickasaws; on the opposite shore they maintained a kind of inn, where Swaney stayed the night. It afforded the rudest kind of shelter, and its hospitality was colored by native superstition. Mrs. Thomas Martin, following the Trace, spent a night there and described it: the Indians were very agreeable to them--gave them a supper of venison, potatoes and coffee, while "Mrs. Colbert," wife of the old chieftain, paraded about, wearing a Paris hat, but barefoot--but would not let them sleep in the house: "They assigned us to another, where slept not less than fifty Indians, many of them drunk, while my husband and others sat up all night. It is not their custom to let strangers sleep in the house with their families."

Leaving here, Swaney pushed on deeper into the wilderness: "He would have to go to the Chickasaw Agency, 120 miles, before he would see a house, or even an Indian wigwam, and would have to lie out one night in the woods or cane brake. . . ." At the Chickasaw Agency he encountered the first white men since leaving Nashville. Even these were, in a certain sense, outlaws. "The Chickasaw Agency was kept by McGee, who was the agent, with Jim Allen as interpreter. Allen was a man of fine address, and was a lawyer who came from Nashville, but failing in business, went off among the Indians. . . ."

Two hundred miles farther on lay the Choctaw Agency: "The route was entirely through Indian country": compared to this, the first half of the journey had been populous. One hundred miles farther still, and he entered Natchez. It was here, in this three hundred mile wide strip of canebrake, swamp and desolation ruled by the Chickasaws and Choctaws, that the danger to travelers lay. The danger was not in the Indians, or rarely. Occasionally a wandering band of Creeks-"great warriors"--cut through the land, but the others were "kind and peaceable. The Chickasaws always boasted that they had never shed the blood of a white man in anger. Allen often told Mr. Swaney that the Chickasaws and Choctaws were the happiest and best people he had ever known. They could not say anything in their native tongue worse than 'skena' (bad) and 'pulla' (mean) and in all his knowledge he never heard of the crime of adultery being committed but once. The punishment in such a case was to cut off the end of the nose of the woman. . . .

Happy Jim Allen! He had lived but a year among these pleasant savages, when his eye grew desirous of one of their virtuous maidens. "The manner of choosing a wife among the Chickasaw Indians was for the swain to make his desire toward a particular maiden known to the chief, and having gained his consent, the suitor would return to his wigwam and there wait until his lady love should be sent to him." In Allen's case the matter had certain complications: his choice had fallen upon no less a person than Susie, daughter of the chief, James Colbert himself. Many braves had been her suitors. Allen, however, paid formal visit to the potentate, made his plea. He then, as custom demanded, retired to his wigwam, closed its flaps and waited there in the darkness while the elders of the tribe debated his request. "He waited until nearly dark, when Susie Colbert made her appearance at his door with a blanket drawn closely around her head, leaving only space enough for her to find her way, and in response to his invitation, walked in and took a seat. This was Jim Allen's courtship and marriage." The union thus formed was fruitful, of a daughter: her name was Peggy Allen. In Swaney's time she had grown into young girlhood: he reported that she was "the prettiest woman he ever saw," and in those days, in the womanless West the fame of a lovely girl spread all through the territory: men would come traveling hundreds of miles, like zealots on a pilgrimage, to settle their longings and look upon her. "Mr. Swaney said it was almost incredible the number of travelers and boatmen who stopped at the Agency to see her, attracted alone by her reputation. She was known to all the boatmen as a great beauty." But she was wilful. Allen's brother, a substantial man, came out from North Carolina to visit them; he tried to persuade Peggy to come east with him; he offered to school her, and launch her out as a belle in eastern society. She refused. Sam Mitchell, the agent in the Choctaw territory, fell madly in love with her. He found no favor with her but he did gain the support of her grandmother, old Chief Colbert's wife. With craft, this beldame invited the girl to visit her in the Indian encampments: she immediately dispatched her, perforce, to Mitchell's cabin, "with eight or ten negroes and as many ponies as dowry." Here was danger of an involuntary bridal, but Peg still showed her spirit. She told Sam Mitchell "she would never marry a drunken white man or an Indian"; she locked the doors of the man's own cabin against him. Baffled, after two weeks Mitchell sent her home again. Allen was proud, but he was also sensible. They were alone in the wilderness. If Mitchell chose to seek vengeance through his Choctaws they had no defense among the Chickasaws: in fact his greater fear was that Grandma Colbert, more spiteful still, might be moved to savage reprisals. But Peggy had another suitor, young Simon Burney, the son of a Natchez planter. She had dallied Simon for years but now, in the uncertainty, she grew more lenient toward him. "He would almost give his life for you," her father told her. So they were married; Peg was whisked downriver to Natchez, away from the dark threat the wilderness had conjured to oppose her beauty. They settled at Natchez; their fate was happy: "Birney amassed a large fortune, and raised and educated a nice family."

Works Cited

http://imahero.com/readingprogram/trailnatchez.html
http://www.tngenweb.org/campbell/hist-bogan/MiamiTrail.html
http://mshistory.k12.ms.us/features/feature30/gsgaines.html
http://mshistory.k12.ms.us/features/feature36/forks_of_the_road.html
http://www.us-census.org/native/choctaw.html
This Reckless Breed of Men
The Trappers and Fur Traders of the Southwest BY ROBERT GLASS CLELAND 1963 NEW YORK ALFRED A. KNOPF
Western Women: Their Land, Their Lives. Contributors: Janice Monk - editor, Vicki L. Ruiz - editor, Lillian Schlissel - editor. Publisher: University of New Mexico Press. Place of Publication: Albuquerque. Publication Year: 1988

http://newdeal.feri.org/guides/tnguide/ch03.htm

http://www.muzzleblasts.com/vol3no6/articles/mbo36-4.html

Studies in American Indian Literature   Series 2
Volume 11, Number 1   Spring 1999 http://oncampus.richmond.edu/faculty/ASAIL/SAIL2/111.html

Stands and Travel Accommodations on the Natchez Trace by Dawson Phelps in the Journal of
Mississippi History, Jan 1949

The Outlaw Years: The History of the Land Pirates of the Natchez Trace. Contributors: Robert M. Coates
- author. Publisher: University of Nebraska Press. Place of Publication: Lincoln, NE. Publication Year:
1986. Page Number: *.

Title: Indian Americans: Unity and Diversity. Contributors: Murray L. Wax - author. Publisher: Prentice
Hall. Place of Publication: Englewood Cliffs, NJ. Publication Year: 1971. Page Number: 51.

http://imahero.com/readingprogram/trailnatchez.html

http://www.tngenweb.org/campbell/hist-bogan/MiamiTrail.html

http://mshistory.k12.ms.us/features/feature30/gsgaines.html

http://mshistory.k12.ms.us/features/feature36/forks_of_the_road.html

http://www.us-census.org/native/choctaw.html

This Reckless Breed of Men

The Trappers and Fur Traders of the Southwest BY ROBERT GLASS CLELAND 1963 NEW YORK
ALFRED A. KNOPF

Western Women: Their Land, Their Lives. Contributors: Janice Monk - editor, Vicki L. Ruiz - editor,
Lillian Schlissel - editor. Publisher: University of New Mexico Press. Place of Publication: Albuquerque.
Publication Year: 1988

http://newdeal.feri.org/guides/tnguide/ch03.htm

http://www.muzzleblasts.com/vol3no6/articles/mbo36-4.html

Studies in American Indian Literature   Series 2   Volume 11, Number 1   Spring 1999
http://oncampus.richmond.edu/faculty/ASAIL/SAIL2/111.html

Stands and Travel Accommodations
on the Natchez Trace by Dawson Phelps in the Journal of Mississippi
History, Jan 1949

End Notes

The Cumberland River is an important waterway in the southern United States. It is 687 miles (1,106 km)
long. It starts in Letcher County in eastern Kentucky on the Cumberland Plateau, flows through
southeastern Kentucky before crossing into northern Tennessee, and then curves back up into western
Kentucky before draining into the Ohio River at Smithland, Kentucky. The Native American name for the
Cumberland River was the Warrito.

In 1748, Dr. Thomas Walker led a party of hunters across the Appalachian Mountains from Virginia.
Walker, a Virginian, was an explorer and surveyor of renown. He gave the name "Cumberland" to the
lofty range of mountains his party crossed, in honor of Prince William Augustus, Duke of Cumberland
whose name became popular in America after the Battle of Culloden (Stewart, 1967

John Murrell (also spelled as Murel and Murrel), a near-legendary bandit operating in the United States
along the Mississippi River in the mid-1800s.

Redbone, Mississippi

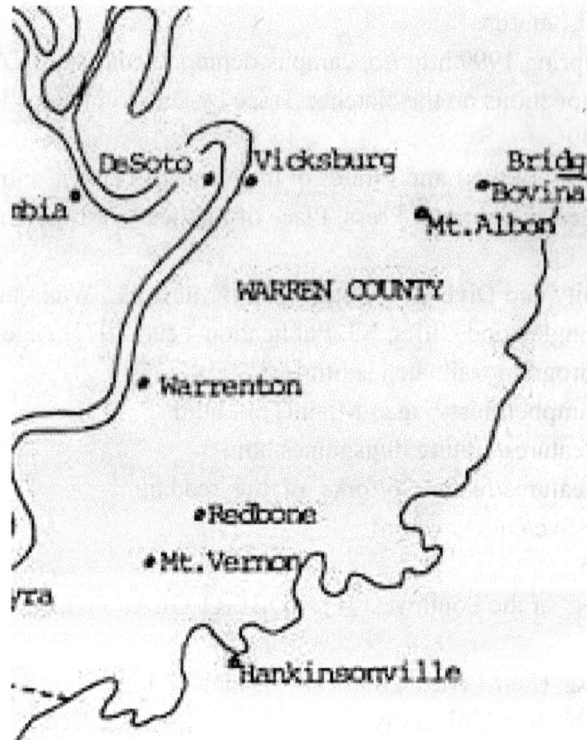

During the 1770s the first white residents of the region that became Warren County settled near the Nanachehaw hills on the Loosa Chitto River. Over the next twenty years the location selected by the original settlers remained popular. By 1800 newcomers had built homes to the north of the Loosa Chitto, along the crude roadway built by the Spanish atop the bluff that ran to the now abandoned Fort Nogales. During the following decade new neighborhoods appeared, where the ridge first approached the river, and at the Walnut Hills. Yet another cluster of farms materialized on a thin strip of high ground bordering the Mississippi adjacent to the uppermost of the Three Islands.

Evidence indicates that people associated the places where they lived with particular families. More than one document speaks of a Gibson neighborhood, for example, and when isolated on a map family groups do appear in clusters. A generation after arriving in Warren County, most members of the Vick family continued to live in the Open Wood neighborhood. The Gibson's gathered in the cane hills region, while the Evans family inhabited the vicinity of Redbone Creek.

Another two hundred or so people lived in the half-dozen villages that dotted the surrounding countryside. They stood as reminders of Vicksburg's humble beginnings. Warrenton, Redbone, Redwood, Bovina, Mt. Albon, Oak Ridge--such places consisted of little more than a church, one or two stores that doubled as taverns, perhaps a blacksmith shop, and maybe a post office. Some hamlets had a cotton gin and warehouse established by a local planter who made his facilities available to friends and neighbors. These hamlets might appear as little more than meeting places within rural neighborhoods, and thus perhaps were not truly urban at all. Yet as a public landing at the river, or a train station, or a simple fork in the road, such locales betrayed an urban function and process that set them apart from surrounding farms and plantations. Like the clearly identifiable cities, most especially Vicksburg, the country villages served as gathering places for rural people and produce, as collectors of goods and information, as points in a chain that stretched upward and outward from farm households to New Orleans, to New York, and finally to the great cities of Europe.

In 1809 the legislature for the Territory of Mississippi responded to the growing white and black population between the Loosa Chitto River and Choctaw Indian lands by organizing Warren County. Within ten years farms could be found in the northernmost corner of the new county. By 1830 farms had become so numerous as to make neighborhoods almost indistinguishable.

Isolation and economic interdependence kept social relations within Warren County's earliest neighborhoods locally and inwardly oriented. Before 1810 only two or three clusters of households, separated by large expanses of uninhabited territory, specked the 400 or so square miles of countryside north of the Big Black River. Within these early settlements people exchanged labor, tools, and produce with one another. They depended on each other for information, for help in times of need, for company. In 1809 a group of farmers along the Bayou Pierre in Claiborne County tried to formalize their interdependence through a "society" organized to promote "the public good individual and public economy," to "bargain contract and purchase for their own use their annual supplies," and to purchase and hold land and slaves. But the objectives listed in the society's charter merely stated the obvious. There was no need for such formality, and the society lasted but briefly. Cooperative interdependence, however, continued.

Of course, more than geography, a shared locale and economic interdependence linked neighboring households. Kinship and friendship also fastened people to one another. Westward migrants tended to travel and settle with associates from their former homes. The Vick and Cook families, for example, together moved to Jefferson County, Mississippi, from Virginia. When after a few years the Cooks moved upriver to Warren County the Vicks soon followed, again settling among their old friends in the Open Wood neighborhood. The Gibson family migrated in several waves from South Carolina, some settling near Natchez, others at Bayou Pierre, with descendants from both branches eventually resting in the same Warren County neighborhood.

Warren County's rural neighborhoods were not, however, peaceable little kingdoms of family and friends happily and harmoniously working together in some cooperative eden. Isolation and need forced people into associations not always to their liking. Those who lived near family and friends, next door to people whom they both trusted and liked, were fortunate indeed. Those who did not, however, still had to live, work, and trade with people whom they did not know very well, or even disliked. No one had the luxury of associating only with friends. Rather, one either did or did not make friends of those with whom one regularly associated. When William Stephens killed a hog that wandered into his field began. Our definition of a neighborhood as a visible cluster of homes will not do, unless we are to assume that they ceased to exist. However, such a conclusion would be misleading. Warren County residents continued to refer to the places where they lived as neighborhoods. If rural neighborhoods persisted as places, at least in the minds of the people, who lived within them, how are we to find them, and how are we to know that the places we find were their neighborhoods? We cannot, exactly, but there is enough evidence to allow us to approximate the location and definition of Warren County's rural neighborhoods as their inhabitants saw them.

Until 1832 the territorial governor, and then the state legislature, appointed all county judges. In that year the new constitution, hailed by historians as typical of the democratic reforms that marked the Age of Andrew Jackson, allowed an electorate of adult free men to choose their local officials. Moreover, it split the authority of the old county court, in which legislative, executive, and judicial power had been combined, between an administrative and legislative board of police and a civil court of probate. Government by planter nabobs was to be no more.

The new constitution did alter county politics. In earlier days local government mirrored informal structures of authority. That is to say, they acknowledged the importance of kinship and neighborhood leadership. In 1820 the state legislature confirmed Jacob Hyland's unofficial position of prominence as head of one of the wealthiest and best-connected families in the county by appointing him justice of the quorum. The next year Hyland's brother-in-law took a place on the bench as judge of probate. Andrew Glass, for several years a partner in business with Hyland's brother, and also connected to the Hyland family by marriage, won the most powerful local elected office, that of sheriff. The three men thus stood atop family, neighborhood, and county. Of course, other neighborhoods had their leaders, and not all could hold public office. But at that time public office meant little, particularly to those who lived at a distance from the county seat. It was no coincidence that Jacob Hyland's plantation abutted the seat of justice. But his position as justice of the quorum gave him little authority in neighborhoods other than in his own, where he was already leader even before he took his place on the bench.

By 1835, the situation had changed. Government wielded authority, and local leaders actively sought public office. Three years following the constitutional convention, William Mills, a Vicksburg attorney with no apparent connections to prominent local families, was elected judge of probate. E. W. Morris, another Vicksburg resident with no connections to leading families, won election to sheriff. Only the new board of police maintained some connection to rural neighborhoods and prominent slaveholding families. John Cowan was closely associated with the Vick family, as was E. G. Cook, whose family had enjoyed power and prestige in the north end of the county since its arrival two decades earlier. Jesse Evans, another elected member of the board of police, belonged to a large family in the Redbone neighborhood near Warrenton. Kinship and neighborhood, however, did not connect board members to each other, or any of them to the judge, or to the sheriff.

BROTHERS AND NEIGHBORS

One warm but windy spring day Benjamin Wailes took a leisurely ride around his neighborhood. From his home at Fonsylvania plantation near the Big Black River he headed southward, over his pasture toward Ivanhoe, an old plantation built by John Stephens forty years earlier, but recently purchased by Wailes for his niece Susan Covington. Susan had lived in the neighborhood as a girl, although she had moved to Natchez when her father died, since then visiting her childhood home infrequently. From Ivanhoe Wailes rode westward to Old Mr. Harris's place, and then on to Doc Hunt's. Finding no one at the doctor's home Wailes ambled through the fields, examining the cluster of Indian mounds south of Hunt's house. Several, he noted "have been ploughed over for a long period and the smaller ones almost obliterated." Wailes continued his tour, heading north at Mrs. Cameron's farm toward the old Valentine plantation. The new owner, a former Vicksburg miller named Austin Mattingly, intercepted the passerby and offered to sell him a load of bricks. The two men settled on a price of eight dollars per thousand before Wailes rode on, passing Mattingly's quarters and barns, near the large artificial pond graced by magnolia trees, and traveling beyond the brick kiln to a shallow creek, which he followed for perhaps two miles to the church. Bethel Methodist, more commonly known simply as Redbone church, attracted a large congregation from the neighborhood on most Sundays. Wailes usually attended, although sometimes he visited Antioch Baptist or, on occasion, if the visiting preacher happened to be a favorite, the chapel at Asbury campground. None was particularly close to Fonsylvania, each requiring a journey of about eight or ten miles round trip. One Sunday Wailes arrived at Redbone after Mr. Drake had already begun his sermon. A large crowd filled the building. Unable to get inside Benjamin listened from a window near the pulpit. While he left his station and wandered through the graveyard, among the "large number of handsome monuments," many of which he thought "exhibit considerable taste." He recognized some of the names, including those of several who, like himself, had come to this Warren County neighborhood from Natchez. From Redbone Wailes followed the road back home.

Methodism in Early Mississippi Territory

Religious groups offer their members social support, opportunities for leadership development, and numerous other nonspiritual benefits. While positive outcomes of church participation are worthy of attention, significant attention has not been placed on potentially negative aspects of church life. This is especially the case in the literature on the Black Church. This article examines the creation and maintenance of power structures (formalized power) and conflict in a Black United Methodist church. Themes derived from qualitative data reveal a number of paradoxes related to power, such as the observation that not all people in positions of power welcome the trappings of power. Also, results indicate that power structures are the result of a nexus between micro and macro factors which operate at both local and nonlocal levels.

Redbone Church

Located near Redbone Rd. along the Mississippi River about three miles north of Vicksburg

Bethel (Redbone) Methodist Church. Warren Co., Miss. Built 1854.
Used as Hospital by Federals at one time during Civil War.

FIGURE 34 PHOTO: BETHEL REDBONE METHODIST CHURCH WARREN CO., MISS. BUILT 1854 USED BY THE FEDERALS AT ONE TIME DURING THE CIVIL WAR.

This is the original cemetery of the Redbone Church and the oldest grave carries date of 1815". Unfortunately I never noticed any familiar Redbone names in the cemetery. Most headstones are broken and lying at the edge of trees and fences. There was extensive damage to several large Oak Trees throughout the cemetery while and impending hurricane made for a short and hasty visit. A large limb from a beautiful Old Oak that had fallen from obvious recent past storm damage can be viewed in the left corner of photo.

FIGURE 35 PHOTO:WELCOME CENTER AT JACKSON MISSISSIPPI BRIDGE

FIGURE 36 PHOTO:HISTORICAL MONUMENT "REDBONE METHODIST CHURCH"

Redbone United Methodist Church Cemetery

FIGURE 37 PHOTO:"A REVOLUTIONARY SOLDIER DAVID GREENLEAF CAN BE FOUND BURIED HERE"

Tobias Gibson South Carolina

Located about ½ of a mile from the Redbone Methodist Church stands a memorial historical marker for Tobias Gibson (1771-1804) he was the founder of Methodism in Mississippi, to which he was appointed in 1800. He was born in Liberty (now Florence) County, South Carolina, and admitted to the conference in 1792. He served circuits in the area, including Holston and North Carolina, until he went to Mississippi. He died at Natchez on April 5, 1804. (See Minutes, 1805.) 121 Tobias was appointed to the Little Pee Dee and Anson Circuit in South Carolina early in 1799. In January, 1800, he was appointed to Natchez, and sometime during the year he made a famous and perilous canoe voyage down the Mississippi and became the founder of Methodism in Mississippi. Jones (Methodism in Mississippi, I, 24 ff.) argues that Gibson reached Natchez late in March of 1799, which was nine months before he was officially appointed. If he gave notice of Asbury's presence in Buncombe County, North Carolina, and it was effective as late as November 1800 it would seem that he must have lingered in the Blue Ridge area for a period before departing for his appointment in Natchez.

FIGURE 38 PHOTO: HISTORICAL MARKER: WHICH REMAINS ON THE OLD RIVER ROAD ABOUT ½ A MILE FROM THE REDBONE METHODIST CHURCH MARKING THE GIBSON HOME SITE, AND WHERE HE WAS ORIGINALLY BURIED.

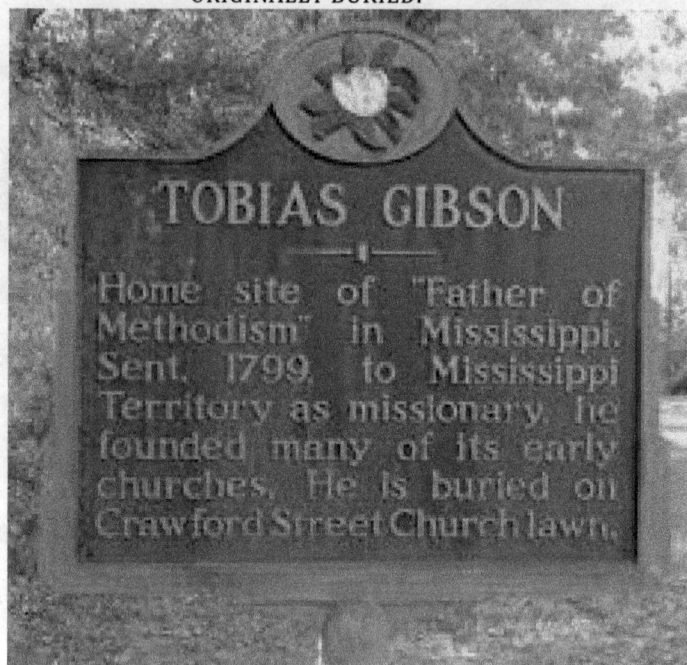

"Tobias went to Lexington in Kentucky, and Jacob Lurton went to the Cumberland Circuit in Tennessee". (See Minutes, 1794.)

During the early 1800s Tobias Gibson, an itinerant preacher sent from South Carolina, brought Methodism into the Natchez area of Mississippi. His ministry covered several hundred miles (Miller, 1966). Due to the lack of trained Methodist ministers and the settlement patterns of colonial America, ministers were responsible for covering large geographic areas. One outcome of this situation was that select individuals residing in the different regions where ministers made their stops were selected to be "class leaders." According to the class leader booklet of the United Methodist Church, "As a present-day class leader you will help a class of fifteen to twenty members shape their daily lives. . . ." (Guidelines, 1992 :5).

John Garvin had been appointed to Savannah and St. Mary's. At this conference Tobias was appointed to Natchez in Mississippi from Charleston in the South Carolina Conference to the Mississippi District of the Western Conference. Since Tobias Gibson had been sent to Mississippi in 1799, eight circuits had been formed, and there were 639 white and 150 colored members there.

The Journal and Letters of FRANCIS ASBURY

The Journal and Letters of Francis Asbury
The Journal - 1771 to 1816
Published in 1958 by
Epworth Press/Abingdon Press
March 1785

Thursday, 20 1787

"I directed my course, in company with my faithful fellow labourer, Tobias Gibson, up the Catawba, settled mostly by the Dutch. A barren spot for religion. Having ridden in pain twenty-four miles we came, weary and hungry, to 0--'s tavern; and were glad to take what came to hand. Four miles forward we came to Howes Ford, upon Catawba River, where we could neither get a canoe nor guide. We entered the water in an improper place, and were soon among the rocks and in the whirlpools: my head swam, and my horse was affrighted: the water was to my knees, and it was with difficulty we retreated to the same shore. We then called to a man on the other side, who came and piloted us across for which I paid him well. My horse being afraid to take the water a second time, brother Gibson crossed, and sent me his; and our guide took mine across. We went on, but our troubles were not at an end: night came on, and it was very dark. It rained heavily, with powerful lightning and thunder. We could not find the path that turned out to Connen's. In this situation we continued until midnight or past; at last we found a path which we followed till we came to dear old father Harper's plantation; we made for the house, and called; he answered, but wondered who it could be; he inquired whence we came; I told him we would tell that when we came in, for it was raining so powerfully we had not much time to talk: when I came dripping into the house, he cried, "God bless your soul, is it brother Asbury? wife, get up." Having had my feet and legs wet for six or seven hours, causes me to feet very stiff. Asbury always desired to go to Mississippi since Tobias Gibson established Methodism there in 1800, but was never permitted by the conference to do so".

Louisiana Kasatchie (Cousatchi/Coushatty) Hills, Bayou and Black Lake Settlements

Louisiana Road Tour through Redbone Country

1931 Road Tour through Redbone Country
Louisiana: A Guide to the State
Book by Louisiana Writers' Project; Hastings House, 1941
Published Jointly By EPWORTH PRESS ABINGDON PRESS London Nashville

Louisiana: A Guide to the State

[1] A plantation in the Natchitoches region was the scene of Harriet Beecher Stowe 's *Uncle Tom's Cabin*. It is a disputed point whether or not Mrs. Stowe ever visited this part of the State, but a spot at Chopin is pointed out as the actual site of the cabin. Kate Chopin, one of the best known short story writers in America in the nineties, lived for a time at Cloutierville. She is the author of *Bayou Folk*. Ada Jack Carver wrote stories concerning the *"Redbones"* of the region, which appeared in *Harper's* and *Century* between 1925 and 1928. Lyle Saxon's *Children of Strangers* (1937) is a novel dealing with Cane River mulattoes.

Key to Points of Interest
SECTION I
Tour
1. Rodessa Oil Field 19a
2. Huey House 15a
3. Giddens' Castle Hill 7b
4. Barksdale Field 18b
5. Site of Caddo Agency House 17b
6. U. S. Pecan Experiment Station 17b
7. Site of Freetown 16
8. Site of Sparta 16
9. Allendale 19b
10. Buena Vista 19b
11. Lands End 19b
12. Rock Chapel 5b
13. Mansfield Battle Park 19b
14. Redbones 16

On the southern shore of Black Lake live many "Redbones" (Louisiana name for a person of white, Indian, and Negro parentage) who, like the mulattoes of Isle Brevelle (**_see_Tour 17b**) live to themselves apart from whites and Negroes. Local traditions vary as to the origin of these people. According to one, they are descendants of early French explorers who intermarried with the Indians; another relates that in the sixteenth century a party of Portuguese sailors, shipwrecked in the Gulf of Mexico, made their way through the wilderness of central Louisiana and settled among friendly Indians. Presumably, these halfbreeds later intermarried with Negroes. Whatever their ancestry, the Redbones are tall and slender, have a reddish complexion, dark eyes, high cheek bones, and straight, black hair. The strange semitransparent appearance of their skin is responsible for their odd sobriquet. Strangers frequently trade and in some instances form friendships with them, but as a whole the group maintains a stoical reserve which cannot be completely broken.

South of Creston La 50 crosses Black Lake Bridge, affording a view of the lake and the surrounding country. Black Lake, and two other near-by lakes, Clear and Saline, are part of the O. K. ALLEN FISH AND GAME PRESERVE, named for the late governor of the State. This preserve comprises an area of 35 square miles and was completed in 1932 with the building of a dam across Saline Bayou.

Tour 17b.

Hagewood--Kisatchie--Junction with US 171; 41.8 *m.*, La 39.

Graveled roadbed.

No accommodations.

This route runs south from Hagewood through wooded upland country. For 22 miles the highway winds through the Kisatchie Division of the Kisatchie National Forest. Beyond the forest are bleak cut-over timber lands inhabited by timber workers, small stock farmers, and squatters.

La 39, branching south from La 6 (*see*Tour 17A) at HAGEWOOD, 0 *m.* (*see*Tour 17A), meanders through sparsely settled timberland. The simple rough board cottages, built of lumber sawed at one of the local mills, are roofed with heart-pine boards split from native timber. Most of the homes have wells dug by hand and the old custom of "witching for water" is still followed. Before a well is dug the local prognosticator surveys the farm with a willow twig or a peach tree limb to indicate, by the bending of the willow, the exact spot at which a vein or spring of water can be found.

At 6.6 *m.* La 39 crosses the boundary of the **KISATCHIE DIVISION OF THE KISATCHIE NATIONAL FOREST** *(build fires in designated fireplaces only; keep grounds clean)* (*see*Tour 15a). In this forest region are stately pines and sandy hills, with occasional outcroppings of sandstone and limestone. Many cold, clear streams flow through rock-walled gorges and over sandstone ledges, forming little rapids and miniature waterfalls. Game is plentiful in the woods; quail, doves, woodcock, some wild turkeys, squirrels, rabbits, deer, and foxes are to be found. Wild honeysuckle, dogwood, wild azaleas, and the climbing yellow jasmine can be seen from February to April; in autumn the red and yellow foliage of oaks, gums, hickories, and maples outline the ridges of the heavily wooded hills. Picnic spots abound.

The **KISATCHIE OBSERVATION TOWER** *(open)*, 19.3 *m.*, is (L) on one of the highest hills in the Kisatchie Forest.

KISATCHIE, 22.3 *m.* (338 alt., 27 pop.), has (R) a consolidated school that serves a large rural community. The village and the Kisatchie Forest were both named for Kisatchie Creek, which flows cast of the town. In John Sibley's report from Natchitoches in 1807 this name appeared as Cossachie, which in Choctaw means "reed river." Left from Kisatchie on unmarked, graveled La 433 to the junction with a dirt road, 1.8 *m.;* L. here to (R) the **KISATCHIE FALLS**, 3.4 *m.* The falls, in reality nothing more than rapids, tumble over limestone and sandstone ledges, their size varying according to the season and the amount of local rainfall. Picnic tables have been erected in a grove of magnolia trees on the banks of the stream. The beauty and quiet of this secluded spot attract visitors from long distances.

At 25.9 *m.* La 39 crosses the southern boundary of the **KISATCHIE DIVISION OF THE KISATCHIE NATIONAL FOREST** *(see above)*.

South of KURTHWOOD, 27.7 *m.* (800 pop.), a sawmill town, La 39 traverses cut-over land. Logging trucks are frequently met on the highway; occasionally an ox team used for skidding or handling logs can be seen. The small houses set at intervals in clearings are generally tenanted by squatters, who are awaiting the day when the second growth of timber will be ready for cutting. In the meantime they get along as best they can, eking out a living from the land and occasionally doing a few days' work for the lumber companies. Most of the land throughout the area is owned by the large lumber companies, and the squatters are charged 50ç to $1 a year to avoid squatters' rights being acquired by the tenants. Some of these people have lived so many years under this arrangement that they customarily regard the property they live on as their own. They improve their places by clearing, burning stumps, and by cultivating additional land; the more enterprising erect new farm buildings. Peculiar difficulties have arisen when these tenants have applied for government assistance for farm improvement.

Although timber work is the chief source of livelihood, many of the inhabitants supplement their incomes by raising goats and other livestock that graze on the free range amid the pines. This country is ideal for cattle, but incomes from livestock are uncertain because of the presence of the modern cattle rustler, who works by night, with the help of improved highways and modern transportation. Cattle thieves drive their large trucks into the grazing area, find a secluded by-road, load the stock and leave for a distant market. About all the owner can find is the spot where the truck left the highway and some of the tracks of his cattle. At times he finds that his cattle have been slaughtered on the spot, which makes apprehension even more difficult, since there is no tell-tale evidence of brands or other marks. In some sections irate livestock owners have organized in an effort to eliminate this hazard to their business. Sometimes a local resident is suspected of rustling, and lively feuds result.

Along the highway in this section are occasional brush arbors, where revival meetings and sometimes regular weekly church meetings are held. The congregations are usually Holiness, Apostolic, or Church of God adherents, although Methodist and Baptist groups also hold services under these arbors.

At 41.8 *m.* is the junction with US 171 (*see*Tour 19b), 0.8 mile north of Leesville.

Brass Ankle Family Summerville, South Carolina

Photos of a Summerville, South Carolina Brass Ankle family. These photos were taken during the 1930s writer's project.

FIGURES 39 PHOTOS: INDIAN MIXED BREED BRASS ANKLE FAMILY NEAR SUMMERVILLE, SOUTH CAROLINA (CONGRESS 1915)

The Burgess Survey

Figure 40 Photo: Elizabeth Burgess The Little "affent girl" was raised by James and Mary Ash/Nash Groves. she later married LC Sweat

Marriage bond issued Dec 22, 1828 in St. Landry Parish by Gideon Sweat giving his "free and voluntary consent to the marriage of my son, (unreadable) with Elizabeth Burgess of the aforesaid Parish." Gideon Sweat's Mark (X) with witnesses (?) Jefferson and James Ray, George King Judge. The document continued with "Leonard Covington Sweat legitimate son of Gideon Sweat and Lettitia Johnson, a native of Opelousas, with Elizabeth Burgess legitimate daughter of (unreadable) Burgess and (unreadable), a native of the Parish of Natchitoches, Gideon Sweat and Issac Ventioner, Security. Thomas Jay/Gay, Esq."

Elizabeth Burgess and Leonard Covington Sweat On Jan. 24, 1829 in nearby Avoyelles Ph., Sweat married Elizabeth Burgess "of Avoyelles Parish, Louisiana. An exact transcription

"Mr. Judge King you will pleaz to grant lisong to Covington Swet to Marry with Elizabeth burgeza a offent girl that I have rased from the age of three months of age a Dauteu of my brother in law. I myself have the sole management of her both curator and parent. These few linz will sirtify that I gave consent this 22 day of December 1828. James Groves. Gideon his X mark Swet, Isaac Ventioner." (James Groves appears to have written the letter and signed his name to it Isaac Ventioner, a brother in law to Leonard C. Sweat........ "Know all men by these presents that Leonard Covinton Sweat, Gideon Sweat and Isaac Ventioner of the State of Louisiana and Parish of Saint Landry are held and bound

Burgess-Sweat-Ash/Nash

In about 1834 a remnant tribe associated with the Muscogee Creek of Alabama, the Pakana Muskogee migrated from the Red River area of east Texas and Louisiana boarder region. This small band of Pakana settled near Onalaska in western Polk County, Texas. The band had were originally living near Fort Toulouse, a few miles north of Montgomery, Alabama, and moved to Louisiana shortly after 1763. See Natchez Trace Figure Map above for reference. Dr. John Sibley Indian agent for the United States who was also Redbone related, reported in 1805 only one hundred and fifty Pakana Muskogees were living on Calcasieu Bayou, forty miles southwest of Natchitoches, Louisiana in the heart of Redbone country. An early chief of the Pakana

Muskogees, Chief Blount, awarded a silver medal for his services as a guide for Gen. Andrew Jackson during the Seminole War in Florida. After the death of John Blount while enroute to Texas via New Orleans, in 1834, the medal was passed to the chiefs of the tribe: David Elliott, Bill Blount, John Blount (grandson of the earlier chief with the same name), and Alex Davis and remains among their people to this day.

In about 1800 John Burgess, a so called Frenchmen closely related to the Redbone families in Calcaseui staked his land in today's western Polk Co., Texas; called the Burgess Survey. In about 1813 there was a great Indian raid, we do not have any details, except that John Burgess and wife Unknown Ash/Nash were killed leaving several orphans who were subsequently taken in and reared by the other Redbone families established in Calacasieu Parish, Louisiana. 1834 the Pakana Muskogees moved to a site on Penwau (according to S. Pony Hill, translated from Creek this means "Turkey") Slough two miles east of its junction with the Trinity River in the area of present Polk County. This location was on a high hill, generally believed to be the peninsula that extends into Lake Livingston and is known as Indian Hill. John Burgess, a supposed Frenchman laid survey on a 640 acres of land along Kickapoo Creek.

FIGURE 41 PHOTO: PAKANA MUSCOGEE INDIAN OF TEXAS

According to legend, John Burgess was married to a member of the Pakana Muskogee, and according to genealogical records and affidavits given; she was a daughter of Thomas Ash/Nash a progenitor forefather of nearly all Louisiana Redbone families. We believe according to affidavits (marriage record of LC Sweat & Elizabeth Burgess by Ventioner and Groves) contains the identity of Elizabeth Burgesses mother as his daughter. Though her name is unknown to us, she would have been the daughter of Thomas and Emily Slater Ash/Nash. Ben Ash/Nash would have been her half-brother and was the son of Thomas and (2) Anna Goings Ash/Nash. That would mean that either Thomas Ash or Emily Slater (see mtDNA results below) was

Pakana, however Thomas Ash's descendant made application the Cherokee Nation; "Thomas Nash was full blooded Indian, by blood." However, Ben Ash, son of Anna Goings was Coushatta associated, perhaps through Hannah Perkins Ash/Nash. Ben also signed old Cherokee settlers treaty, and the treaty of Dancing Rabbit "Penashes". The family lore was always Creek Muscogee.

According to affidavits given, Elizabeth was raised by James and Mary Polly Ash/Nash Groves at Glass Window trading Post, Vernon Parish, La. Both Isaac Ventioner and James Groves witness that Elizabeth born about 1813 was an "affent girl" (sic), "the legitimate daughter of my wife's brother in law." These statements would suggest that Elizabeth's mother was in fact the daughter of Thomas Ash/Nash and (1) Emily Slater. The couple obviously died shortly after arriving in Texas at the Burgess survey.

John Burgess had invited other tribal members from his wife's clan to relocate to their survey in Texas, from Louisiana Red River region. There was a "Widow Burgeff" listed in the 1810 Opelousas census records next door to Thomas Ash, Gibson Johnson, Gideon Gibson, Thomas Goyens and Benjamin Ash and Jean Baptists Lafitte who we believe to be the Pirate, Jean Lafitte. The "widow" Burgess could have been daughter of Thomas Ash/Nash, widow of John Burgess survey.

The property was inherited by Burgess's wife and subsequently by other members of the tribe and became a permanent home for the Pakana Muskogees in Polk County. In 1859 Texas Governor Hardin R. was appointed James Barclay to serve as agent for the Muskogees, as well as for the Alabama and Coushatta who lived in Polk County. Responsibility for the Muskogee was included also in the duties of agents appointed for the Polk County Indians in 1861-65, 1867, 1868, and 1872. On November 12, 1866, the Texas legislature passed an act granting the Polk County Muskogee, 320 acres of land.

Unfortunately the land was never purchased, and they continued to live on the John Burgess Survey without title. The population of this Pakana Muskogee community declined slowly almost from the date of the tribe's first appearance in Polk County: fifty were counted in 1859; forty-two were reported in 1882. The remaining probably died off as a result of Illness and absorption by the nearby Alabama and Coushatta probably were the main reasons for the Muskogee's population declines. In 1899, persuaded by Creek Indians from Oklahoma, Chief

John Blount and many of the Polk County Muskogees went to the Creek Nation in Oklahoma to live. Only a few-less than ten-Pakana Muskogees remained in their settlement on the John Burgess Survey.

FIGURE 42 PHOTO: AN OLDER ELIZABETH BURGESS SWEAT

Our Redbone families continued to live in Polk Co., Texas. After the infamous Rawhide Fight, Leonard Covington Sweat husband of Elizabeth Burgess moved to Polk Co., Texas and his family soon followed. Leonard C. Sweat's Y-DNA matched perfectly to the Goyens, Williams, Warwick, Powell (Osceola), and one genetic distance from the Richard Perkins line, of Spesutie, Maryland. Leonard C. Sweat was the son of Gideon "Gadi" (1812-1882) and Letitia Johnson (1795-1854) both born in Burke Co., North Carolina and died in Louisiana. The Johnsons were early settlers to the Kisatchie area of Louisiana around Natchitoches. They appear to have arrived with the group of Talimala Band of Apalachicola who were reserved land there by the French. After the Louisiana Purchase the U.S. Congress denied the Indian reserve and the majority of Indians relocated to the Kisathcie Hills area where later, they also were denied land claims and the ones who remained eventually burned out by white settlers.

FIGURE 43 PHOTO: BENJAMIN ASH/NASH AKA "BEN ASH/ES" SIGNED CHEROKEE OLD SETTLERS TREATY, THE TREATY OF DANCING RABBIT "PENASHES" AND GAVE PERMISSION FOR "WHITE MEN TO SETTLE ON "COUSHATTY LAND" IN TEXAS CHARACTER REFERENCE. HE WAS DESCRIBED BY FAMILY MEMBERS AS VERY TALL, THIN AND ONLY WORE MOCCASINS THOUGH BOUGHT SHOES HUNG NEAR HIS DOOR, PURCHASED BY HIS SON FOR HIM, HE REFUSED TO WEAR THEM.

FIGURE 44 PHOTO: OLLA W NASH ON RIGHT SON OF WM. HARRISON GRANDSON OF BENJAMIN ASH/NASH B. 1895 D1925 KILLED ON A WAGON LOADED WITH LOGS AT SMITHS FERRY TYLER TEXAS

FIGURE 45 PHOTO: LULA NASH NEW'S CHILDREN, DAUGHTER OF BIG JOSEPH ASH/NASH AND MARTHA ANN WILLIAMS GRANDCHLDREN OF BEN ASH/NASH.

FIGURE 46 PHOTO: WILLIAM HENDERSON, SON OF BIG JOSEPH & MARTHA ANN WILLIAMS, GRANDSON BENJAMIN ASH AND HANNAH PERKINS ASH/NASH, ASH/NASH

Though Benjamin would not have been a descendant to the Burgess Survey, he was obviously a vital part of the Coushatta Indian Community through his wife, Hannah Perkins and related families. In a Texas character certificate dated 1834-1836, Ben Ashes "Head men of the Coushatta does give permission for the White men to settle on Coushatty land" and though he was married to Hannah Perkins, only after his half-brother William Ash/Nash died. It has been erroneously assumed and reported that the document pertaining to Hannah Perkins Ash/Nash was that of Benjamin and not his half-brother William Ash/Nash. "Hannah Nash is to be allowed to move about East Tx. to return to her people, her husband is dead" permission by Sam Houston. The Texas handbook and other historians are inaccurate when they claim this was "Ben Ash" (b 1801-1888) who had died. Hannah Perkins Ash/Nash Ash/Nash was married first to "Ben's" half-brother William. It would have been William Ash (1795-1830) who was killed. Hannah was the daughter of Nimrod Perkins he was a Revolutionary War Veteran and Betsy Waters (not "Laughing Waters"). A picture of Mahala Ash/Nash Turner the daughter of Hannah Perkins and William Ash can be seen here. Little else is known of Nimrod, he is suspected to also be of the Richard Perkins line.

FIGURES 47 PHOTOS: HEADSTONES FOR MATILDA SWEAT MASON ASH/NASH AND BENJAMIN ASH/NASH CEMETERY NO ZULCH, MADISON, TEXAS. LAST VISIT IN 2015, THE CEMETERY IS POOR CONDITION AND IT IS NEARLY IMPOSSIBLE TO LOCATE SOME GRAVES. IT IS ON PRIVATE PROPERTY AND PERMISSION MUST BE OBTAINED TO GAIN ACCESS. ALSO, A FOUR WHEEL DRIVE IS RECOMMENDED DURING MOST OF THE YEAR

FIGURE 48 PHOTO: MATILDA "TILLY" SWEAT MASON ASH/NASH AND SON GUIDE EMANUEL ASH/NASH. MATILDA WAS THE DAUGHTER OF ELIZABETH BURGESS AND LC SWEAT. THEY SETTLED ON BENJAMIN ASH/NASHES LAND AT NO. ZULCH, MADISON CO., TEXAS WHERE SHE IS BURIED WITH BENJAMIN ASH/NASH.

Some descendants of John Burgess Survey

Leonard Covington and Elizabeth Burgess Family

Elizabeth Burgess, daughter of **Unknown Ash/Nash** *(E. Slater/Thomas Ash/Nash[2], Unknown/John the Indian Trader[1])* and **John A. Burgess** married **Leonard Covington Sweat,** son of **Gideon "Gadi" Sweat** and **Lettitia "Letty" Johnson,** on 22 Dec 1828 in St. Landry Parish, Louisiana. Leonard was born on 8 Dec 1812 in Bayou, St Landry Parish, Louisiana and died after 1872 in Jasper, Jasper County, Texas.

Mr. Sweat was evidently of strong character and a leader in the community. He participated in the famous Rawhide Fight in Vernon Parish, La. about 1850 and led a posse of vigilantes in cleaning up the "Jayhawkers" who plagued the area during the Civil War plaguing the area with their robbery and murder. Children of Leonard "Uncle Linn" and Elizabeth Sweat who moved to Texas following the Rawhide Fight.

FIGURE 49 PHOTO: "UNCLE LINN" SWEAT AT GLASS WINDOW CEMETERY, VERNON PARISH, LOUISIANA. HE STILL HAD THE AXE HANDLE USED BY GRANDFATHER LC SWEAT IN THE RAWHIDE FIGHT, AKA RAGE STAND HILL, GLASS WINDOW TRADING POST, VERNON PARISH, LOUISIANA.

Noted events in his life were:
- 1870 US Fed Census: Madison Co., Texas.
- Military: 27th La. Infantry, 23 Mar 1862.

Children from this marriage were:

Mary Sweat was born about 1832 in St. Landry Parish, Louisiana and died in 1870 in Trinity Co., TX about age 38. Mary married **Sylvester Curtis**.

Leonard Covington Sweat, Jr. was born on 10 Dec 1835 in Pitkin, Vernon Parish, Louisiana, died on 18 Dec 1931 in Vernon Parish, Louisiana at age 96, and was buried in Glass Window Cemetery, Vernon Parish, La. Leonard married **Mary C. Groves** (d. 24 Dec 1902).

Henry Sweat was born about 1837 in Ten Mile Creek, Rapides Parish, La.

Elizabeth Sweat was born about 1841 in Ten Mile Creek, Rapides Parish, La. and died about 1918 about age 77. Elizabeth married **Zeddie Gibson**.

Missouri Sweat was born about 1843 in Ten Mile Creek, Rapides Parish, La. and was buried in Post Oak Cemetery, Franklin, Robertson Co., Tx.

Martha Sweat was born about 1843 in Opelousas Parish, Louisiana and died in 1885 in Franklin, Robertson Co., TX about age 42.

Matilda "Tilly" Sweat was born about 1847 in Rapides Parish, Louisiana, died in 1898 in Texas about age 51, and was buried in Nash Cemetery, No. Zulch, Madison, TX. Matilda married

137

Unknown Mason about 1860 in Louisiana. Matilda next married **Emanuel Command Nash/Ash/Ashes** (d. 10 Jul 1947) on 12 Dec 1883 in Robertson, Texas.

William Sweat was born about 1851 in Ten Mile Creek, Rapides Parish, La. and died about 1925 about age 74. William married **Janey Singleton**.

Gady Sweat was born about 1858 in Ten Mile Creek, Rapides Parish, La. and died after 1872 in Texas.

Nancy Elizabeth Sweat was born on 21 Feb 1872, died on 23 Apr 1943 at age 71, and was buried in Glass Window Cemetery, Vernon Parish, La. Nancy married **Charles Steven Wise** (d. 27 Nov 1940).

Louisa Sweat was born about 1848 in Ten Mile Creek, Rapides Parish, La.

Sarah Sweat was born about 1851 in Ten Mile Creek, Rapides Parish, La. and died about 1888 about age 37. Sarah married **Frank Pinson**.

4. Mary Sweat *(Elizabeth Burgess [2], John [1])* was born about 1832 in St. Landry Parish, Louisiana and died in 1870 in Trinity Co., TX about age 38. Mary sweat married *Sylvester Curtis* their children are:

Children from this marriage were:
i.	**Macenia Curtis** was born about 1852.
ii.	**Vienna Curtis** was born about 1854.
iii.	**Steven Curtis** was born about 1857.
iv.	**Leonard Curtis** was born about 1859.
v.	**Missouri Curtis**.
vi.	**Phoebe Curtis** was born about 1864.

Sylvester Curtis. Sylvester was born about 1828. **Richard Curtis, Jr**. First Baptist Minister in Mississippi. He was born in Dinwiddie County, Virginia, on May 20, 1756; son of Richard Curtis, Sr. and Phoebe, widow of **William Jones**. **Richard Curtis, Sr.**, and family (there was a stepson, John Jones, who married Anna, daughter of William Brown on 28 Jun 1768, and five sons and three daughters) resided in 1775 on the Great Pee Dee River, near the mouth of Black River, South Carolina, but came to the Natchez Country in 1780, where Richard Curtis, Sr. died near Cole's Creek on November 10, 1784. Accompanying Richard Curtis, Sr. to the Natchez Country were 3 sons, a stepson (John Jones) and 2 sons-in-law, three of whom later became pioneer citizens of Amite County: (1) son Richard, Jr. and his wife Pattie; (2) Son **William Curtis** and his wife; (3) and daughter Hannah Curtis, wife of John Courtney. **Richard Curtis, Jr.,** who had been licensed as a Baptist Minister in South Carolina in 1778, began to preach throughout the Natchez Country but especially in the Salem Community near Cole's Creek. In 1795 he ran afoul of the Spanish authorities for preaching and officiating at the marriage of his niece, Phoebe Jones to David Greenleaf, and he was forced to return to South Carolina, where he was ordained in 1796. He returned to the Mississippi Territory in 1798, and as Moderator helped to organize in due and ancient form Salem Baptist Church on Cole's Creek in Jefferson County as a regular Baptist Church, the first in Mississippi.On May 9, 1806, Rev. Richard Curtis, Jr., assisted by Rev. Thomas Mercer, Rev. James Courtney from South

Carolina, **Rev. Isaac Jackson** from New Providence Baptist Church and **Rev. Jonathan Curtis** from Salem Baptist Church, constituted the Ebenezer Baptist Church on Beaver Creek in Amite County and was the first Pastor. Among the charter members were Mary Curtis, and his brother-in-law, John Courtney, both with letters from Salem Baptist Church on Cole's Creek. **Mary Curtis** (wife or daughter?) dismissed by letter on October 1, 1808. **Rev. Richard Curtis, Jr.**, was Pastor of New Hope Baptist Church in Adams County, Mississippi (organized in 1800 and was the second Baptist Church in Mississippi), and a messenger to the Mississippi Baptist Association in 1808-1811. **Rev. Richard Curtis, Jr.**, was disallowed a claim of settlement on Beaver Creek in Amite County in 1802, because the land was not improved, but was granted 320 acres there in 1808. He is listed as a citizen of Amite County in the Census of 1805 and 1810. (A relative also named **Richard Curtis** is listed in the Census of 1810 and 1816.) Rev. Richard Curtis, Jr. died of cancer on Beaver Creek in Amite County, Mississippi on October 28,1811, and is buried in the yard of what was years later the residence of Dr. W. b. Kinnabrew, about 1/2 mile from Ebenezer Baptist Church, and there is a marble obelisk in the churchyard. John Courtney, brother-in-law of Richard Curtis, Sr., was appointed delegate from Ebenezer Baptist Church of Amite County, Mississippi on January 31, 1807, to attend the organization meeting of the Mississippi Baptist Association at Cole's Creek Church. He settled with his wife, **Hannah Curtis**, and 7 children on 666 acres on Beaver Creek, Section 30, Township 1 north, range 3 east in November, 1802. Brother **Benjamin Curtis**, brother-in-law John Stampley, a Baptist Minister, and half-brother **John Jones** and their families settled in the Cole's Creek area of the Mississippi Territory. (The author of the above, who remains anonymous, inserted following note. jtd) The second Baptist Church organized in Mississippi was located at the confluence of Big Bayou Pierre and Little Bayou Pierre in Claiborne County, Mississippi. This area is not in the city limits of Port Gibson, Mississippi. The second Baptist Church in Mississippi was organized in 1798, in Claiborne County, Mississippi and was known as Bayou Pierre Baptist Church. It ceased to exist in 1825. Will of RICHARD CURTICE, SENIOR Book 1, Transcript Original Spanish Records on file. Noted events in his life were: 1850 Census: Rapides Parish, Louisiana.

5. **Leonard Covington Sweat Jr.** (Elizabeth Burgess [2], John [1]) was born on 10 Dec 1835 in Pitkin, Vernon Parish, Louisiana, died on 18 Dec 1931 in Vernon Parish, Louisiana at age 96, and was buried in Glass Window Cemetery, Vernon Parish, La. Research Notes: Enumerated 1880 Vernon Parish, La. Census

Leonard married **Mary C. Groves**, daughter of **James Jr. Groves** and **Nancy Perkins**. Mary was born on 21 Sep 1840, died on 24 Dec 1902 at age 62, and was buried in Glass Window Cemetery, Vernon Parish, La.

Children from this marriage were:

> i. **James Henry "Bud" Sweat** was born about 1860 in Natchitoches Parish, La. James married **Ella Wales**.
> ii. **Emma Sweat** was born on 11 Feb 1861, died on 1 Feb 1876 in Vernon Parish, Louisiana at age 14, and was buried in Glass Window Cemetery, Vernon Parish, La.
> iii. **Lee Sweat** was born on 2 Apr 1864, died on 10 Mar 1910 at age 45, and was buried in Glass Window Cemetery, Vernon Parish, La. Lee married **P. Caroline**

"Dollie" Hall (d. 15 Jul 1959).

iv.   **Laura V. Sweat** was born on 22 Jul 1866, died on 15 Mar 1888 in Vernon Parish, Louisiana at age 21, and was buried in Glass Window Cemetery, Vernon Parish, La. **William Penn Sweat** was born on 25 Dec 1869, died on 13 Nov 1956 at age 86, and was buried in Glass Window Cemetery, Vernon Parish, La. William married **Alma Chester** (d. 16 Mar 1965).

v.   **Nancy Elizabeth Sweat** was born on 21 Feb 1872, died on 23 Apr 1943 at age 71, and was buried in Glass Window Cemetery, Vernon Parish, La. Nancy married **Charles Steven Wise** (d. 27 Nov 1940).

vi.   **Almarinda E. Sweat** was born on 29 Mar 1874, died on 19 Jan 1875 in Vernon Parish, Louisiana, and was buried in Glass Window Cemetery, Vernon Parish, La.

vii.   **Mary C. Sweat** was born on 24 Oct 1876, died on 16 Feb 1898 in Vernon Parish, Louisiana at age 21, and was buried in Glass Window Cemetery, Vernon Parish, La. Mary married **James Pinkney Groves** (d. 5 May 1940).

viii.   **Annette Sweat** was born on 8 Jan 1878, died on 8 Feb 1902 in Vernon Parish, Louisiana at age 24, and was buried in Glass Window Cemetery, Vernon Parish, La. Annette married **A.B. Slatten**.

ix.   **Andrew J. Sweat** was born on 28 Mar 1883, died on 20 Feb 1888 at age 4, and was buried in Glass Window Cemetery, Vernon Parish, La.

6. Henry Sweat *(Elizabeth Burgess [2], John [1])* was born about 1837 in Ten Mile Creek, Rapides Parish, La.

Noted events in his life were:
• 1850 Cesus: Rapides Parish, Louisiana.

7. Elizabeth Sweat *(Elizabeth Burgess [2], John [1])* was born about 1841 in Ten Mile Creek, Rapides Parish, La. and died about 1918 about age 77. Elizabeth married **Zeddie Gibson**.

8. Missouri Sweat *(Elizabeth Burgess [2], John [1])* was born about 1843 in Ten Mile Creek, Rapides Parish, La. and was buried in Post Oak Cemetery, Franklin, Robertson Co., Tx.

Noted events in his life were:
• 1850 Cesus: Rapides Parish, Louisiana.

9. Martha Sweat *(Elizabeth Burgess [2], John [1])* was born about 1843 in Opelousas Parish, Louisiana and died in 1885 in Franklin, Robertson Co., TX about age 42.

10. **Matilda "Tilly" Sweat** pictured above *(Elizabeth Burgess ², John ¹)* was born about 1847 in Rapides Parish, Louisiana, died in 1898 in Texas about age 51, and was buried in Nash Cemetery, No. Zulch, Madison, TX. Matilda married **Unknown Mason** about 1860 in Louisiana. Matilda next married **Emanuel Command Nash/Ash/Ashes,** son of **James Nash/Ash/Ashes** and **Mary "Polly" Perkins,** on 12 Dec 1883 in Robertson, Texas. Emanuel was born on 18 Dec 1843 in Rapides Parish, Louisiana, died on 10 Jul 1947 at age 103, and was buried in Mt. Zion Cem., Trinity Co., TX.. Noted events in his life were: He appeared on the census in 1850 in Rapides Parish, Louisiana. He appeared on the census in 1870 & 1880 in Madison Co., Texas.

- He applied to the Cherokee Nation citizenship court on 11 Jul 1896.

Children from this marriage were:

- **FIGURE 50** PHOTO: EMANUEL "COMMAND" NASH HUSBAND OF (1) NANCY SIMMONS ALLEN, (2) MATILDA "TILLY" SWEAT MASON, AND (3) SENA GOYENS

-

FIGURE 51 PHOTO: GUIDE E. NASH, SON OF "COMMAND" AND MATILD SWEAT MASH ASH/NASH

i. **Guide Emanuel Nash/Ash/Ashes** was born on 22 Aug 1885 in Madison Co., TX., died on 28 Jun 1967 at age 81, and was buried in Mt. Zion Cem., Trinity Co., TX. Guide married **Missouri Lacey Goins** (d. 19 Apr 1963) on 18 Sep 1909 in Madison Co., TX.

ii. **Caion Nash/Ash/Ashes** was born on 10 Dec 1887 in Louisiana, died on 23 Oct 1889 at age 1, and was buried in Nash Cemetery, No. Zulch, Madison, TX.

iii. **Gussie Nash/Ash/Ashes** was born on 4 Apr 1890 in Texas, died on 20 Mar 1896 at age 5, and was buried in Nash Cemetery, No. Zulch, Madison, TX.

iv. **Gadi** died young mentioned in the 1896 Cherokee Application affidavit of genealogy.

v. **Will Nash/Ash/Ashes** was born on 26 Dec 1893 in Louisiana and died on 18 Nov 1915 at age 21.Will married Effie Thomas (d. 21 Aug 1930).

vi. **Robert "Rob" Nash/Ash/Ashes** was born on 23 Sep 1895 in Louisiana, died on 17 Nov 1988 at age 93, and was buried in Mt. Zion Cem., Trinity Co., TX. Robert married Dessie Jeafrey/Jeffries (d. 18 Mar 1997) on 3 Jul 1925. Some her family of Jaffries are buried at Nash Cemetery No Zulch, Madison Co., Tx. though nothing else is known of them.

vii. **John Nash/Ash/Ashes** was born about 1897 and died about 1904 about age 7

FIGURE 52 PHOTO: NORTH ZULCH ASH/NASH SETTLEMENT & CEMETERY.
THIS OAK TREE IS ALL WHICH REMAINS OF THE HOME PLACE, CEMETERY IN THE BACKGROUND. FIRST SETTLED BY BENJAMIN "BEN" ASH/NASH INHERITED LATER BY NEPHEW BROTHERS STEVE AND EMANUEL "COMMAND" ASH/NASH.

11. William Sweat *(Elizabeth Burgess [2], John [1])* was born about 1851 in Ten Mile Creek, Rapides Parish, La. and died about 1925 about age 74. William sweat married **Janey singleton** their kids are:

i. Siney Arddue Sweat 1874 – 1969
ii. James Edward Sweat 1876 – 1895
iii. William Vorce Sweat 1878 – 1897
iv. Troy Leonard Sweat 1879 – 1919
v. Mary Addie Sweat 1882 – 1901
vi. Mattie Gardia Sweat 1884 – 1969
vii. Vodie Sweat 1885 – 1963
viii. DeWitt Sweat 1888 – 1963
ix. Ordean Sweat 1890 – 1980
x. Warner Sweat 1892 – 1976

12. Gady Sweat *(Elizabeth Burgess ², John ¹)* was born about 1858 in Ten Mile Creek, Rapides Parish, La. and died after 1872 in Texas. Likely shot with his father Leonard in an ambush and was killed. Leonard made it back to near Crocket according to Cheryll Perkins. The ambush was the result of a feud with Nash & Keefer families?

13. Nancy Elizabeth Sweat *(Elizabeth Burgess ², John ¹)* was born on 21 Feb 1872, died on 23 Apr 1943 at age 71, and was buried in Glass Window Cemetery, Vernon Parish, La. Nancy married **Charles Steven Wise,** son of **William Wise** and **Corrine Hunt.** Charles was born on 26 Aug 1878, died on 27 Nov 1940 at age 62, and was buried in Glass Window Cemetery

14. Louisa Sweat *(Elizabeth Burgess ², John ¹)* was born about 1848 in Ten Mile Creek, Rapides Parish, La. Noted events in her life were: 1850 Cesus: Rapides Parish, Louisiana.

15. Sarah Sweat *(Elizabeth Burgess ², John ¹)* was born about 1851 in Ten Mile Creek, Rapides Parish, La. and died about 1888 about age 37. Sarah married **Frank Pinson.**
Vernon Parish, La.

Fourth Generation (Great-Grandchildren)

> 16. Macenia Curtis (Mary Sweat 3, Elizabeth Burgess 2, John 1) was born about 1852.
> 17. Vienna Curtis (Mary Sweat 3, Elizabeth Burgess 2, John 1) was born about 1854.
> 18. Steven Curtis (Mary Sweat 3, Elizabeth Burgess 2, John 1) was born about 1857.
> 19. Leonard Curtis (Mary Sweat 3, Elizabeth Burgess 2, John 1) was born about 1859.
> 20. Missouri Curtis (Mary Sweat 3, Elizabeth Burgess 2, John 1).
> 21. Pheobe Curtis (Mary Sweat 3, Elizabeth Burgess 2, John 1) was born about 1864.

22. James Henry "Bud" Sweat (Leonard Covington Sweat Jr. 3, Elizabeth Burgess 2, John 1) was born about 1860 in Natchitoches Parish, La. James married **Ella Wales**. Ella was born on 25 Aug 1859. The child from this marriage was:

> i. **Gracie Berton Sweat** was born about 1869 in Natchitoches Parish, La.

23. Emma Sweat (Leonard Covington Sweat Jr. 3, Elizabeth Burgess 2, John 1) was born on 11 Feb 1861, died on 1 Feb 1876 in Vernon Parish, Louisiana at age 14, and was buried in Glass Window Cemetery, Vernon Parish, La. General Notes: Dbl Stone with sister Almarinda Sweat.

24. Lee Sweat (Leonard Covington Sweat Jr. 3, Elizabeth Burgess 2, John 1) was born on 2 Apr 1864, died on 10 Mar 1910 at age 45, and was buried in Glass Window Cemetery, Vernon Parish, La. Lee married **P. Caroline "Dollie" Hall**. P. was born on 24 Nov 1871, died on 15 Jul 1959 at age 87, and was buried in Glass Window Cemetery, Vernon Parish, La. Children from this marriage were:

   i. **Willie Jackson Sweat** was born on 23 May 1895, died on 23 May 1928 at age 33, and was buried in Glass Window Cemetery, Vernon Parish, La.

   ii. **Ida Sweat** was born on 1 Mar 1901, died on 29 Mar 1987 at age 86, and was buried in Glass Window Cemetery, Vernon Parish, La.

   iii. **Ida** married **Houston Townley** (d. 25 Oct 1962).

   iv. **Henry Sweat** was born on 31 Oct 1905, died on 29 Nov 1968 at age 63, and was buried in Glass Window Cemetery, Vernon Parish, La.

   v. **Andrew Jackson Sweat** was born on 28 Mar 1908, died on 15 Mar 1987 at age 78, and was buried in Glass Window Cemetery, Vernon Parish, La. Andrew married Hazel Wiley (d. 27 Jul 1976)

   vi. **James W. Sweat** was born on 31 Aug 1892, died on 19 Aug 1896 at age 3, and was buried in Glass Window Cemetery, Vernon Parish, La.

   vii. **Sam H. Sweat** was born on 14 Jun 1897, died on 3 Nov 1964 at age 67, and was buried in Glass Window Cemetery, Vernon Parish, La.

25. Laura V. Sweat *(Leonard Covington Sweat Jr.* [3]*, Elizabeth Burgess* [2]*, John* [1]*)* was born on 22 Jul 1866, died on 15 Mar 1888 in Vernon Parish, Louisiana at age 21, and was buried in Glass Window Cemetery, Vernon Parish, La.

26. William Penn Sweat *(Leonard Covington Sweat Jr.* [3]*, Elizabeth Burgess* [2]*, John* [1]*)* was born on 25 Dec 1869, died on 13 Nov 1956 at age 86, and was buried in Glass Window Cemetery, Vernon Parish, La. William married **Alma Chester**. Alma was born on 30 Dec 1873, died on 16 Mar 1965 at age 91, and was buried in Glass Window Cemetery, Vernon Parish, La..

27. Nancy Elizabeth Sweat *(Leonard Covington Sweat Jr.* [3]*, Elizabeth Burgess* [2]*, John* [1]*)* was born on 21 Feb 1872, died on 23 Apr 1943 at age 71, and was buried in Glass Window Cemetery, Vernon Parish, La. Nancy married **Charles Steven Wise,** son of **William Wise** and **Corrine Hunt**. Charles was born on 26 Aug 1878, died on 27 Nov 1940 at age 62, and was buried in Glass Window Cemetery, Vernon Parish, La..

28. Almarinda E. Sweat *(Leonard Covington Sweat Jr.* [3]*, Elizabeth Burgess* [2]*, John* [1]*)* was born on 29 Mar 1874, died on 19 Jan 1875 in Vernon Parish, Louisiana, and was buried in Glass Window Cemetery, Vernon Parish, La. General Notes: Dbl stone with sister Emma Sweat.

29. Mary C. Sweat *(Leonard Covington Sweat Jr.* [3]*, Elizabeth Burgess* [2]*, John* [1]*)* was born on 24 Oct 1876, died on 16 Feb 1898 in Vernon Parish, Louisiana at age 21, and was buried in Glass Window Cemetery, Vernon Parish, La.Mary married **James Pinkney Groves,** son of **Linson P. Groves** and **Lettie M. Johnson**. James was born on 1 Jan 1875, died on 5 May 1940 at age 65, and was buried in Glass Window Cemetery, Vernon Parish, La..

30. Annette Sweat *(Leonard Covington Sweat Jr.* [3]*, Elizabeth Burgess* [2]*, John* [1]*)* was born on 8 Jan 1878, died on 8 Feb 1902 in Vernon Parish, Louisiana at age 24, and was buried in Glass Window Cemetery, Vernon Parish, La. Annette married **A.B. Slatten**.

31. Andrew J. Sweat *(Leonard Covington Sweat Jr. [3], Elizabeth Burgess [2], John [1])* was born on 28 Mar 1883, died on 20 Feb 1888 at age 4, and was buried in Glass Window Cemetery, Vernon Parish, La.

32. Guide Emanuel Nash/Ash/Ashes *(Matilda "Tilly" Sweat [3], Elizabeth Burgess [2], John [1])* was born on 22 Aug 1885 in Madison Co., TX., died on 28 Jun 1967 at age 81, andwas buried in Mt. Zion Cem., Trinity Co., TX. Guide married **Missouri Lacey Goins,** daughter of **William Collins Goins** and **Amanda "Mandy" "Aunt Candy" Lavina Samford,** on 18 Sep 1909 in Madison Co., TX. Missouri was born on 23 Jul 1886 in Polk Co., TX., died on 19 Apr 1963 at age 76, and was buried in Mt. Zion Cem., Trinity Co., TX.. She was married (1) Austin Ausberry Ash/Nash, son of Calvin and Jane E. Raegan who was killed crossing a bridge when his horse bolted and threw him off instantly killing him. Children from this marriage were:

    i.   **Maxine Nash/Ash/Ashes** was born on 16 Sep. Maxine married **Arvle Woodrow Stringer**

    ii.   **Viva Viola Nash/Ash/Ashes** was born on 15 Feb 1910 in Brazos County, Texas **Audey "Bill" Nash/Ash/Ashes** was born on 2 Aug 1911 in Madison Co., Texas,

    iii.   **Mary Bracie Nash/Ash/Ashes** was born on 28 Jul 1914 in Trinity Co., Texas, died in 1917 at age 3, and was buried in Mt. Zion Cem., Trinity Co., Texas.

    iv.   **Vivian Christine Nash/Ash/Ashes** was born on 27 Jul 1916 in Trinity Co., Texas.

    v.   **Robbie Looney Nash/Ash/Ashes** was born on 30 Aug 1918 in Trinity Co., Texas.

    vi.   **Lois Faye Nash/Ash/Ashes** was born on 21 Jun 1921 in Trinity Co., Texas

    vii.   **Guy "Sambo" Nash/Ash/Ashes** was born on 30 May 1928 and died in Burke, Angelina Co., Texas. He died Dec. 7, 2011.

    viii.   **Angus Arden Nash/Ash/Ashes** was born on 28 Jun 1931 in Angelina Co., TX, died on 28 Jun 1931, and was buried in Mt. Zion Cem., Trinity Co., TX.

33. Caion Nash/Ash/Ashes *(Matilda "Tilly" Sweat [3], Elizabeth Burgess [2], John ')* was born on 10 Dec 1887 in Louisiana, died on 23 Oct 1889 at age 1, and was buried in Nash Cemetery, No. Zulch, Madison, TX.

34. Gussie Nash/Ash/Ashes *(Matilda "Tilly" Sweat [3], Elizabeth Burgess [2], John ')* was born on 4 Apr 1890 in Texas, died on 20 Mar 1896 at age 5, and was buried in Nash Cemetery, No. Zulch, Madison, TX.

35. Will Nash/Ash/Ashes *(Matilda "Tilly" Sweat [3], Elizabeth Burgess [2], John ')* was born on 26 Dec 1893 in Louisiana and died on 18 Nov 1915 at age 21. Will married **Effie Thomas**. Effie died on 21 Aug 1930. Children from this marriage were:

i. **Maude Marie Nash/Ash/Ashes** was born on 8 Nov 1912. Maude married **Preston Childress** on 18 Oct 1929. Maude next married **Frank Morgan** on 30 May 1969

FIGURE 53 PHOTO: GUIDE E. ASH/NASH DESCENDANT OF BURGESS SURVEY WITH WIFE MISSOURI GOYENS ASH/NASH, ASH/NASH BOTH DESCENDANTS OF BENJAMIN ASH AND HANNAH PERKINS ASH/NASH, ASH/NASH. AT THEIR HOME IN BURKE, ANGELINA CO., TEXAS

36. Robert "Rob" Nash/Ash/Ashes *(Matilda "Tilly" Sweat [3], Elizabeth Burgess [2], John [1])* was born on 23 Sep 1895 in Louisiana, died on 17 Nov 1988 at age 93, and was buried in Mt. Zion Cem., Trinity Co., TX. Robert married **Dessie Jeafrey** on 3 Jul 1925. Dessie was born on 1 Apr 1909 and died on 18 Mar 1997 at age 87. Children from this marriage were:

  i.   **R. D. Nash/Ash/Ashes** was born on 19 Mar 1929, died in Feb 2007 at age 77, and was buried in Mt. Zion Cem., Trinity Co., TX
  ii. **G. E. Nash/Ash/Ashes** was born on 18 Sep 1927, died on 10 Jan 1956 at age 28, and was buried in Mt. Zion Cem., Trinity Co., TX.
  iii. **John** Nash/Ash/Ashes was born on 17 Mar 1929 and died on 9 Apr 1991 at age 62. John married Aline Landers in May 1948. John next married **Norma Mosely** on 19 Jan 1968.
  iv. oyce Nash/Ash/Ashes was born on 24 Jan 1931 and died on 21 Oct 1988 at age 57. Joyce married **Nick Baustert**.
  v.   onald Ray Nash/Ash/Ashes was born on 10 Oct 1932. Donald married **Claudia Nash/Ash/Ashes** on 27 Feb 1959.

FIGURE 54 PHOTO: LtoR ED ((1)NANCY SIMMONS ALLEN)), GUIDE ((2) MATILDA "TILLY" SWEAT)), ELI ((1) NANCY SIMMONS ALLEN)) HALF-BROTHERS; SONS OF EMANUEL COMMAND NASH

37. John Nash/Ash/Ashes *(Matilda "Tilly" Sweat [3], Elizabeth Burgess [2], John [1])* was born about 1897 and died about 1904 about age 7

Fifth Generation (Great Great-Grandchildren)

38. Gracie Berton Sweat *(James Henry "Bud" Sweat [4], Leonard Covington Sweat Jr. [3], Elizabeth Burgess 2, John [1])* was born about 1869 in Natchitoches Parish, La.

39. Willie Jackson Sweat *(Lee Sweat [4], Leonard Covington Sweat Jr. [3], Elizabeth Burgess [2], John[1])* was born on 23 May 1895, died on 23 May 1928 at age 33, and was buried in Glass Window Cemetery, Vernon Parish, La.

40. Ida Sweat *(Lee Sweat [4], Leonard Covington Sweat Jr. [3], Elizabeth Burgess [2], John [1])* was born on 1 Mar 1901, died on 29 Mar 1987 at age 86, and was buried in Glass Window Cemetery, Vernon Parish, La. Ida married **Houston Townley**. Houston was born on 16 Jun 1900, died on 25 Oct 1962 at age 62, and was buried in Glass Window Cemetery, Vernon Parish, La.. Children from this marriage were:

> i. **Henry Townley** was born on 31 Oct 1905, died in Nov 1968 at age 63, and was buried in Glass Window Cemetery, Vernon Parish, La.
> ii. **Jackie Jackson Townley** was born on 25 Jun 1924 and died on 15 Mar 1987 in Glass Window Cemetery, Vernon Parish, La. at age 62.
> iii. **Tilley Gertrude Townley** was born on 1 Jun 1920, died on 15 Mar 1987 at age 66, and was buried in Glass Window Cemetery, Vernon Parish, La.

41. Henry Sweat *(Lee Sweat [4], Leonard Covington Sweat Jr. [3], Elizabeth Burgess [2], John [1])* was born on 31 Oct 1905, died on 29 Nov 1968 at age 63, and was buried in Glass Window Cemetery, Vernon Parish, La.

42. Andrew Jackson Sweat *(Lee Sweat [4], Leonard Covington Sweat Jr. [3], Elizabeth Burgess [2], John[1])* was born on 28 Mar 1908, died on 15 Mar 1987 at age 78, and was buried in Glass Window Cemetery, Vernon Parish, La. Andrew married **Hazel Wiley**. Hazel was born on 16 Jan 1914, died on 27 Jul 1976 at age 62, and was buried in Glass Window Cemetery, Vernon Parish, La.. The child from this marriage was:

> i. **Helen "Doris" Sweat** was born on 7 Dec 1937, died on 7 Feb 1977 at age 39, and was buried in Glass Window Cemetery, Vernon Parish, La.

43. James W. Sweat *(Lee Sweat [4], Leonard Covington Sweat Jr. [3], Elizabeth Burgess [2], John [1])* was born on 31 Aug 1892, died on 19 Aug 1896 at age 3, and was buried in Glass Window Cemetery, Vernon Parish, La

44. Sam H. Sweat *(Lee Sweat [4], Leonard Covington Sweat Jr. [3], Elizabeth Burgess [2], John [1])* was born on 14 Jun 1897, died on 3 Nov 1964 at age 67, and was buried in Glass Window Cemetery, Vernon Parish, La.

45. Maxine Nash/Ash/Ashes *(Guide Emanuel Nash/Ash/Ashes [4], Matilda "Tilly" Sweat [3], Elizabeth Burgess 2, John [1])* was born on 16 Sep. Maxine married **Arvle Woodrow Stringer,** son of **Doc Willis Stringer** and **Corene "Rosie" Stephens**. Arvle was born on 9 Dec 1914 in Diboll, Angelina Co., TX.

46. Viva Viola Nash/Ash/Ashes *(Guide Emanuel Nash/Ash/Ashes [4], Matilda "Tilly" Sweat [3], Elizabeth Burgess [2], John [1])* was born on 15 Feb 1910 in Brazos County, TX and died in Aug 1943 in San Angelo, Tom Green Co., Texas at age 33. Viva married **Cyllis Hollis**. Cyllis

died in San Angelo, Tom Green Co., Texas.

47. Audey "Bill" Nash/Ash/Ashes *(Guide Emanuel Nash/Ash/Ashes [4], Matilda "Tilly" Sweat [3], Elizabeth Burgess [2], John [1])* was born on 2 Aug 1911 in Madison Co., Texas, died on 19 Oct 1981 at age 70, and was buried in Garden Of Memories, Lufkin, Angelina, Texas. Audey married **Brink Stringer,** son of **Doc Willis Stringer** and **Corene "Rosie" Stephens**. Brink was born on 4 Dec 1911, died on 6 May 1986 at age 74, and was buried in Garden Of Memories, Lufkin, Angelina, Texas.

48. Mary Bracie Nash/Ash/Ashes *(Guide Emanuel Nash/Ash/Ashes [4], Matilda "Tilly" Sweat [3], Elizabeth Burgess [2], John [1])* was born on 28 Jul 1914 in Trinity Co., TX, died in 1917 at age 3, and was buried in Mt. Zion Cem., Trinity Co., TX.

49. Vivian Christine Nash/Ash/Ashes *(Guide Emanuel Nash/Ash/Ashes [4], Matilda "Tilly" Sweat [3], Elizabeth Burgess [2], John [1])* was born on 27 Jul 1916 in Trinity Co., TX. Vivian married **Hollis**. Vivian next married **Carl Johns**.

FIGURE 55 PHOTO: JEFF, GUIDE AND AMANDA "MANDY" ASH/NASH

50. Robbie Looney Nash/Ash/Ashes *(Guide Emanuel Nash/Ash/Ashes [4], Matilda "Tilly" Sweat [3], Elizabeth Burgess [2], John [1])* was born on 30 Aug 1918 in Trinity Co., TX, died on 6 May 2008 in Lufkin, Angelina Co., TX at age 89, and was buried in Old Union Cem., Angelina Co., TX. Robbie married **Leonard Stringer,** son of **Doc Willis Stringer** and **Corene "Rosie" Stephens,** on 26 Dec 1936 in Lufkin, Angelina Co., TX. Marriage status: married. Leonard was born on 8 Dec 1914 in Lufkin, Angelina Co., TX, died in Nov 1999 in Lufkin, Angelina Co., TX at age 84, and was buried in Old Union Cem., Angelina Co., TX.

51. Lois Faye Nash/Ash/Ashes *(Guide Emanuel Nash/Ash/Ashes [4], Matilda "Tilly" Sweat [3], Elizabeth Burgess [2], John [1])* was born on 21 Jun 1921 in Trinity Co., TX, died on 18 Oct 1923 at age 2, and was buried in Mt. Zion Cem., Trinity Co., TX.

52. Guy "Sambo" Nash/Ash/Ashes *(Guide Emanuel Nash/Ash/Ashes [4], Matilda "Tilly" Sweat [3], Elizabeth Burgess [2], John [1])* was born on 30 May 1928 in Angelina Co., TX. Guy married **Margie Ruth Watson**.

53. Angus Arden Nash/Ash/Ashes *(Guide Emanuel Nash/Ash/Ashes [4], Matilda "Tilly" Sweat [3], Elizabeth Burgess [2], John [1])* was born on 28 Jun 1931 in Angelina Co., TX, died on 28 Jun 1931, and was buried in Mt. Zion Cem., Trinity Co., TX.

54. Maude Marie Nash/Ash/Ashes *(Will Nash/Ash/Ashes [4], Matilda "Tilly" Sweat [3], Elizabeth Burgess 2, John [1])* was born on 8 Nov 1912. Maude married **Preston Childress** on 18 Oct 1929. Maude next married **Frank Morgan** on 30 May 1969.

55.   Jack Evin Nash/Ash/Ashes *(Will Nash/Ash/Ashes [4], Matilda "Tilly" Sweat [3], Elizabeth Burgess [2], John 1)* was born on 12 Jun 1915.Jack married **Della Unknown**. Jack next married **Sudie Garrison** on 26 Nov 1934.

56.   R. D. Nash/Ash/Ashes *(Robert "Rob" Nash/Ash/Ashes [4], Matilda "Tilly" Sweat [3], Elizabeth Burgess 2, John [1])* was born on 19 Mar 1929, died in Feb 2007 at age 77, and was buried in Mt. Zion Cem., Trinity Co., TX.

57.   G. E. Nash/Ash/Ashes *(Robert "Rob" Nash/Ash/Ashes [4], Matilda "Tilly" Sweat [3], Elizabeth Burgess 2, John [1])* was born on 18 Sep 1927, died on 10 Jan 1956 at age 28, and was buried in Mt. Zion Cem., Trinity Co., TX. General Notes: Sgt. U.S. Marine Corps. Waorld War II Korea

FIGURE 56 PHOTO:ROBBIE LOONEY ASH/NASH STRINGER. DAUGHTER OF GUIDE E. & MISSOURI LACEY GOYENS, ASH/NASH/ASH/NASH. NAMED FOR GREAT UNCLE JOHN LOONEY GOYENS WHO WAS NAMED FOR THE JOHN LOONEY TEMPORARY CHIEF OF THE CHEROKEE.

58.   John Nash/Ash/Ashes *(Robert "Rob" Nash/Ash/Ashes [4], Matilda "Tilly" Sweat [3], Elizabeth Burgess 2, John [1])* was born on 17 Mar 1929 and died on 9 Apr 1991 at age 62. John married **Aline Landers** in May 1948. John next married **Norma Mosely** on 19 Jan 1968.

59.   Joyce Nash/Ash/Ashes *(Robert "Rob" Nash/Ash/Ashes [4], Matilda "Tilly" Sweat [3], Elizabeth Burgess 2, John [1])* was born on 24 Jan 1931 and died on 21 Oct 1988 at age 57. Joyce married **Nick Baustert**.

60.   Donald Ray Nash/Ash/Ashes *(Robert "Rob" Nash/Ash/Ashes [4], Matilda "Tilly" Sweat [3], Elizabeth Burgess [2], John [1])* was born on 10 Oct 1932. Donald married **Claudia Nash/Ash/Ashes** on 27 Feb 1959.

Sixth Generation (3rd Great-Grandchildren)

61.   Henry Townley *(Ida Sweat [5], Lee Sweat [4], Leonard Covington Sweat Jr. [3], Elizabeth Burgess 2, John [1])* was born on 31 Oct 1905, died in Nov 1968 at age 63, and was buried in Glass Window Cemetery, Vernon Parish, La.

62.   Jackie Jackson Townley *(Ida Sweat [5], Lee Sweat [4], Leonard Covington Sweat Jr. [3], Elizabeth Burgess [2], John [1])* was born on 25 Jun 1924 and died on 15 Mar 1987 in Glass Window Cemetery, Vernon Parish, La. at age 62.

63.   Tilley Gertrude Townley *(Ida Sweat [5], Lee Sweat [4], Leonard Covington Sweat Jr. [3], Elizabeth Burgess 2, John [1])* was born on 1 Jun 1920, died on 15 Mar 1987 at age 66, and was buried in Glass Window Cemetery, Vernon Parish, La.

64. **Helen "Doris" Sweat** *(Andrew Jackson Sweat [5], Lee Sweat [4], Leonard Covington Sweat Jr. [3], Elizabeth Burgess [2], John [1])* was born on 7 Dec 1937, died on 7 Feb 1977 at age 39, and was buried in Glass Window Cemetery, Vernon Parish, La.

.

Village of the Long King Burgess Survey Texas Trails, and Traces

BATTISE TRACE. The Battise Trace was one of the trails radiating from the village of Long King, who was the principal chief of the Coushatta Indians in Texas during the early 1800s. This trace connected Long King's Village in southern Polk County with Battise Village, near the mouth of Kickapoo Creek on the Trinity River in San Jacinto County. From Long King's Village the Battise Trace extended northwestward on the east side of the Trinity River in Polk County, went across Garner's Prairie south of Blanchard, led through the headwaters of Penwa Slough, and then crossed Caney Creek, Sandy Creek, and Kickapoo Creek. Next, the trail turned southeast near Onalaska, crossed the Trinity River near the mouth of Kickapoo Creek at a point where Duncan's Ferry (later Patrick's Ferry) was established, and proceeded to Battise Village in San Jacinto County. The Coushatta Trace then crossed the Trinity at the same place, and Patrick's Ferry continued to be used until the development of automobiles and a state system of roads and bridges.

The trail between Long King's Village and Battise Village is mentioned in surveyors' field notes for land surveys in western Polk County. A typical entry related to the Battise Trace may be found in the field notes for the Thomas Burrus Survey, which refers to "a road leading from the Long King's Village to the Baptiste (Battise) Village."

KICKAPOO TRACE. The Kickapoo Trace was a trail leading from the village of the Kickapoo Indians in the area of present Frankston in northeastern Anderson County to the John Burgess survey in the area of western Polk County. The trail followed a route southward near the site of present Neches and Slocum in Anderson County, across present Houston County fifteen miles east of Crockett, through the area of Trinity County eight miles west of Groveton, and then across the present western boundary of Polk County to merge with the Coushatta Trace in the John Burgess survey on Kickapoo Creek. The length of the Kickapoo Trace was ninety miles. The trail was apparently used by the Kickapoo Indians to contact Coushatta Indians along the Trinity River and to get to the Coushatta Trace for travel to the interior of Texas. Although a creek in western Polk County was named Kickapoo Creek, there is no evidence that members of the Kickapoo tribe ever established a village in this area.

Settlements to be continued...

The Lost State off Franklin, now Franklin, Tennessee; Watuaga Petition 1790's

Tensas, Alabama Indian Old Fields between Biloxi and Old Mobile and the Natchez Trace, see figure map above. Strother/Strawther, Hall, Sizemore, McGilvary, Massacre at Ft. Mims

St. Catherine and Cole's Creek Settlements

No Man's Land-Land Owners-Chief Bowels Cherokee

Taensa area, Arkansas and Ft Kaskaskia Missouri Territory

Rapides Parish Settlement-Talamala Band of Apalachicola

A Settlement of great consequence; The Collins Settlement at Attakapa and Opelousas District, Lousiana 1770's.

Calcasieu Settlement-Ten Mile and Bearhead Creek

St. Martin Parish from Georgia and South Carolina

Glass Window Trading Post and Rage Hill Stand (Rawhide Fight) about 1850

Baratarian Island -Battle of New Orleans

Gone To Texas. Redbones move into Texas and "invent" the Texas cattle culture.

Newton Settlement

Nacogdoches

Trinity River Settlement

Madison Co Settlement (Nash & Williams)

Galveston the Simon Goyens and Wm Taylor White aka "LaBlanc" family descendants inherited Galveston Island until it was eventually sold off in the early 1910s.

Camps on the old Opelousas Beef trail Ashworth, Taylor, Drake, LaBlanc and others.

Angelina, Burke Diboll and Big Thicket Texas

The Historic Red-Bone Riot at Ten Mile

Figure 57 Photo: L to R Josh "Jock" Perkins, Elmer Willis, Solomon Doyle, Mae Ashworth Willis, Nora Ashworth Griffin, Shelby Ashworth Unknown Location probably Bearhead Creek, Louisiana

Calcasieu Parish, On Christmas Eve 1881

By L.L. Harris

as told to him by Mrs. Isles, the mother of his wife, Eliza Isles Harris, and daughter of Joseph Moore, Sr.

Anyone who does not believe that extremity develops outstanding character rather than defeating progress never came in contact with frontier Louisiana.

Along in the early 50's, a son of the house of Moore, County Mayo, fled from the wrath of an Irish nobleman, whose dog he had killed. Shipping aboard a freighter, he worked his 3 week passage to America as a cabin boy, and in time became a citizen of Rapides Parish, Louisiana.

About the same time, a young doctor suddenly left one of Virginia's best homes and sought safety in that same isolated section lying between the Calcasieu and Sabine Rivers. Here, the culture that both had known drew the fugitives together and their common interests multiplied.

Up from the South had drifted the more venturesome, more nomadic sons of the descendants of Acadia and here they had lodged along the creek banks and developed under the horny handed nursing of the frontier into hard riding, hard fighting, self-reliant men. Out of the West had come Alabama, Choctaw, and Coushatta's, bringing as their contribution toward the making of this strange part of the State of Louisiana the stoicism, the cunning, the vindictiveness, and the smoldering, sensitive pride of the Indians.

Unique to this section of Louisiana and the by-product of its conglomerate ingredients, persisted a clan through whose veins ran the blood of Spanish and India, into which had seeped the traces of outlaw and renegade element that for generations had nested up in the rough hills, but ever and above every other racial heritage, the Indian prevailed and the traits and character of the Indian predominated. These people were known as "Redbones" and- always ready and quick to fight and kill- their resentment flashed most fiercely at the merest suggestion that anywhere in their past had Negro blood played a part in shaping "Redbone" tradition.

The vast unfenced, unclaimed area of Southwest Louisiana afforded range for the thousands of head of cattle and sheep and the scattered settlements afforded domicile for the types of men who follow the calling of the open range. Factional friction and strife fomented like home brew in this new country where the laws were largely to meet the conditions that each day brought forth and wee enforced by the men who made them- or died in the attempt.

As a young man, Joseph Moore, the young Irishman aforementioned, had taken a school in this section, made one of the best teachers west Louisiana ever knew. Then came the Civil War and his enlistment with the Army of the South. During his period of service he swam the Mississippi River at Vicksburg in the discharge of his duties as a Confederate spy. On his return to civilian life he followed merchandising in several localities, until the winter of 1881 found him in partnership with his early friend, the young Virginian, Dr. Hamilton, and serving a scattered population for a large, weather-browned store called Westport, but better known and generally spoken of as "Ten Mile".

Near this store was a settlement called "Rawhide" where dwelt a considerable number of Redbones. Back in the early 30's bad blood had led to a deadly fight at Rawhide between the Redbones and the white settlers in which the mixed bloods had been victorious by virtue of their overwhelming numbers. All during the half century that followed hatred between these rival factions had smoldered like a sleeping volcano, ready to burst into a violent eruption at the slightest provocation. At a community-wide meeting during harvest time Gordon Musgrove who was present, and who possessed a bitter and caustic tongue, stoked the fire by leaving the meeting-house suddenly with the remark, "The smell of nigger always did make me sick".

But it was at a mid-winter horse race at the finish of which it was quite generally accepted an unfair decision had been given, that furnished the tinder on which the friction of a slurring remark started the flame to flickering end which later burst forth in the famous "Ten Mile Fight".

Sympathy and money of the white men had followed Buck Davis' horse in the race, but a contested decision had favored the animal ridden by Henry Perkins, a Redbone. The rivalry was keen, arguments were ugly, and no one knew just how the actual encounter was averted, but the day ended and the factions drifted apart, glowering at each other, finally leaving for their homes, bristling and snarling, but with no hair in their teeth.

On the night of Dec, 23rd, a week after the horse race, the Redbones from miles around gathered at a big dance at Bob Wray's house for which the renowned fiddle of old Uncle Rube- a darky- supplied with the electromotive force. A rough board dance in those days could no more be held without "red licker" than it could without a fiddle, and "red licker" could not course down congenial throats without their feudal grievance welling up to possess heart and soul of vindictive men spoiling for a fight.

An inverted dry-goods box occupied one corner and thereon sat enthroned 2 kegs, 1 of wine, and 1 of whiskey, and beside the box next the fireplace sat Old Uncle Rube with his fiddle-joint rulers over the conviviality of the throng of merry makers. As the evening advanced the leaders gradually assembled around the box throne partook freely of its libations, and drifted inevitably into the topic of threatened hostilities. Simon Miracle, prominent and influential among the Redbones, habitual dispenser of the festive fluid, and representative of the "Big Store", as Moore's store was called, in that lucrative capacity diplomatically discouraged the plan or plot which involved an outbreak at Ten Mile, as that would jeopardize the cherished source of income. Instead, he proposed and advocated the plan of waylaying their enemies at Chincquapin Gully, as nearly all of them including the Musgroves, the Davis' and the older and younger generations of Lacaze passed the Gully on their way to the Big Store. This plan, Simon pointed out, was far better as the victims could be shot from ambush without danger and no one would know who did it.

Freely and confidently they talked, all unmindful of old Uncle Rube who was sawing valiantly on his fiddle and beating time with his feet, apparently oblivious to everything but his own paramount part in the success of the evening. But if the solemn faced old darky, eyes closed and swaying to his music, missed a word of what passed at the throne that night it was nothing more potent than an order for drinks. His best friends were of the opposing faction an while the faithful old fiddler and his lame mule were seen to jog sleepily in at their sagging gate and out to the grass-thatched lean-to stable half an hour after the strains of "home Sweet Home" had sobbed from his weary fiddle, none saw them slip silently through the gap into the woods behind the lot, and none saw them slip stealthily back in again after the 10 mile circuit just as the sun broke over the trees a couple hours later.

So it happened that however many skulking forms may have lain under cover of brush piles or crouched behind tree trunks the next morning, no shots were fired at Chincquapin Gully and the customary Christmas Eve crowd straggled in by various neighborhood roads and trails leading to the Big Store. No place in the world ever knew nerves to be tuned like fiddle strings with less evidence through and about the Big Store that day. As was their custom, a few Redbones had come in and they hung around near the hitch rack or leaned against the trees in the midst of which the Big Store had been built. Occasionally one would come in quietly and make a purchase.

About 10 o'clock Gordon Musgrove rode in, tied his horse at the hitch rack, and sauntered up the steps of the wide gallery, passing a cheerful greeting to Buck Davis who stood leaning against one of the posts chewing tobacco. The talk of the 2 men soon turned to the horse race and whether by design or chance it was as Marion Perkins, older and larger brother of the erstwhile rider of the winning horse, stepped out with a new cattle whip in his hand, that Musgrove said, "You won that race clean, Buck, and if I'd bin ridin' instid of you, I'd a-had that money or I'd whipped Henry Perkins".

It was a straight challenge and Marion Perkins did not hesitate. Tossing his cattle whip to the floor, he faced Musgrove and said, coldly, "mebbe you want to whip his brother now".

Like a pair of 5 point bucks, the men charged at each other. The hatred of generations put fury and force into every blow that left the shoulder and few failed to find solid targets. It was a man's fight with no rules, science or quarter. Each man sought to keep his back toward the building and each instinctively circled when driven toward the open front door of the Big Store; the crafty, crouching, cat-like movements of the Indian contrasted with the lighter, fleeter bolder attach of the fighting French timber-jack.

A solid blow to the face sent Musgrove crashing against the wall but as if bouncing back from the impact the agile, well-knit form leaped into the air and launched a slashing kick which landed squarely on the unguarded jaw of the heavier man, Marion Perkins.

Staggering from the terrific force of that driving force, Perkins yielded himself to its impact and dove toward the nearest post as if to leap to the ground, but catching a brace against it he drove himself back toward Musgrove, ducking under a savage swing and grasped the Frenchman about the waist, lifted him off his feet and hurled him to the floor, driving his own head into the pit of the under man's stomach as they fell. With the breath knocked out of him by the fall Musgrove was unable to retain the hold he had secured around Perkin's neck and the larger man lost no time in taking full advantage he had gained by gripping his prostrate opponent between his knees and driving his heavy fists into the unyielding face pillowed on the rough floor.

Just as Musgrove's vicious kick landed, a rangy horse jogged around the front of the Big Store and the steel gray eyes of John Watson, it's rider, took in the situation at one flashing glance. Seeing nothing alarming in the fight at that stage, he had wheeled his horse casually toward the hitch rack, not however, without permitting a move to escape him and when, in the next instant, the 2 men crashed to the floor Watson leaped clear of his saddle, throwing his reins to a popping-eyed Negro lad as he snapped- "Heah, boy, hold my horse."

Bounding up the steps in 2 jumps, Watson reached the gallery and strode up to the men where even Redbone stoicism failed to conceal the exultant brutality of Perkins.

If there was a "best man" in all the reaches of that rough and tumble country, it was John Watson. Tall and rangy like the horse he rode, broad of shoulders and narrow of hip, with muscles bulging across his back with every panther-like move of his synchronized body, he seldom wore a coat and carried about him the air of always stripped for action. From the Calcasieu to the Sabine rivers, there was not one boy who had reached the age of 10 years who had not heard with awe of the quick, deadly accuracy of John Watson's heavy single-action. 45.

Intoxicated with the joy of the killer Perkins saw nothing but the battered, blinded face beneath him.

Watson, not failing to sense in full the mercilessness of the victor in his victory, saw no silk glove case before him. Gauging his stride, he swung a kick that lifted Perkins clear of his victim and slammed him against the corner post of the store gallery. Before the man could gain his knees, Watson seized him by the shoulders and hurled him sprawling into the dust half-way to the hitch rack. Before attempting to rise, Perkins looked dazedly about to see what Goliath had stormed so disastrously into his hour of glory. Watson stood idly by at ease on the edge of the gallery, but there was no mistaking the incisiveness of his tone as he drawled, "you stay tar till I tell you to git up".

As Perkins landed in the open roadway, Joe Moore came from the store and bent over the quivering form of Musgrove. Turning to Watson he said, calmly, "looks as if that fall had knocked all the wind out of Gordon". Then addressing Davis, he said, "Buck, get a horse and ride over to Dr. Hamilton".

Although the whole encounter had been crowded into 3 or 4 minutes of time, every man about the place was on the scene as Musgrove began to get his breath and staggered to his feet. Just then Doc Hamilton rode up to the west door of the Big Store, returning from a country call made in Vernon Parish. Having seen the Dr. approaching, Moore and Watson had gone to meet him as he entered the back door of the store, for they realized that it was time for straight thinking and steering a steady course. Outside, only the fact that Perkins was under orders of

John Watson saved him from mob violence, but the actual presence of that cold-eyed executive could have added nothing to the inviolate status of the still prostrate Redbone.

Ten minutes later the 3 men walked out to where Perkins still lay unjurt where he had fallen. A circle opened for them as Moore said, "get up, Marion, and go inside." Looking quickly at John Watson, Perkins made no move until Watson nodded his approval, and no man spoke as the 4 disappeared through the doorway. Leading the way to the back of the store, Dr. Hamilton turned to Mr. Perkins and said, "go upstairs, Marion, and keep quiet and don't show yourself. We will see that you are safe." Again glancing at John Watson, Perkins caught the quick nod, and did as he was told.

Half an hour later, old Bob Perkins, father of Marion and Henry, rode up to the Big Store and walked in. He had heard of the fight and that his boy was held prisoner inside. His face was tense and set as he approached Joe Moore. Dr. Hamilton, suave, courteous, cool, moderator of all the back country, a fair man and of unflinching courage, beckoned to old man Bob to follow him into a quiet corner. There he laid the situation briefly but squarely before the aggressive father. As he did so he poured a glass of his best wine and extended it to old Bob as he said soothingly, "Mr. Bob, we have assured Marion we would see that he is not harmed, and now that you have come and can go with him, we will send a boy for his horse and keep the crowd occupied in front while he slips out the back door and gets away. Where shall we say that you will meet him?"

Pushing back the glass of offered wine, Old Bob straightened up and with all the cold arrogance of his ancestors replied; "Doc Hamilton, this is no time for drinking! My boys has done run away for the last time. Nothin' but a Rawhide fight will do now".

Turning on his heel, he strode swiftly the length of the store and out to his horse, mounted, drove his spurs viciously into the horse's flanks as the animal wheeled from the hitch rack, and dashed through the trees to where a group of his kind awaited the outcome of his interview. There he ordered a runner to take all speed to the Miracle settlement with the inflaming report that the white men wee holding Marion a prisoner in the store and were going to kill him; that they should gather all their forces and guns and ammunition, and come at once to

159

fight it out. Little did the men at the Big Store suspect the lurid lie that old Bob had sent back to his people and the sinister program that he had inaugurated. Even when the approaching cavalcade of Redbones was reported to them they continued unperturbed in the casual, carefree ways of the Holiday season. It was only when the yapping babble of high-pitched female voices grew plain did the gathering menace compel recognition of the fact that the Redbones had taken to the warpath.

The Redbone women remained in the background hiding behind trees and keeping up a continual turmoil Most of their men, likewise, kept within shelter of the grove, dodging about from tree to tree. A few of the bravest, however, rode boldly up to the hitch rack and advanced to the building on foot. All were armed and all were fighting mad.

Simon Miracle, Bob Perkins and Matt Dail disarmed suspicion by climbing the steps and approaching the door as though on a peaceful mission. But as Louis Lacaze stepped out of the store door behind Joe Moore and started towards his horse, Simon Miracle instantly threw his gun on him, and was balked in his purpose only by Moore's quick action in springing between and shouting, "for God's sake! Simon, don't do that."

The esteem and respect in which Joe Moore was held by the community, white, black, and mixed, saved the life of Lacaze. Miracle lowered his gun and Louis re-entered the store. As Moore followed a roar went up from the disappointed Redbones. The store doors were slammed shut and barricaded. All this transpired with such swiftness that several white men were caught and kept outside.

Those inside the Big Store at the time and upon whom devolved its defense, were Joe Moore, Dr. Hamilton, John Watson, Louis Lacaze, Sam Nolen, Hugh Saunders, and Moore's 3 sons- Mayo, aged 15; Dan, aged 13; and young Joe, aged 11 years. Young Joe was later in life to become District Attorney for Southwest Louisiana, and later, still, Federal District Attorney for all the Western part of the state. The Big Store was the supply base for a large territory in the way of arms and ammunition, so the little garrisons did not lack for means of support.

Marion Perkins had been watching developments from a window upstairs, and at the first outbreak he came down into the main store. Moore immediately unbarred the back door and allowed him to go unmolested.

The Historic Redbone Riot at Ten Mile

The first shot fired that day was fired by Marion Perkins and that immediately after his peaceful release from the protection of the white men. That shot killed a quiet, inoffensive non-participant in the race riot- a man named Dikes, who had come- innocently and unarmed- to the Big Store to do his holiday shopping. After Perkins had shot and fatally wounded the man in cold blood, Dikes fell sagging and groaning against the side of the building, and in that condition and over his pleading that he was already a dead man, old Bob Perkins beat him over the head with his gun.

Young Joe Moore, crouching against the inside of the wall, plainly heard the man pleading and the attack by old Bob, and announced to his co-defenders that Mr. Bob had killed a man. This ghastly outrage was the casting die in favor of a fight to the finish without quarter and as old Bob gloatingly returned to the front of the store he was filled with buckshot from the men in the store. The penalty he had earned was paid while his hands were still hot with its earning.

Gordon Musgrove was another who failed to get inside before the doors closed and during Marion Perkins' mad rushes he came upon Musgrove and shot him several times and left him for dead, lying in a pool of his own blood on the ground. After Perkins had hurried away in search of other victims on whom he vent his murderous wrath, Matt Dial, coming across Musgrove perceived signs of life and fired a shot into the prostrate form after which he seized a piece of rough scantling and beat the helpless body until he was sure that no life remained.

During a lull in the fighting, Joe Moore peering cautiously through the side window thought he saw Musgroves' eyelids quiver and on the chance that life still lingered he risked the life of his 13 year old son, Don, by sending him out to investigate. The plucky boy returned and reported that the man still breathed. The defenders immediately sent out 2 of their number, under cover of a terrific volley of shots, and brought their comrade inside. In spite of the desperate condition in which his assailants had left him Musgrove eventually recovered- a worthy example of the wonderful hardihood of the men who shaped the destiny of that rough frontier.

Through the hours that the fight lasted Mayo, Dan and Young Joe Moore stood valiantly by their elders, loading guns, drawing and carrying to the men at their stations upstairs and down whatever they desired from the stores of ammunition, cherry bounce, cider or whiskey. Just as

Young Joe stooped before a barrel to fill a glass of cider, a bullet crashed through the window, whizzed over his bent body and embedded itself in the wall beyond.

Simon Miracle, openly embittered at having yielded his chance to kill his man early in the conflict, stealthily ranged from one vantage point to another, seeking a chance to retrieve himself. Seeming to feel that his comrades had outdone him he became bolder and less cautious until, in a reckless effort to place an effective shot, he exposed himself to the quick aim of Louis Lacaze, the man he had tried to kill on the gallery, and as he himself fell dead his shotgun exploded, tearing a big hole in the ground as it fell from his lifeless hands. And the treachery which he had planned the night before had earned its swift reward.

With this loss, the 2 bravest men of the entire Redbone clan were gone and with them the boldness and aggressiveness of the besieging forces. From this time on none of the attacking party showed himself in the open, but a constant bombardment was kept up from behind nearby trees, Even a shadow passing across a window drew a volley of shots from the alert gunmen.

The leading spirit of this typical Indian warfare was Hiram Miracle, the blustering bravery of Marion Perkins having waned with the unexpected death of his father and the too evident fact that the notches were not all to be cut out on the Redbone guns who had lost the horse race, thought his chance to escape had come and dividing his attention between running and looking back for the pursuers he feared might follow, he was retreating westward when he bumped into a sturdy sapling with a glancing blow which crushed a bottle of whiskey in his hip pocket. Just at that moment a volley of shots put more speed into his heels. Feeling the flask's contents trickling down his leg- and thinking it was blood from a wound- he forgot caution and hung all his faith on speed. Shaping his course like a bee to a his hive, he burst the half-open gate from its leather hinges as he fled into the house yard of Doc Hamilton, yelling, "I'm kilt! I'm kilt!" But Mrs. Hamilton knowing well the danger which would accrue if he were seen taking refuge in her house refused him entrance and urged that he continue his flight into the adjacent swamp and lie down behind a large log that had fallen close to the hog trail below the lot.

When it became evident that the tactics of Hiram and his followers meant a long-drawn out fight, the straight line of John Watson's lips and his steel-gray eyes narrowed and he took his stand by the broken window upstairs looking out over the infested grove. Soon a shirt sleeve showed for an instant at the side of a tree. Instantly, his big .45 barked and a chip flew from the bark of the tree while the smoke of the shot half concealed the darting form as it sought shelter behind a larger tree almost in line and a rod further from the window whose defender needed no further identification. Another crashing report; another flying chip; another retreating form.

After the advance firing line had thus been dislodged, man by man, some with punctured hat brim and some with creased skin, Hiram Miracle feeling the importance of silencing that deadly window, risked a lightening quick shot whose aim had been carefully gauged before his intention and a narrow slab of his side were revealed. But he was not quick enough for when he snatched himself back into his shelter it was with the stinging sensation that told him he was hit. And only with the greatest difficulty did he keep his feet as he backed, slowly backed away, keeping his tree carefully in that unerring line of fire.

Steadily the retreat continued and the shooting abated. Shortly the clatter of hoofs told that the fight for the day was over. As soon as they could be reasonable sure that no skulking Redbone lurked for a final shot, the men came cautiously out of the Big Store.

Dr. Hamilton sought out Uncle Rube and instructed him to saddle his mule and take a roundabout route to the Stevens' house where he could secure a fast horse; then as soon as he felt it was safe to do so to push on to Sugartown and summon reinforcements in anticipation of renewal of the fight the next day.

The call was answered by William Iles, Kid Singleton, Jess Iles, John Neely, and Bill McDonald who rode through the night and immediately on arrival relieved the exhausted garrison and continued on guard all day Christmas.

The night after the fight passed without incident. The Big Store and all its approaches were picketed while day was breaking. Early in the morning a plan was adopted for forestalling a possible renewal of hostilities. The situation was serious. The white settlers were scattered; the roads and trails were for the most part through timbered country and a guerrilla warfare could soon wipe out every white family in the outlying districts. In all the territory lying between the Calcasieu and the Sabine there was no man who had earned the fuller respect of all men for deliberate thinking and whose decrease were known among whites, blacks, and Redbones to carry up true and accurate to the letter of their making than those of Soulange Lacaze, father of

Louis, Belezaire and Joe. When the rugged pioneer's word was given for the fulfillment of an obligation, or for the enforcement of an agreement, no man had ever known Soulange to depart a hair's breadth from his promise. And so it was of unanimous vote that the white men on this Christmas morning chose him to carry the flag of truce into the insurgent camp of the Redbones.

Riding calmly up to the home of Hiram Miracle without a glance to the right or left, Soulange called upon the men to come out. The men did not come out, but after a brief interval during which the lone rider sat motionless and waited, the women came slowly from the house, saluted their visitor respectively and reported that the men were all away from home.

Not deigning to dispute their statement, the ambassador replied coldly and clearly so that his voice could be heard throughout the house behind them, "as you like. I will tell you then my business". Leaning forward slightly in his saddle he continued slowly in a voice that was deep and quiet- "I warn you all now, that if a hair of a white man's head is hurt anywhere in these settlements, as long as I am here we will make a black burn of you."

Wheeling his horse toward the gate, he tapped his broad chest with the butt of his whip, and continued in a tone of the very mildness of which told every one of his hearers how deadly earnest he was: I will see to it that there isn't seed of a Redbone left this side of the Sabine River".

The women shrank closer together as their eyes bulged and remained fixed on the stern face above them. Then after 2 attempts to speak, one of the women faltered out: "M-Mister Soulange, w-w-we don't want t-t-trouble. We wa-want peace."

Without moving a muscle or letting hi piercing gaze release his transfixed listeners, the stately horseman answered with the ring of chilled steel in his voice, "We want peace- and we're going to have peace!"

After a few seconds, during which it seemed that even the dark green leaves of the big magnolia above his head dared not move, Soulange Lacaze pressed a knee gently to his horse's side and without further sign, wheeled and rode down the grass-grown trail and into the shadows of the trees that seemed to close behind him.

And while the old man lived his peace was never broken

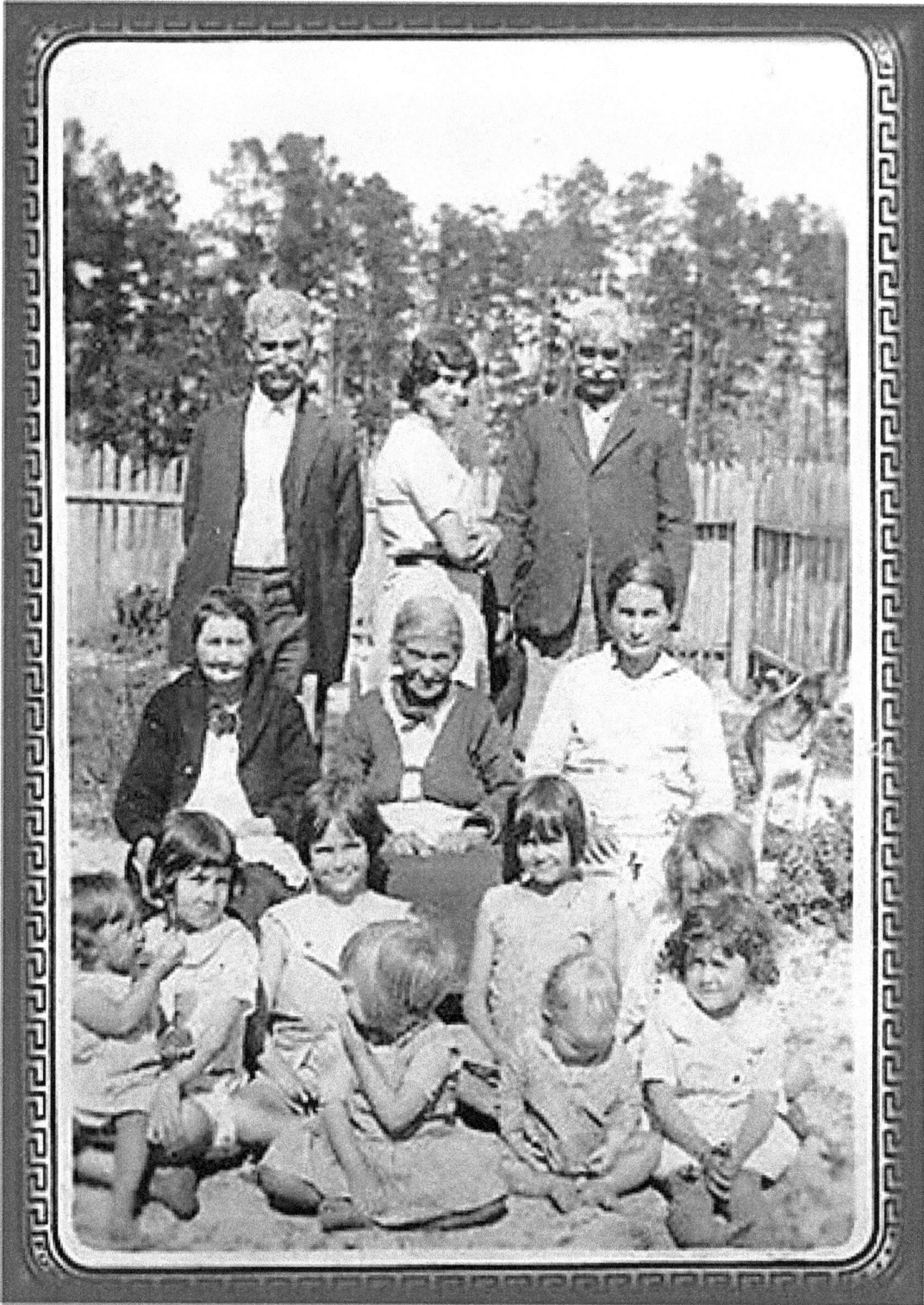

FIGURE 58 PHOTO: WM MOSES AND LOUISIANA HOOSIER GOINGS

The Buckskin Curtain of Indian Country

By Scott Sewell

An article in National Geographic I saw spoke of the "Rebirth of a Sioux Nation", and highlighted the emergence of a growing nationalism and sense of peoplehood among the Oglala Lakota, a perspective that views the outside world of modern America and its people as "other", and Lakota tradition and language as truly important to their survival as a people. This is all undoubtedly true, but what is the true measure of peoplehood? On the vast Pine Ridge reservation, a people who a century ago were predicted to be "gone", "assimilated", and "Americanized" by the 21st Century are in their own view as Lakota as ever, and many of the younger generation are questioning the legitimacy of the social order that has reigned on the reservation for generations, just as their parents and grandparents have. A questioning of the entire construct of race and identity is happening across our modern society.

This sense is not new among the Oglala Lakota for those who were there or remember the struggles of the 1960's and 70's and of the seismic effects of these times on the minds of many Indian people across America, as a sense of the potential for rebirth and renewal of Indian identity emerged from the heart of the urban Indian ghettos and windswept reservations. In a sense the Lakota have never loss their grip on their identity as a people who have been corralled but not broken, challenged but not defeated, and who walk in peace and holiness even as the rates of murder, suicide, neglect, and poverty on the reservation far exceeds those any other communities, and for some family's conditions are at times worse than those for many third world countries, smack in the heart of the American Midwest. The same could be said in some ways of east L.A., Appalachia, or countless other areas.

When I saw the cover of the National Geographic showing a young Lakota charging across the plains on horseback in silhouette on a crest of a hill, I thought of people who I hadn't seen and years, some of whom I had found out during the last decade through the Indian grapevine had left this world, usually in a violent way. As I perused the pages, I saw many faces and names of old friends and people who I knew well then, and had ran with twenty years ago when I was a young man brimming with energy and active in sobriety workshops, cultural renewal, and language preservation, in the cities and the reservations of the west. The article

167

made me think about how much change even a young man of 40 years like me has seen, and how sometimes when one is 'steadily' watching something, one may not see the slower changing developments happening for just this reason. Sometimes a snapshot, such as this article in National Geographic, contrasted with the Pine Ridge I remember from decades ago, or the half century ago of some of my teachers and elders, shows how fast some things change.

As I think of the Indian Country of a century ago described by the oldest elders to me over the years in Indian church camp houses, sweat lodges, and Corn Dance arbors, compared to what I see daily in my life here in Cherokee Nation and Oklahoma this past decade, I see things unfolding that few have reason to speak of, and fewer even see. A sense of Indian-centric identity, at least culturally speaking certainly continues to grow among people choosing to identify as Native American and affiliate with the cultural traditions of various tribes, whether or not they have actually lived in those tribal communities.

These strongholds where ancient communal rhythms and traditions are facts of daily life, where people go to sweat lodge with the new moon and life is not a Norman Rockwell painting, places where commodities are food, checks from relatives in faraway cities are gas money, and tribal gatherings and connections the most important activity on the social calendar aren't the place of Dances with Wolves' scenes, noble savages and dreamcatchers. It is the real world of community survival.

The mainstream of the American society really knows little more about what is happening behind the "Buckskin Curtin", the invisible line that separates the people of 'Indian Country' from other Americans, than do many of the politicians who influence the creation of the state and federal Indian policies and procedures that partially determine the present and coming generations of Indian people's quality and way of life. Under the current conditions of governmental policies and practices, the social lives of many of the persons who are enrolled in federally recognized tribes, especially here in Oklahoma, is one that is not actively resisting the forces of assimilative social and economic inclusion, always touted as "beneficial" to Indian people and communities. Economic development and other such endeavors have become the forefront of tribal goal setting and endeavors, even as small percentages of budgets are earmarked for the (in most cases) social institutions based on the 'differences" in the Indian cultural heritage from Euro-American majority that surround the small and often rural communities where truly traditional Indian life survives in the Sooner state.

American governmental policies promise success to young Indians, even as it takes youths away from building social institutions that have been historically important for tribal survival, to serve in the military far from the Oklahoma tribal or reservation communities where their presence (and the crucial generational reinvestment that they and their children represent) is lost to the larger Indian community. Often with little commentary, the 'patchwork' of sovereign trust lands that are the reality for all but the largest reservations allows for a steadily increasing non-Indian population "on the rez".

As anyone who attends powwows and community events in Oklahoma or the eastern U.S. can tell you, there is no shortage of powwows and the like today anywhere in the country, but fewer and fewer people will be seen there who can be differentiated from the general population. Many of the feathered and enthusiastic participants at these events attest to an adherence to traditional values, customs, and a sense of self –identified 'Indianess', even as the intermarriage rate to persons of a 'different' race is highest among today's Native American population according to the U.S. Census. (See http://www.npr.org/2011/03/31/134421470/native-american-intermarriage-puts-benefits-at-risk for more information on how these increasing situations impact on the tribes of the northern plains and other areas).

The Office of Management and Budget defines the concept of race as outlined for the United States Census as not "scientific or anthropological". It takes into account "social and cultural characteristics as well as ancestry", using "appropriate scientific methodologies" that are not "primarily biological or genetic in reference. Another words, the idea of who is, and is not an "Indian" is more hotly debated as ever, even in the face of declining blood quantum degrees and increasingly self-identified "Indians" who are not connected with tribal communities or Indian population centers.

Not known by most people, if not for the geographical and social isolation of many of the dozen or so large reservations, especially in the northern plains, intermountain west, and south western region, most tribes would be like the vast majority of the Oklahoma and eastern U.S.

tribes enrolled members; indistinguishable physically from the general population (regarding phenotypical appearance) and in many cases knowing and practicing little if any of the 'traditional' culture of the tribe, with blood quantum degrees in increasingly small fractions. A tribal community identity, language and cultural preservation, and other aspects of tribal life are independent of concepts of race as understand to westerners, but with a swelling mainstream (and in many cases now not white necessarily) pressing in on geographic isolation of many tribal populations, ancestral genetic diversity (and in most cases non-Native American) increases.

As a case in point, in her life time my (late) 'Auntie' Mary Frances Johns, a Miccosukee born in the everglades in the early 1900's, saw many families of Seminole and Miccosukee transition from "Full-blood" traditional, primarily native language speaking persons living in all Indian settlements, to the situation faced by her grandchildren, much like the children of Miccosukee Tribal Chairman Buffalo Tiger; persons of several racial/ethnic ancestries and unable to attend traditional religious green corn ceremonies due to this. Unfortunately from my observations of many 'federally recognized' Indians that I share my daily life with, few want to see what is happening around them, the continuing erosion of "Indian blood" as defined through the lens of blood quantum, the loss of the few remaining identity markers that make them in anyway different from the surrounding mainstream population.

Tribal governments continually changing political/economic strategies emerge to deal with hard-to-accept social change (unfortunately for politicians and social conservatives of any 'race' an unending ever-changing reality), and political infighting increases as blood quantum amounts on tribal members CDIB cards continue to plunge, even as various multi-'tribal' ancestries increase in an individual or family, and every year more tribes switch from a 'blood-quantum' roll, to a descent roll. 'Descent roll' enrollment is a situation in which descent from an ancestor on a past roll is the requirement for current enrollment, no matter how small the blood quantum for example, Cherokee Nation of Oklahoma citizens of 1/2000 blood quantum…I'm not kidding. Currently the Cherokee Nation of Oklahoma has over 300,000 enrolled members, 9 out of ten of which have blood quantum amounts in the 1/100's or less, and who in most cases know little or nothing of the language, culture, etc. of the Cherokee. I don't say this as a criticism, only reporting the realities I see among friends and family in Cherokee Nation.

The Buckskin Curtain of Indian Country

If I have seen anything that could put what is happening into a brief statement it is that "ISOLATION=Indian Identity (genetics, language, culture)" and that when social isolation is lost, so is most of the wide spread native traits you find in large tribal populations. The history of Europe over the last few millennia reflects this same process of how with the end of social isolation, massive change ensues, often with the loss of previous identity markers, as any genetic and linguistic map of Europe shows, only in regions with geographical features like mountains, swamps, and islands are the remnants of the earliest Europeans found. Social identity does not equal genetic identity though, for the process of synthesis that destroys also creates and social hybridity often chooses aspects of past identities to enshrine as "defining" features, as groups like the Lumbee, Melungeons, and other hybrid peoples show.

Though genetic research of the past decade has shown that many modern non-federally groups who identify as Indian socially have little Native American genetic ancestry, it has not slowed the struggles by many to secure federal acknowledgement by the BIA and Congressional legislation. On the other hand, millions of Americans have a significant amount of American Indian ancestry, even as they keep this aspect of their 'racial' and cultural identity at arm's length for the most part. I am speaking about the Native American genetic heritage of the millions in America of Hispanic descent, primarily Mexican and other Latin American extraction. Though few Academicians and NO tribal leaders want to admit it, there is more "American Indian" DNA in an east L.A. neighborhood than there is in the entirety of many of eastern Oklahoma tribes, though political realities ("Indian Sovereignty") says that treaty obligations to tribes means that the 'unique' government to government relationship between tribes and the United States government means that they will still be "Indian Tribes" even when the 'highest' blood quantum degree in the tribe are in the 1/100's. (A situation faced by several tribes in Oklahoma and the Northeastern United States)

Anecdotally speaking, if you go to the 'Indian hospital' in any little rural Northeast Oklahoma town, you see 95% of the people there are clearly phenotypically Caucasian in appearance (many being enrolled members of tribes from the area like Cherokee, Delaware, Shawnee, Modoc, Peoria, Wyandotte), and are receiving free medical care, even while hundreds of thousands of southwestern United States American citizens of 'Chicano' ancestry are dying of diseases and health issues DIRECTLY tied to their American Indian ancestry. For many people in Indian Country, the American Indian Movement and other organizations and personalities statements about colonialism and the like are just posturing and political hyperbole, but in many cases they are pointing our situations that haven't yet come to the awareness of the greater Indian community.

Over the last few years 'Direct To Consumer' genetic ancestry testing has led to many revelations about aspects of identity that would have otherwise been unknown. Modern genetics is another world from the rooms full of dusty records used to track the blood quantum degrees of modern Indian America, and its reality is not tied to 200 years or more of US government and Bureau of Indian Affairs 'paper-pushing' and supposed benevolent social control of "its tribes", often practiced social policies bent on suppression/isolation/annihilation of Indian identity (people), and exploitation of this continents wealth to make contemporary America a world leader. Despite Americas place as a superpower and arbitrator of affairs of nations world-wide, America's prominence and financial success which its American Indian communities for the most part do not share in (or in many cases, like the Hopi, Mohawk, Miccosukee, and others even want to share in if it means a loss of the communal identity and life ways held preeminent by these communities.) Even as our often neglected cousin to the south continues to be awash in blood and dysfunctional and crippling corruption directly traceable to the American hunger for drugs, Billions of dollars flow to the Middle East while the cancer of the drug trade spreads steadily.

Almost without comment the Latin American genetic heritage of the great new world civilization cradle continue to spread across the North American social landscape, a new reckoning of 'Indian' will emerge during this century, as most Americans ancestral heritages continue to mingle to a degree never known before. From what I can see, a time will come in 50 years when the membership of the Cherokee Nation of Oklahoma will be over a million people most of whom will be of truly miniscule fractions of Cherokee or even Indian ancestry, and the general population will be of American Indian ancestry as much through 'Latino' ancestry as through any 'native' to the continental United States.

The families of many of my relatives can attest to the current realities of the impact of Latinos on the average American experience; my own, my brother, several cousins, my ex-wife, and countless friend's marriages to persons of Hispanic/ Mexican ancestry right now attests to the unfolding nature of identity today. as one of my heroes, the Cherokee Nation's favorite son and sage Will Rogers said a century ago, "i don't know but what I read in the papers", and as I try to 'read between the lines', and this is something that is not too often reported on unless there is some money in it for somebody; Change isn't 'coming' to Indian Country and America for that matter, it is here, now, and with bells on as the saying goes. The question is who is benefitting from the changes occurring?

Certainly the new found monies flowing into tribal communities is affecting them surely, but for example, is money from the new, huge (Hard Rock) Cherokee Casino in Catoosa Oklahoma going to help the struggling traditionalist and stomp dancers of the nearby Kenwood and other "Cherokee full-blood" areas to preserve the social institutions (and yes, I will say it, necessary self-imposed isolation) to STAY Cherokee deep into this next century? I am not wanting to sound judgmental of the tribal, state, or federal government, none of these governments, peoples or communities are "to blame" for the ever present and unchanging reality of social change, but as someone of Creek and Cherokee Native ancestry (among my many ancestries, like most people), i think that if the Basque, Jews, Roma, and other "old world" populations can develop cultures and identities that can 'adapt and survive'.

I truly do hope for Americas sake that for the beautiful and culturally-vulnerable peoples and communities I have come to know and love in my life, the Euchee, Cheyenne-Arapaho, Natchez, Pottawatomi, Kickapoo, Kialegee, and, though few realize it, the Maya (yes there are many Maya in Tulsa and OKC), that the modern notions of diversity, inclusion, multiculturalism, and ' economic development' are not necessarily new to Indian communities, and are not necessarily the answer to "the Indian problem" as it was once known, and that new strategies should and must be considered for the preservation of what remains of distinct native American communities

FIGURE 59 PHOTO: LTOR, ALPHA GIBSON, BELLA ALLEN MATHEWS, LULA ALLEN REED LTOR, CHARLIE NASH, PINKNEY ALLEN, JESSE (JESUS) MARIA GARZA ALL STEP CHILDREN OF EMANUEL COMMAND NASH (1) NANCY SIMMONS ALLEN (2) MATILDA "TILLY" SWEAT (3) SENA GOINS NASH FELDER MORGAN SWILLY, RAPIDES PARISH, LA. TO NO ZULCH, MADISON CO., TEXAS

Redbone Progenitor Families
Doyle to Drake Marriage

Drake Doyle Marriage Relations

The origins and ancestry of some progenitor Redbones continues to be debated. Unlike the dominant European practice, the families appear to have inherited European surnames both matrilineal[3] and patrilineal[4]. The most common surnames having been inherited from Northern European origin by way of traditional descent as well as by adoption, enslavement through indentures, and familial association with extended European kin, rather than being wholly acquired on these shores. The most common surnames are:

ACOSTA, ANDERSON, ALLEN, ARCHER, ASHWORTH, BANKS, BARNES, BASS, BALL, BELL, BENNETT, BERRY, BLOODWORTH/BLUDWORTH, BOWLIN/BOLIN, BROOKS, BUNCH, BURGESS, BUTCHER/BOTCHER, BUXTON, CARTER, CHAVIS, CHERRY, CHOAT, CLARK, CLIFTON, COLBERT, COLE, COLLINS, CLOUD, COOD/TY, COOPER, COWARD, DAVIS, DEAN, DIAL/DYAL/DOYALL, DYESS, DRAKE, DRODY/DRODDY, DURANT, EMANUEL/MANUEL, ESTESS, EVANS, FAVOR/leFAVRE, GARNETT, GARDNER, GHANO, GIBBS, GIBSON/GYPSON, GOINS, GOIE/GOY/S, GRIFFIN/ITH, HARMON, HALL, HICKS, HOLLIS, HARDY, HOWARD, HYATT, IVY/IVEY/IVIE, JACKSON, JAMES, JEFFRIES/JAEFRY, JOHNS, JOHNSON, LeGRANDE/LAGRAND, LEE, LITTLE, LOONEY, MADDOX, MIRACLE/MERKLE, MARTIN, McILVARY, MINGO, MITCHELL, MONIAC, MOORE, MULLINS, MUSOUTH CAROLINAGROVE, NASH/ASH, NELSON/NEILSON, ORE, PALMER, PERKINS, PINDER, POWELL, PRIEST/PEACE, REES/CE, ROBERSON/ERTSON, ROLFE, ROSS, SAMPSON, SEVIER, SHERRILL, SI/YMMONS, SIMMS, SIZEMORE, SMILING, SMITH/E, STAR, STROTHER, STRINGER, SWEAT, TALBOT, TAYLOR, TILLEY, TIPTON, THOMPSON, TORRY/IE, TURNBULL, UTIE/UTI, VALENTINE, VICKERS, WAITIE/WATEY, WARD, WARE, WARREN, WARWICK/RICK, WATER/s, WEATHAFORD, WEAVER, WILLIAMS, WILLIS, WILSON, WING, WISBY,WISE, Y-BARVO/BO,YOUNG.

This is not intended to be a completed list, there are families which I am sure intermarried but that I have neglected to mention, or are not known to me. There are some surnames included here which have not in the past been recognized but share in our genealogical

---

[3] ˌmatrəˈlinēəl,ˌmā-/ *adjective*: **matrilineal**; of or based on kinship with the mother or the female line
[4] pat·ri·lin·e·al/ *adjective*: **patrilineal;** of relating to, or based on relationship to the father or deSouth Carolinaent through the male line.

ancestry, and are carried by some of our Mixed blood Indian families. Some families are associated through marriage, and as such did not include their entire family surname as Redbone.

Through genealogy, DNA and common history we are piecing our families back together, one by one. With each family we re-assemble through conventional and non-conventional genealogical and historical research we are finding each day that the theories of ethnologists, anthropologists and historians of the past, were neither all completely correct, nor completely incorrect concerning the Redbones' ancestral origins and ethnic cultural admixtures.

Scientists found that there are exactly as many skin pigment colors to the various races of this world as there are different colors of soil [dirt]. Stacy R. Webb, Natchitoches, Louisiana 2003

The Marriage Certificate

This all starts with a marriage certificate recorded in 1822 among the archives at St. Landry Parish Louisiana. It is certificate #46 and reads:

> "To all whom these may concern Know ye, that the Revd. Joseph Willis one of the ministers of the Gospel, is hereby authorized and empowered to join together in the holy bonds of Matrimony, John Dyal & Rachel Drake both free people of color of the aforesaid Parish."

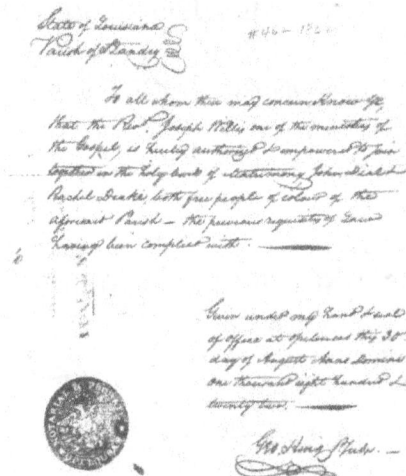

Figure 60 Document: Marriage Certificate Doyle and Drake (Johnson, Drake Cousins 1980)

Though recorded as Dial, Dyal and Dyol in some records, the families were known also as Doyle, interchangeable, and will hereafter be referred to as Doyle.

As we examined this one document I began to pull the pieces of nearly 400 years of genealogy and interrelatedness together, which sparked an epic example of our families, and their clan's Multi ethnic and Amerindian heritage. I cannot tell the story of our *Doyle* and *Hill* family without also telling the whole story, which is the way Redbone heritage goes, with endless loops of common ancestors.

Please remember that in some cases, we are only guessing as to birth and death years, some ancestors there is little documented information and so one must estimate the variables, and calculate the most appropriate dates with the information at hand. We encourage corrections and additions.

The Groom's Family

John Jackson Doyle (Mary Perkins/Thomas [5], M.Mixon/John Joshua [4], E.Hill/James [3], L.Hastings/Thomas [2], H. Blackwell/Isaac Malcom [1]) born about 1803 in Opelousas Parish, Louisiana and died 14 Oct 1877 in Rapides Parish, Louisiana and was buried at Occupy #1 Cemetery in Glenmora of the said parish. He married *Marie Rachel Drake* (genealogy and details of the Drake family continued below under Bride's Family). They had at least the following children:

- *Solomon* born 1824-1870 m. Agnes "Agg" Buxton
- *Jackson John* born 1825 m. Nancy Mancil
- *Mary S*. born 1826
- *Aaron* born 1830-1900 m. Serena Wilson, this family will also be presented in the upcoming *Goins Book* Chapter by Marilyn Baggett Kobliaka.
- *William* born 1834 m. Cecil Ann Ashworth
- *James* born 1835 m. Martha "Polly" Farrell
- *John* born 1835, *Willis* born 1838 m. Kissiah Perkins
- *Thomas* born 1840 m. [1] Adeline Miracle [2] Lavicia Perkins
- *Martha* born 1842
- *Isaac* born 1847 m. Sarah Perkins.

Figure 61 Photos: #1 James Doyle 1847 to 1940 son of Aaron and Serena Wilson Doyle #2 Francis "Sissy" Buxton wife of James Doyle[5]

John, the groom was the son of ***Thomas Doyle*** *(M.Mixon/Joshua [4], E.Hill/James [3], L.Hastings/Thomas [2], H. Blackwell/Isaac Malcom[1]).* He was born about 1770 in Craven, now Pendleton District, South Carolina and died about 1860 in Rapides Parish, Louisiana. Thomas married [1] ***Mary Willis Johnson*** (she married first to ***Isaac Johnson***) and, [2] ***Mary Perkins*** *(M.Black/Wm Joshua "Old Jock" [3], M. Sherrill/Richard Jr. [2], Richard [1])* she was born about 1764 in Williamsburg, Virginia and died, probably Rapides Parish, Louisiana; she married ***Thomas Doyle*** on 23 Sep 1811 in Opelousas Parish, Louisiana. ***Mary Willis Johnson Doyle*** married [1] ***Isaac Johnson*** and was also the mother of ***Francis Johnson*** who married ***Sarah Gibson/Gypson*** (Pezzullo n.d.) and ***Gibson Johnson*** who married ***Sarah Anderson,*** all Redbone progenitors born in Craven County, South Carolina and migrated later to the Tensaw area of the Creek Indian Old Fields near Old Mobile Alabama and the Apalachee Indian Village, and then to St. Landry Parish, and Rapides Parish, Louisiana. See inset map Natchez Trace for referenced geography. Also see Johnson, Hill, Sizemore, Strother/Strawthers and others in Tensas, Indian

---

[5] Courtesy, Claudia and Stevie Doyle.

Old Fields. The family later attempted to settle among the Apalachee Indian Reserve set aside by the French Government in 1767, Rapides Parish, Louisiana. ***Thomas Doyle*** and [1] ***Mary Perkins*** had at least the following children:

- ***John J.*** born 1830 m. Marie Rachel Drake
- ***Aaron*** born 1798
- ***Louis M.*** born 1808
- ***Thomas*** born 1809
- ***Henderson Hill***

To the union between ***Thomas*** and [2] ***Mary Willis Johnson*** (*Rachel Bradford/Revd. Joseph Willis[2], Mary Unknown/Aggerton[1]*) was born the following children: ***Mary Doyle*** born about 1826 in Indian Old Fields near Old Mobile, Alabama she married ***William Strother/s*** born July 1817 in Louisiana and died 1850 in Rapides Parish, Louisiana. The Strother Family descended from the ***William Strother*** and ***Dorothy Savage*** family of Orange County, Virginia to Hancock County Georgia then to Alabama and Louisiana.

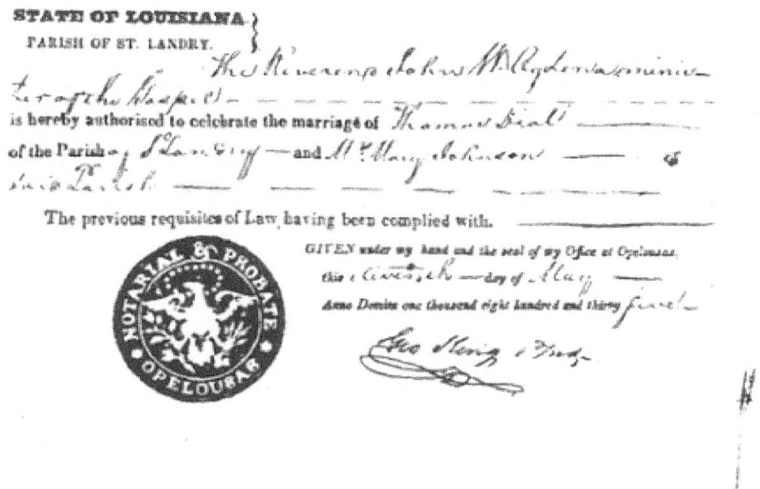

Figure 62 Document: Thomas Doyle marriage certificate to Mary Willis Johnson 1835, St. Landry Parish, and Louisiana. (Johnson 1980)

Groom's Grandparents

The groom was the grandson of ***John Joshua Doyle*** (*Elizabeth Hill/James [3], Thomas [2], H. Blackwell/Isaac Malcom[1]*) born in about 1743 and died 1845 in Kentucky, he married ***Mary***

Mixon (*Mary Bird/ Samuel ², John ¹*) born 1753 in Pee Dee, Craven, South Carolina and died 1778 Craven Co., South Carolina. Little is known of this couple, they had at least one other child, a son, **Aaron Doyle** who married the aunt of the bride, **Elizabeth Aurelisa Drake** *(Charity Chavis/John Aaron Sr. ¹)* in Rapides Parish, Louisiana; more about this couple below. **John Joshua** also married [2] **Unknown.**

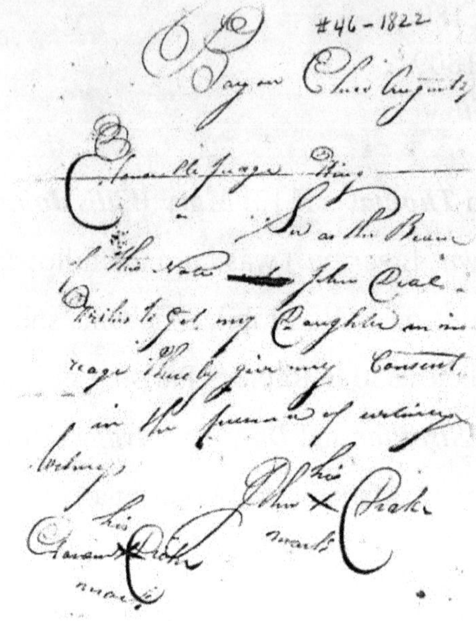

Figure 63 Document:Accompanied Marriage Bond Documents Doyle/Drake Marriage John Aaron Drake gives Permission #46 1822 Bayou Choupique, Calcasieu Louisiana. [6]

Mary Mixon (*Mary Bird/ Samuel ², John ¹*) was the daughter of **Samuel Mixon** *(Mary Russell/John Mixon¹)* born about 1726 Cheraw, South Carolina and died 1860 in Tollgate, Marion Co., Alabama and [1] **Mary Bird** *(Sarah Empson/Thomas Bird¹)* born about 1726 in Cheraw, Chesterfield, South Carolina and died 1769 in North Carolina. **Mary Bird** was the daughter of **Thomas Bird,** born 1685 in Wilmington, New Castle, Delaware and died 1726, and **Sarah Empson** born 1687 in Goole, New Castle, Delaware and died 1741 in Wilmington, New Castle, Delaware. **Samuel Mixon** *(Mary Russell/John Mixon¹)* was noted with **Revd. Joseph Willis** and served in the American Revolutionary War with "Marion's Men" who fought alongside the famous Colonel Francis Marion, also known as the "Swamp Fox" South Carolina Militia who accomplished extraordinarily against the British. **Samuel Mixon** next married [2]

---

[6] (Johnson, Drake Family Cousins 2005)

Keziah Smith born 1755 and died in 1794 in Darlington District, Kershaw County, South Carolina. *Samuel Mixon* next married [3] *Clarissa Slone*. Samuel reared many children with all his wives and was a known Indian Trader among the Cheraw, Catawba, and Cherokee Indians. Some of his wives and children were concurrent.

MARION'S MEN

In May of 1780, the city of Charleston surrendered to the British. In August of that same year, Lord Cornwallis defeated the Americans at Camden, South Carolina, and the southern region of the colonies was for all practical purposes, under British control. But the Pee Dee region of South Carolina an area stretching from the Santee to the Pee Dee Rivers, a rebellion continued. According to James William Dobein, who gave a contemporary account; a public meeting was held, and they resolved unanimously to resist the British. Dobein in his accounts also describes the populace of the region as "a people who at all times during the war abhorred either submission or vassalage." Col. Francis Marion was sent by the Continental Army to act as leader of the militia. From 1780 through 1782, the ragged band known as "Marion's Men" continually harassed the British, cutting off their supply lines and costing them dearly in both manpower and ability to conduct war on other fronts and contributing greatly to the eventual defeat of the British.

This group under the "Swamp Fox" is often credited with development of guerrilla warfare learned from the Native Americans during the French and Indian Wars. A favorite strategy was to repeatedly attack and fall back, drawing the British deeper and deeper into the swamps where they had a distinct "home field advantage." According to Dobein, an early historian who, as a fifteen year old boy, served with Marion, the band had a group of marksmen who were adept at picking off the enemy soldiers. The British were offended by the fact that this was not the way "gentlemen" conducted war. In response, Marion and his supporters freely acknowledged that they were not "gentlemen", but were fighting the only way they could and playing the hand they were dealt. In Gwen Bristow's fictional account a character says "*quite a few of us can't read...but every man of us can shoot the eye out of a squirrel at the top of a pine tree!*" That may be a bit of braggadocio, but certainly they were effective at what they did.

These were not regular members of the Continental army with some claim or hope of compensation from the Continental Congress. They were untrained, unpaid volunteers who were conducting their own war, using whatever weapons they had or could capture. Some, obviously Mixed Blood Indians whose skills at these type military warfare was common, and known to them, unlike the British who had little understanding of the type of warfare. Dobein related that local blacksmiths made saws into swords, and other unconventional means of obtaining, and building weapons. Letters from Marion to General Greene with the regular army continually note the lack of supplies and even report that at times some planned actions could not be carried out because his men had no ammunition. Meals were what they could scavenge and what their families and friends could supply and, there are records that Samuel's father, *John Mixon*, as well as *Samuel* himself supplied beef for the group and supplies were woefully inadequate. Reportedly, they often subsisted on sweet potatoes and water. They were not a formally organized group which remained consistent. Instead, they came and went, sometimes joining in battle and sometimes staying home with their families and Dobein reports there were occasions on which Marion almost despaired of their return, but at last and always, the militia returned, back to the camps in the swamps and back to the privations of their war. When Col Marion visited a regular army camp on one occasion, Col Otho Williams described them as "*Col. Marion, a gentleman of South Carolina, attended by a very few followers, are distinguished by small leather caps and the wretchedness of their attire.*"

We know that these men were "Marion's Men" not because they are listed as members of the continental army but because following the war people in South Carolina who were acutely aware of what they had accomplished made an effort to find out who they were and provide documentation of their contribution. So these are our ancestors, not "gentlemen", but rather something better I think and examples of the everyday heroism of a rag tag bunch of ordinary people who helped in the founding of this country.

Of The Redbones…"*When the war broke out several of them enlisted in Hampton Legion, and when the legion reached Virginia there was a great outcry among the Virginians and the troops from other States against enlisting negroes.*" Sen. Wade Hampton

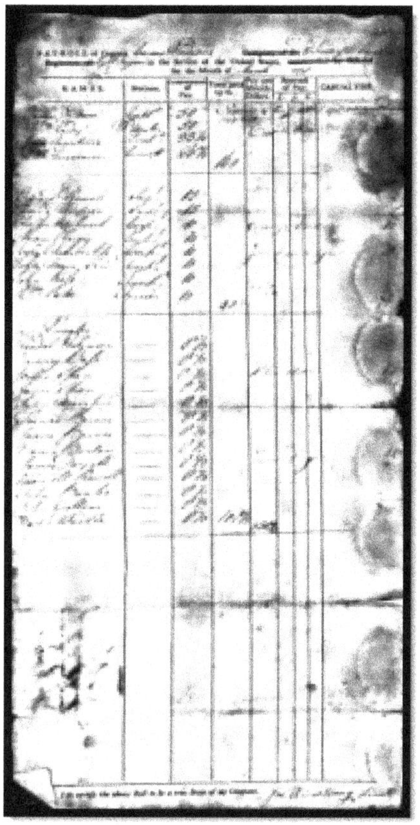

Figure 64 Document: Sharp's of No. Carolina Light Dragoon's March 1778 Pay-Roll: Capt. Cosmo Medici, Wm. Hardy, Louis Armstrong, Privates: Edward Powell (Sergt.), Illegible Thompson (Sergt), Charles Upchurch (Corprl), Abram Hargis (Corpl), Joel Chamberless (Corpl), John Marr Sr. (Corpl), John Rolf (illegible), Wm. Tate (farrier), Randal Robinson, Drury Bass, Willis Span, James Span, John Marrfield, Thomas Barnes, James Barnes, James Buxton, James Doyall, Mancill Powell, John Banks, Illegible Waddle Listed in Casualties Column, James Doyall, Willis Span. (Department 1775-1783) (Webb 2006).

Groom's Great-Grandparents

John Doyle was the great grandson of *James Doyle/Doyall (I. Hastings/Thomas², H. Blackwell/Isaac Malcom¹)* born 1715 in Beauford, North Carolina and died 1778 at Fort Moultrie, SC and *Elizabeth Hill* born about 1717 in Craven County South Carolina and died in 1820 in St. Landry Parish, Louisiana. Little is known of *Elizabeth Hill* however the following has been suggested: *(Mary Nelson/Samuel ¹, Elizabeth Williams/Samuel ², Elizabeth Strong/John Benjamin ³, Elizabeth Proctor/John ², Mary Symmonds/George ¹)*. The couple had at least the following children:

- *Tapley "Tap"* born 1760 in Beaufort, NC. and died 1852 in St. Landry Parish, Louisiana perhaps he married *Jane Hardy* (Isle of Wright family at Basse's Choyce) they settled first at

Stone Gap, Franklin County Tennessee with Old Jock Perkins families, and then later settled in Jackson and Augusta counties Georgia and owned a trading business with his father-in-law called "Hardy & Doyal Co.," *Tampley/Tapley "Tap/Tamp" Doyle* is reputed to have come down the Natchez Trace with a wave of Redbones from the Chickamauga Indian Village (then part of Grainger County, Tennessee) and the birth place of *Chief Redbone* born about 1700 in what is now Ypsilanti, Talbot County with a group of Redbones lead by progenitor *Thomas Nash/Ash (Betsy Goins/Thomas Nash/Ash [1], Unknown/John Nash [1])* "The Indian Trader" at Ft. Blackmore to Ft Cumberland and River among the Cherokee, Delaware of Powell Mountain, Nottoway, Catawbas and Cheraw's.[7] This group lead by Thomas Nash/Ash and "Tap" Doyall is believed to have originated among the Saponi and Rappahannock Indians of Talbot's Choyce, Delaware and removed to this area of Georgia, in the mid to late 1600's. Later, Thomas Nash, James Groves and Tap Doyle would settle around Walnut Hill, Vernon Parish, Louisiana where the Bloody Raw Hyde Fight took place in about 1850. This area was also known as; Burton's Station where a stage coach that greatly influenced travel in the area ran between Alexandria, Louisiana and Texas, Burton's Station also served as an important Indian trading post but as well the recreational center with a tavern, and nearby race track and the well-remembered battle ground of the Raw Hyde Fight which was named "Rage Stand Hill." It was also a gathering-place for militia, muster, enlistment and posse recruitment. Another popular spot in the vicinity was "Black Jack Hill" named for a so called Black man named *Jack Hill*. Whom I suspect was a brother or close relations to *Elizabeth Hill*, Tap's mother.

- *James* born 1746 in Craven Co., South Carolina and died about 1778,
- *John Joshua* born 1746 in Craven Co., South Carolina and died in 1778 m. Mary Mixon,
- *Edward* born 1758 in Fairfax Co., Virginia and died in 1833 at Blount, Alabama,
- *Keziah* born 1768 in Pee Dee, South Carolina and died 1829 in Bayou Choupique, Calcasieu Parish, Louisiana m. James Ashworth this couple had the following children:
  - *Elizabeth* born about 1777 she m. Hugh Nelson
  - *James II* born 1779 died 1870 m. Mary Perkins
  - *Jesse* born about 1790 he m. Sarah Perkins
  - *Mary Polly* born 1792 died 1862 m. George Perkins
  - *William* born about 1793 m. Deliada Gallier
  - *Moses* born 1799 m. Anna Bunch *(Rhoda Mosley/Drury [1])*
  - *Aaron Burr* born about 1803 died 1863 m. Mary Bunch
  - *Sarah* born about 1807 m. Jacob Hayes
  - *Tapley Abner* born about 1809 died 1859 m. [1] Rosalie Gallier, [2] Lavina Goins *(Eliz. Betsy Perkins/James Goings)*.
- *John Anderson* born 1769 in Stokes County, NC. and died in 1853 at Mill Creek Cabell Co., Virginia,
- *Aaron*

---

[7] (George Washington, Valley Forge, Pennsylvania 1777)

- *Thomas*

James Doyle also served in the Revolutionary War and was a listed at a casualty, on March 5, 1778 North Carolina's 3rd. Regiment of Light Dragoons, he was listed as a casualty and his rank was Private. Not much else is known of *Elizabeth Hill* except that she arrived in Louisiana as a widow, and lived to be very elderly and a suggested genealogy which has not been confirmed. But according to Verna Thompson of the Truth Seekers, *The Ashworth Puzzle,* she provides court documents dated November Term 1833, Parish of St. Landry, Elizabeth Doyle *"a free woman of color"* petitions three of her sons; Taply "Tap", Thomas and Aaron.

Pg. 2 "To the Honorable the Judge of the fifth judicial district, in the western circuit division of the State of Louisiana, holding Court, in and for the Parish of St. Landry The petition of Elizabeth Dial a free woman of color, residing in the said Parish respectfully sheweth – That your petitioner is in extreme old age, being one hundred and three years old, and very sickly so much so as to be utterly unable to work, and is extremely poor, and in a starving condition. That she has children to wit: Taply Dial, Thomas Dial, and Aaron Dial all residing in said Parish, and all three in good circumstances, and able to support her, but that they all, unmindful of their duty as her children have refused and still do refuse to afford your petitioner any assistance whatever, although she has repeatedly requested them to do so, so that she is compelled to apply to the laws of her country to coerce them to fulfill their natural obligations towards her --- She therefore prays that said Taply Dial, Thomas Dial and Aaron Dial, all free men of color, may be cited as the law directs, to appear before your Honorable Court to answer to this petition, that they may be condemned and adjudged jointly and severally to furnish your petitioner with an alimony suited to their ability to pay and to her necessities, either in clothing and food or in money as your Honorable Court may judge proper – She prays for general relief and or in duty Etc. Thos S. Lewis Attry for petitioner Filed 8 Sept 1832 Henderson Taylor Clerk" [8]

Groom's Maternal Lines

John Doyle (*M.Perkins/Thomas[5], M.Mixon/John Joshua [4], E.Hill/James [3], L.Hastings/Thomas [2], H. Blackwell/Isaac Malcom[1]*) was the great grandson of the well-known progenitor and pioneer family of old Colonial record. *Wm. Joshua "Old Jock" Perkins* (*Mary"Ester" Sherrill/Richard Jr [2], Richard[1]*) of Accomack County, Virginia. Old Jock was born about 1732, and when he was two years old in September 1734, he was bound to James Gibson [9] along with a brother, *Jacob Perkins* no last name or parentage given for either boy, just

---

[8] (Thompson 2015)
[9] (Accomack Co., Virginia Orders 1731-36, page 133)

"Ester Perkins." Regardless, Joshua "Parkins" purchased 125 acres in Bladen County, North Carolina at Wilkerson Swamp, a branch of the Little Pee Dee River adjoining land entered by **Benjamin Davis** before October of 1761. Old Jock sold that land in 1770 as part of a larger 250 acre tract, the other half owned by his nearly identical yDNA match **Robert Sweat**, father of **William**, **Ephraim** who married **Olive Perkins**, **Gilbert** who married **Francis Smith** (couple mentioned below in case) and **Mary** who married **Isaac Perkins, Jr.** (*Hannah Sweat/Isaac, Sr.*[4], *Mary Black/Wm Joshua "Old Jock"*[3,] *Mary "Ester" Sherrill/Richard Jr*[2], *Richard*[1]) and perhaps more. **Robert Sweat** had originally purchased the tract of land from **Philip Chavis** in 1768. The location of this property is situated on the border of Robeson County, NC, near the lines of present day Marlboro, and Dillon Counties, South Carolina.

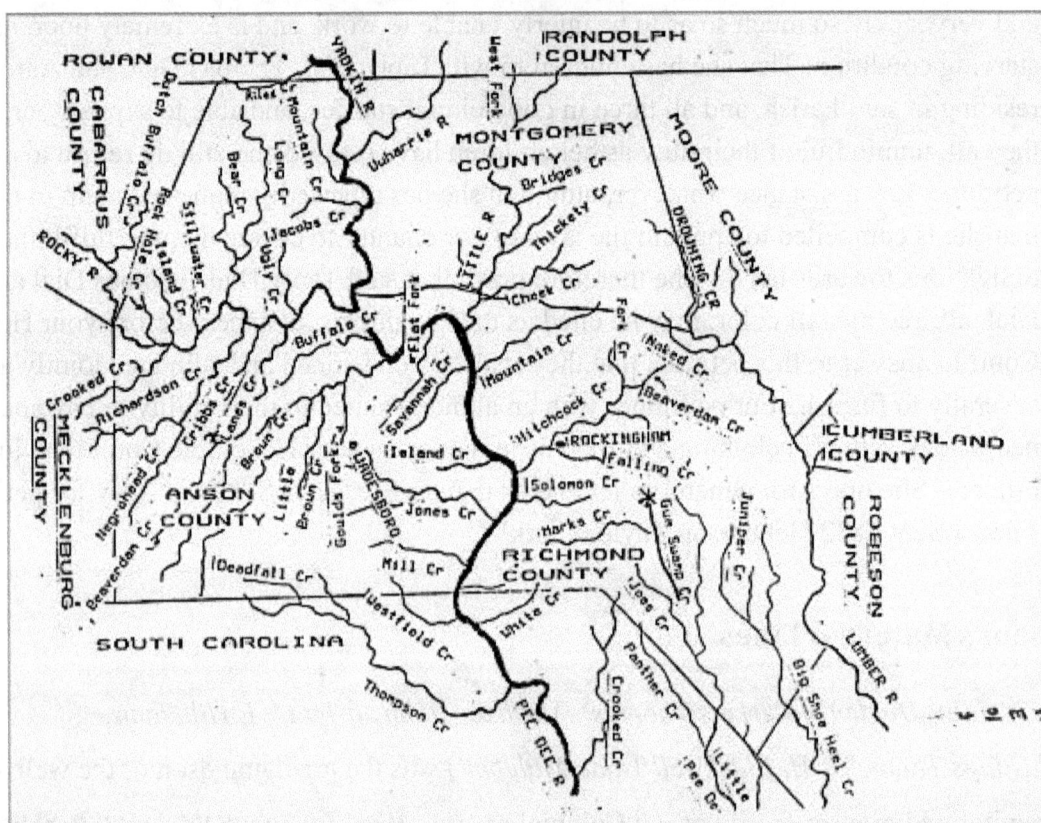

Figure 65 Map of border South Carolina, and North Carolina Pee Dee River, and Robeson Rowan, etc. Counties

These families are reputed to have been progenitor of the people known as Melungeon, who are most famously represented by a group of descendants at Vardy Community on Newman's Ridge, Tennessee, and the Melungeon Heritage Association which hosts a large

Union gathering every year at various location these families lived, migrated to and grew their Mixed Blood Indian families. Some of these families migrated between Louisiana and Tennessee, Kentucky, West Virginia, Ohio (Caramel Indians), Indiana (Louisiana Hoosier and Wm Moses Goings families from Tennessee, to Indiana to Louisiana), Oklahoma and Arkansas visiting one another and continuing to marry among one anther from the late 18th to the mid-19th century. About the time of the great removals and later Civil War reconstruction I mark a great decline in mutual recognition of the groups. Several, if not most of the remnant Mixed Blood clans across the board are heavily related to the people known as Redbones and share several genealogical lines, and DNA to date. Here is an example of our group's travels, and migrations and relationships between one another. I would say our families certainly didn't allow geography and the harsh conditions of pioneer travel to hinder kinships between their clans. A late migration of Redbones in 1828 led by Mayo which Scott Sewell and his cousin Steven Pony Hill have researched and written about, at length, rejoins their Muscogee Creek family in Texas, and Louisiana. [10]

No. 1533, District Court, St. Landry Paris, **Delaney Taylor wife of John Bass vs Gilbert Sweat,** Filed Aug. 27, 1829 Lewis & Lesassier & Bowen Attorney for Plaintiff

> ***"Joshua Perkins*** *a free man of color, being duly sworn to testify in the aforesaid case under the order aforesaid Saith----"He is seventy one years old in November next and was born on Little Pee Dee River in the present State of South Carolina in what is now, he is informed called Marion District. Has known **John Bass** and **Delaney Taylor** his wife the Plaintiffs from childhood---sometimes has not seen them for several years at a time---Has known the Defendant ever since he was a boy---Sometimes they were separated for several years together--then came together again---the Defendant was born in South Carolina on Pedee River, near to the place where witness was born----Was in her lifetime, acquainted with Frances Smith dec'd---first became acquainted with her about the year 1777 in South Carolina in the same part of the country where he lived--- Thinks he never saw said **Frances Smith** dec'd until after she went off with the Defendant-----Never saw **John Barney Taylor** but once that he recollects, and that was when he went with the Defendant to carry off the aforesaid **Frances Smith** dec'd ---It was in the year 1777 he believes---in the same part of the country where he was born--- fourteen or fifteen miles distant----Always understood that the aforesaid **Frances Smith** dec'd was the wife of **John Barney Taylor**---they always passed in that part of the*

---

[10] In late 1857 or early 1858 a large number of families left the Choctawhatchee River area of northwest Florida and journeyed west to Rapides Parish, Louisiana. These families, often described as "mixed-bloods" joined an older settlement of Willis, Goins, Perkins and Sweat Redbone families. (Hill 2005)

country as man and wife---and when Defendant went off with her---she was spoken of as **John Barney Taylor's** *wife---It was in the year 1777 that witness went with the Defendant to assist him in carrying off the aforesaid* **Frances Smith** *dec'd, when they went to the house where she was, they found a man there who witness was told was* **John Barney Taylor** *the husband of said* **Frances Smith** *dec'd ---Witness lent the Defendent a horse to carry off the aforesaid Frances Smith dec'd ---When witness and Defendant first went to the house and found Taylor there, they went off and afterwards got the aforesaid Frances Smith dec'd out and she went off with the Defendant---At the time the aforesaid Frances Smith dec'd went off with the Defendant, John Barney Taylor was alive---never saw him since---never heard he was dead---I was old acquaintance of the defendant--- knew him from boyhood--has sometimes lived near him and has been for several years without seeing him---Always friendly with Defendant---never knew of the marriage of the aforesaid* **Frances Smith** *dec'd with the Defendant---Thinks from the intimacy that has always existed between them, that if there had ever been any marriage, he should have known of it--Has lived near Defendant in South Carolina, North Carolina & Tennessee, came with , live Defendant when he left Tennessee and came on to Big Black River in Mississippi near him there and removed to Opelousas, about the same time that the Defendant did. Has seen him frequently since he lived in Opelousas---and been at his house---Arrived in Louisiana twenty six years past---Never knew or heard of the death of* **John Barney Taylor** *---Has heard it spoken of that the Defendant and said* **Frances Smith** *dec'd were not married--Always believed so himself---and believes that such was the impression with all those who knew them well and for a long time---Is no relation of the Defendant--The Defendant is he believes about seventy three or four years of age.......*

Cross examined by Plaintiff Counsel---

"Thinks he heard that **John Barney Taylor** *went off with the army about fifty three years ago---Never seen him since---thinks he has heard that said* **Taylor** *was killed or died in the Army---but is not sure---Witness was then about seventeen years old---Heard it said that Defendant and* **Frances Smith** *dec'd had afterwards got married -- was not present himself.." Examined by Defendants Counsel---Says that he has heard that Troublefield (?) married them---Does not know that said Troublefield had any authority to marry any person---Said Troublefield was not as Witness thinks a Justice of the peace or Judge, but was a son (?) of a preacher he believes....*
Joshua Perkins(X) his mark

Sworn and subscribed to by making His ordinary mark at Opelousas in The Parish of St. Landry this 25th Day of May in the year 1830 Before me Henderson Taylor Justice of the Peace Acting in & for the Parish of St. Landry The foregoing testimony is to be read on the trial of the case of John Bass & wife vs Gilbert Sweat--No. 1533 the district court of St Landry --subject to all legal exceptions except as to the time, place and manner of taking the same--Opelousas May 25th 1830. Thomas H. Lewis Pffs. atty. R. Garland Atty. for defendant." [11]

Old Jock was listed as Mulato [12] taxable in Washington County[13], Tennessee in 1787 and died there in 1801. Old Jock married **Mary "Polly" Black** who was thought to have been born in Scotland about 1730 and was likely an indentured servant; she died in South Carolina though little else is known of her. Some details of her features are gleaned through the various documents and court testimonies; she was a white woman, who had black hair and stunning blue eyes.

Figure 66 Map: Washington "District" County, later known as the Lost State of Franklin. The original settlers leased the land from the Cherokee Indians along the river, and established their own government known as the Watuaga Petition. Many of our ancestors are also documented

---

[11] (Jackson 1995)

[12] Mulatto: from Spanish mulato, small mule, person of mixed race, mulatto, from mulo, mule, from Old Spanish, from Latin mulus. The term mulatto, originated with the racial policies of European colonizers in the Americas, originates from the Spanish caste system. Because civil rights and responsibilities were based directly on the degree of European blood that a person had, such classifications were highly elaborated, and minor distinctions in ancestry were carefully recorded. While these terms have highly precise definitions, in actual practice they were often used based on impressions of skin color rather than definite knowledge of ancestry

[13] In 1776, Washington District was created as part of North Carolina, comprising what eventually became the state of Tennessee. In 1777 Washington County, Tennessee was created and in 1779 Sullivan County was created from part of Washington. By 1796 Washington County had attained approximately its current size and shape with Unicoi County finally being created in 1875 from part of Washington and Carter counties.

living in the Lost State of Franklin (Washington County, Tennessee), 1796 census Willis, Ivey, Goins, "Ashurst" Ashworth, Perkins, Jeremiah Bass, "Smiely (Smiley), Waters to mention a few. Many of these men, Sherrill, King, Reeves, Rober/tson, Morris (Choctaw), Sevier, Davis, Clark, Cooper, Hawkins, Mitchell (Gypsy), Morris, Vaugh (Van) (Creek), Tipton, Choat/e (Choctaw & Chickasaw), Williams, Simpson, Moore and David Crocket would also sign the Watauga Petition, 1776.

Petition of the Inhabitants of Washington District

"There is a cemetery, now in DuPont State Forest (Transylvania Co., North Carolina where there are Ashworth, Mitchell, Moore, and the Thomas families buried there, Transylvania County fronts with Greenville Co., South Carolina in the mountains." [14]

INCLUDING THE RIVER WATAUGAH, NONACHUCKIE, &C., 1776

In 1772, the white settlements south of the Holston River, although acknowledged to be an unorganized part of North Carolina, were without any form of government. In 1772, they "exercised the divine right of governing themselves," forming a "written association and articles for the management of general affairs. Five Commissioners were appointed, by the decision of a majority of whom all matters in controversy were settled..." The Articles of the Watauga Association are apparently not extant, but it is known that they" in convention assembled, elected as Commissioners, thirteen citizens. They were John Carter, Charles Robertson, James Robertson, Zach. Isbell, John Sevier, James Smith, Jacob Brown, William Bean, John Jones, George Russell, Jacob Womack, Robert Lucs and William Tatham."[15]

In 1775, the Wataugan's secured their lands by purchasing it from the Cherokee Nation, and by August 1776, had petitioned North Carolina for recognition of their government, now termed "Washington District." The following petition is undated, but is believed to have been signed in 1776. The original, located in the North Carolina State Archives at Raleigh, states "Received August 22, 1776." [16]

To the Hon. the Provincial Council of North-Carolina:
The humble petition of the inhabitants of Washington District, including the River Wataugah, Nonachuckie, &c., in committee assembled, Humbly Sheweth, that about six

---

[14] According to Scott Withrow, 2015
[15] (J.G.M. Ramsey 1853)
[16] (ibid.)

years ago, Col. Donelson, (in behalf of the Colony of Virginia,) held a Treaty with the Cherokee Indians, in order to purchase the lands of the Western Frontiers; in consequence of which Treaty, many of your petitioners settled on the lands of the Wataugah, &c., expecting to be within the Virginia line, and consequently hold their lands by their improvements as first settlers; but to their great disappointment, when the line was run they were (contrary to their expectation) left out; finding themselves thus disappointed, and being to inconveniently situated to move back, and feeling an unwillingness to loose the labour bestowed on their plantations, they applied to the Cherokee Indians, and leased the land for a term of ten years, before the expiration of which term, it appeared that many persons of distinction were actually making purchases forever; thus yielding a precedent, (supposing many of them, who were gentlemen of the law, to be better judges of the constitution than we were,) and considering the bad consequences it must be attended with, should the reversion be purchased out of our hands, we next preceded to make a purchase of the lands, reserving those in our possession in sufficient tracts for our own uses, and resolving to dispose of the remainder for the good of th community. This purchase was made and the lands acknowledged to us and our heirs forever, in an open treaty, in Wataugah Old Fields; a deed being obtained from the Chiefs of the said Cherokee nation, for themselves and their whole nation, conveying a fee simple right to the said lands, to us and our heirs forever, which deed was for and in consideration of the sum of two thousand pounds sterling (paid to them in goods,) for which consideration they acknowledged themselves fully satisfied, contented and paid; and agreed for themselves and their whole nation, their heirs, &c., forever to resign, warrant and defend the said lands to us, and our heirs, &c., against themselves, their heirs, &c.

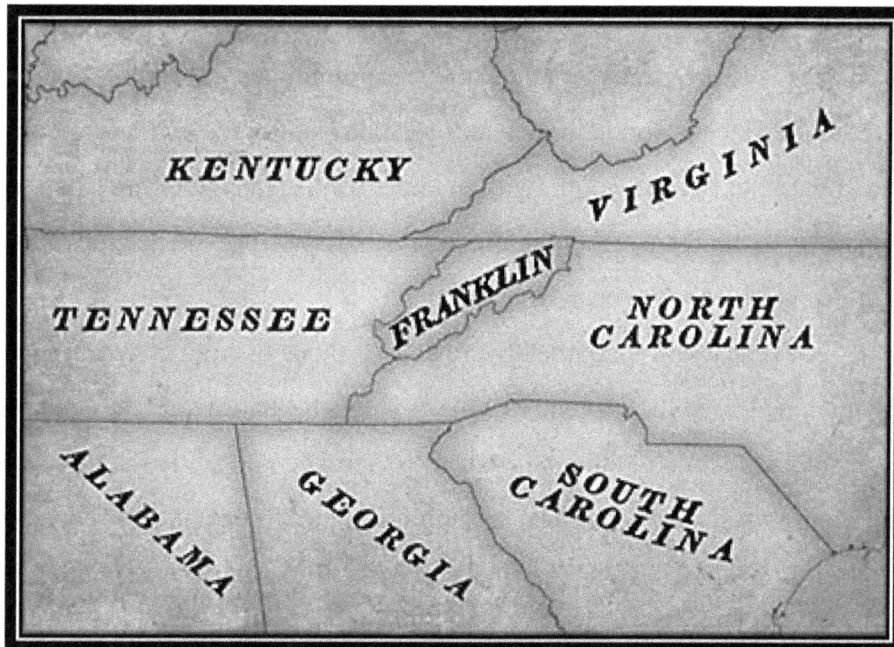

FIGURE 67 MAP: THE LOST STATE OF FRANKLIN, NOW TENNESSEE

The purchase was no sooner made, than we were alarmed by the reports of the present unhappy situation between Great Britain and America, on which report, (taking the new united colonies for our guide,) we proceeded to choose a committee, which was done unanimously by the consent of the people. This committee (willing to become a party in the present unhappy contest) resolved (which is now in our records) to adhere strictly to the rules and orders of the Continental Congress, and in open committee acknowledged themselves indebted to the united colonies their full portion of the Continental expense.

North Carolina formally agreed to accept the Washington District (The Lost State of Franklin, as it is now known) government, authorizing it to send representatives to the Provincial Congress in Halifax, NC on 12 Nov 1776 (in session until 18 Dec 1776). Those representatives included Charles Robertson, John Carter, John Haile and John Sevier from "Washington District, Watauga Settlement." Jacob Womack was also elected, but did not attend. A year later, at its Nov 1777 session, the general assembly of North Carolina approved the formation of Washington County, assigning it the boundaries of most of present-day Tennessee:

> "Beginning at the north-westwardly point of the County of Wilkes [North Carolina], in the Virginia line; thence, with the line of Wilkes County, to a point twenty-six miles south of the Virginia line; thence due west to the ridge of the Great Iron Mountain, which, heretofore, divided the hunting-grounds of the Overhill Cherokees, from those of the Middle Settlements and Vallies; thence, running a southwardly course along the said ridge, to the Uneca Mountain, where the trading-path crosses the same, from the Valley to the Overhills; thence, south, with the line of this state adjoining the State of South-Carolina; thence, due west to the great River Mississippi; thence, up the same river to a point due west from the beginning." [17]

In 1792, several family members were among those taxable in Washington County, Tennessee which had been the epicenter of the Watuagah Petition and descendants of those families known to have bought the land from the Cherokee and settled there in hopes of establishing their own state of Franklin. Though it was not to be and is now part of Tennessee and just south of Johnson City. The families enumerated include: Yates, Millagen, Simerly, Waters, Wilson, Waggoner, Gentry, Cook, Jones (over age), Snider, Guinn/Goins (James was

---

[17] (ibid.)

over age), Ford, Heatherly (over age), Perkins, Lindsay (over age), Wilder, Baker, Ashurts (Ashworth), Wallas, Graves, Snider, Kane, Hendrick, Peters, Green, Shoults, Bass, Arnold, Johnson, Burton, Coates, Price, Moore, Humphreys, Garland, Carriger (?), Driggar, Ivy, Bowers, Nasie/Narie/Nanie (?), Cobb, Herr, Tipton, Redmon, Worley, Newland, Kite, Lincoln, Gilbert, Drury, Helton, Robison, Starness, Milagen, Hooker.

WASHINGTON COUNTY LIST OF TAXABLES

A List of the Taxable Property of Alex Andrew Greers Company in the Year 1792

Name	Land	Pole	Name	Land	Pole
Jacob Hendrick	300	1	Samuel Tipton	550	1
J. Michael Smith Peters	750	1	John Garland	200	1
Thomas Dunkeon		1	Steven Redmon	100	1
Aleson Greer		1	John Price		1
Christian Shoults Joner		1	John Worley	100	1
Jeremiah Bass		9	John Nowland		1
Jacob Hedrick, Junr	?	1	John Lacy		1
Valentine Sevier, Junr		1?	Ephraim Murry		1
Richd. Cox		1	Isaac Kite	200	2
Joseph Brown		1	Joseph Green	400	3
John Arnold		1	Christopher Peters		1
Thomas Greers		1	Isaac Lincoln	350	1
Robt Johnston		1	John Gillum		1
John Carter		3	James Wright		1
Charels Burden		1	Abraham Helton		1
Jarret Burden	100	1	Michael Dary		1
James Price	275	1	Arnold Helton		1
Solomon Holbett	233	1	John Musgrove		1
Elisha Humphreys	125	1	Humphrey Garland		1
John Parker Moore		1	John Robison	50	1
Christian Shooths Sen		1	Christian Stoner		1
Gutredge Garland	130	1	James Hilsapps	100	1
Godfrey Carriger Sen	2727	1	Andw Green Senr	2150	4
Nicholas Carriger	500	1	Robert Hooker		1
Mihael Carriger		1			
Godfrey Carriger Juns					
Lanelow Carter	2930	6			
William Duggar	200	1			
James Ivy	100	1			
Old Miller	150	1			
Leonard Bowers	50	1			
Peter Nave	150	1			
Abraham Nave		1			
Abraham Sevier	100	1			
Joseph Sevier		2			
Valentine Sevier Sen.	350 1000	1			
Phar Cobb	500	10			
Joseph Large		1			
John Haas "Kerr"	1	1			
Isaac Tipton		1			
Thomas Tipton		1			

FIGURE 68 1792 DOCUMENT: WASHINGTON COUNTY LIST OF TAXABLES (LORIDANS N.D.)

194

WASHINGTON COUNTY LIST OF TAXABLES

- 1792 -

A list of Taxable Property taken by Rich'd White for the year

	Land	Free poles	Slaves
Samuel Yates		1	—
James Milsaps	200	1	—
John Simerly	200	1	
George Waters WALTERS		1	—
John Wilson sen.	60		— 1
David Waggoner	572	1	— 3
Joseph Gentry	110	1	
William Wilson	—	1	0
John Wilson 2nc	70	1	0
William Cook	—	1	—
Mathew Waggoner	—	1	2
Lewis Jones sen. over age	100	—	—
Adam Snider	115	1	0
Champness Guinn	—	— 1	0
James Guinn over age	250		—
Joseph Ford (over age)	600 375	1	1
Evin Heatherly over age	95	0	0
George Perkins	200	1	0
Mathew Lindsay over age	176	0	0
Joab Wilder do	50	0	0
William Baker		1	0
John Ashurst	100	1	0
Aaron Wallace	—	1	0
James Graves	—	1	0
Samuel Wilson	225	1	0
Peter Snider	132	0	0
Peter Kane		1	0
Amt Carrd over —			
Edward Smith over age	600		

note: 2 pages of Richard White's List misplaced. not copied here. see original

FIGURE 69 DOCUMENT: WASHINGTON COUNTY LIST OF TAXABLES (LORIDANS N.D.)

195

Old Jock Perkins was a wealthy plantation owner known far and wide for his fine racing and pacing horses, iron works plantations and the familie's mysterious origins. He claimed to be "Portuguese Guinea" a fact that his descendants would later defend in a Johnson County, Tennessee court, accusing their neighbors of calling the Perkins "Negros" in the case of Joshua F. Perkins vs John R. White in 1857. Though the trial was lengthy and involved several witnesses for defendant, and plaintiffs, all testimony given by witnesses was in accordance with "perceived" notions of ancestry, and varied opinions from Portuguese, to Negro, to Cherokee Indian. What was the most interesting of the testimony were the testimonies given by the following witnesses who give accounting of first-hand what Old Jock had told to them and or others concerning his ethnic origins;

Nicholas Smith of Johnson Hampton that he "heard Old Jock Perkins refer to himself as Guineagree" **Mary WHITE** who "personally knew Jac Perkins" said "he was referred to as Guinea", **John D. SHUFIELD** *"Joshua's father and uncles of a dark color. The **GRAVES** dark. Heard my step grandfather say he knew the grandfather of plaintiff on Peedee in S.C. and he was called a free man in that place", **Richard WHITE** testified "he was a blue gum negro", *Jacob Perkins* "darker than **Joshua**. The mother of Joshua said the GRAVES were Portuguese and her brother Guineagree Privileges", **Lewis LEWIS** testified "Saw old Jake PERKINS, Joshua's father at mill. Guinea.... God d---d negroes. Jack PERKINS hair was wooly as wool on a sheep's back."

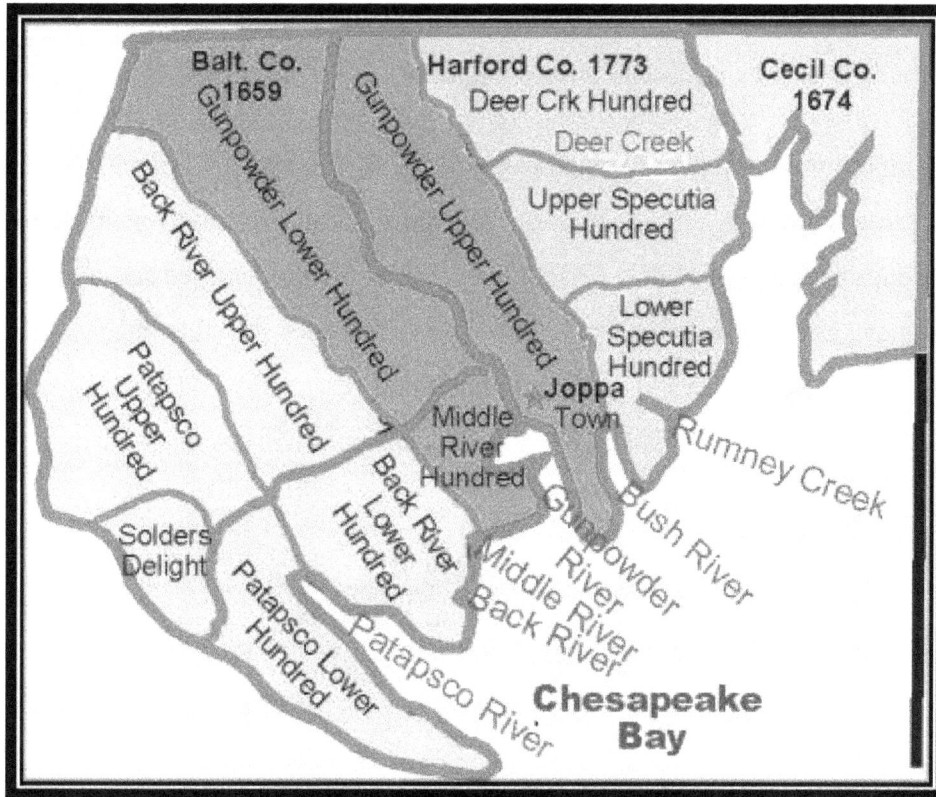

Figure 70 Map: Specutie 100 and surrounding land owned by Nathaniel Uite, Maryland. Perkins, Mixon, Clark and Sherrill's.

Spes-Utie

The origin of the Perkins family at this point is worth of noting several facts with regard to **Richard Jr.** (Mary Utie/Richard [1]), Old Jock's father who married **Mary "Ester" Sherrill**, known patriarch couple and source for contributing "ethnic" origin of the family. Richard Perkins owned land in the first settlement known as "Specutie/a/Spesutie/a 100" name In Latin meaning "Utie's hope"[18] of early 1630's Swan Creek, Baltimore Maryland.

"In 1634 the first settlers set sail on the Ark and the Dove for Lord Baltimore's new colony Maryland. Beginning in 1658 a few souls ventured north of St. Mary's and secured the first land grants in Baltimore County (what is now Harford County). The land in those grants hugged the shoreline in the area around Romney Creek to Swan Creek As vessels came into the Chester

---

[18] The name Spesutie is derived from the Latin for Utie's Hope, 17th century Manorial Grant to Colonel Nathaniel Utie. "About 1649, Col. Utie came from Virginia to explore the upper bay region and find a place to settle. In 1658, Bearson's Island, located a few hundred yards south of Havre de Grace, was granted to Nathaniel Utie. He changed the name to Spesutie, using the Latin Spes-Utie, meaning Utie's Hope. The spelling was later changed to Spesutia as it is known today."(Wright 1967)

River from England or France or Guinea, they passed close to this old house and the messages brought over from the mother country made the sails of the ships a doubly welcome sight."[19]

With several references to ships from Portugal, Guinea, and France, arriving at ports near the Swan Creek, Spesutia land made an obvious port of entry for many people of various origins, cultures, religions, and very likely class statues. Slaves and indentured servants from all over the Portuguese and Spanish Empires would have been off loaded into the tobacco rich plantations of the area. Later, runaway slaves, and freed indentured servants would be accepted, and protected in some cases by the local Indians. They would easily mix with the Indian tribes and cause many generations of Mixed Blood descendants.

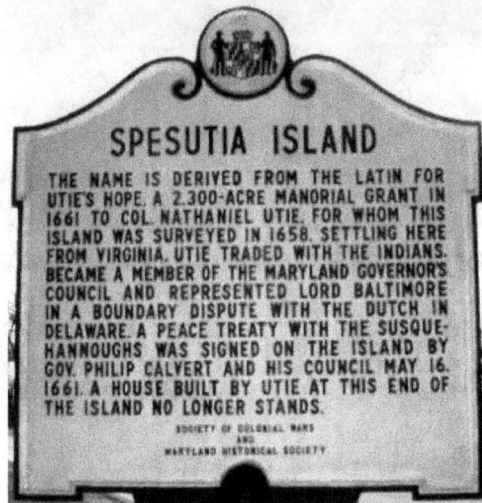

Figure 71 Map: Spesutia Island Historical Marker

Oxford was laid out in accordance with the "Act for the erection of necessary towns" in 1684, and in 1707 the county-seat was moved to that thriving town. The last session of the court at ' 'Yorke" was on the 17th day of June, 1707, and the first session at Oxford was held on the eiqth of August following. Oxford became a port of entry and to its harbor vessels came from England, Guinea, Barbados and the ports along the Atlantic Coast. [20]

Bohemia[21] [i] River now located in Cecil County situated between Delaware Bay and Chesapeake Bay was also home to the Susquehannough Indians and *Nathaniel Utie* born 1635 in

---

[19] (Earle 1821)

[20] (Earle 1821)

[21] Bohemianism is the practice of an unconventional lifestyle, often in the company of like-minded people,

Jamestown. Nathaniel had come to Maryland with a group of Puritans exiled from Virginia in 1649. Utie sometimes spelled Utye first settled at Providence, just outside modern day Annapolis. Spesutia Island is a 1,500 acre island in the Chesapeake Bay in Harford County, Maryland, 5.5 miles southwest of Aberdeen. Spesutia Narrows bounds the island on the west and the bay bounds it on the north, east and south. The island is part of Aberdeen Proving Ground now, and is off limits to the public. The island was originally used by the Indian tribes of the area to hunt bear, and on some of the older maps of the area represent the Island with a bear head symbol.

Lord Baltimore had established a large tobacco plantation just inland from the coast, but when he handed out land grants to the Puritan settlers Utie became the largest land holder in what was then, Baltimore County. He was instructed to inform the Dutch, whose settlements along the northeastern Atlantic coast extended south into Delaware, that Lord Baltimore had decided many of their colonies were now in Maryland. The Dutch were not completely delighted to turn over all their holdings to Lord Baltimore, which resulted in the eruption of the two decades long series of conflicts known as the Anglo-Dutch Wars. Of course, because Utie was the messenger for Lord Baltimore he also became notoriously despised as such. Many Dutch complained of his high handedness but was often and variously described as mutinous, seditious, violent, boisterous, stormy, blustering, irritating, and frivolous.

When Utie received the grant for the little island in the Chesapeake, he called it Spes-Utie, which combines the Latin spes, meaning hope, with his own surname, which basically means he called the island "Utie's Hope." Utie thought the name would encourage settlers to stay on his lands. The island was also known as "Spesutia." Utie brought settlers to the Upper Chesapeake, and built a house on the island called Spesutia Manor. At some point, he married a woman named Mary Mapletoft Ward, who was the widow of one of Utie's settlers.

---

with few permanent ties, involving musical, artistic, or literary pursuits. In this context, Bohemians may be wanderers, adventurers, or vagabonds.

This use of the word bohemian first appeared in the English language in the nineteenth century to describe the non-traditional lifestyles of marginalized and impoverished artists, writers, journalists, musicians, and actors in major European cities.[1] Bohemians were associated with unorthodox or anti-establishment political or social viewpoints, which often were expressed through free love, frugality, and—in some cases—voluntary poverty. A more economically privileged, even aristocratic or wealthy, bohemian circle is sometimes referred to as haute bohème[2] ("high bohemians").[3]

The term Bohemianism emerged in France in the early nineteenth century when artists and creators began to concentrate in the lower-rent, lower class, Romani neighborhoods. Bohémien was a common term for the Romani people of France, who were mistakenly thought to have reached France in the 15th century via Bohemia,[4] at that time the only protestant and therefore heretic country among Western Christians.

Mary Mapletoft Ward Utie died in 1665; she was stabbed to death. According to Maryland court records, Mary was stabbed repeatedly in the upper arm on September 30th, 1665 and died five days later on October 4th, at Spesutia Manor. According to her husband, the stabbing was done by one of their slaves, a man named Jacob. Jacob, with only the slenderest pretense of a trial, was condemned to be drawn and hanged, and this sentence was carried out in St. Mary's City a few months later. Slavery had just been legalized in Maryland in 1664. As a slave owner, Utie was in possession of several potential murder suspects who were legally considered subhuman and could not defend themselves against any allegations he might make against them. He had no neighbors, and if one of his other slaves should happen to witness anything, they couldn't testify against him in court. (Pezzullo n.d.)

In early 1666, Nathaniel Utie remarried, this time to Elizabeth Carter, the daughter of John Carter of Virginia. Elizabeth received 1/3 of her father's estate as a wedding gift, and according to John Carter's will, she would inherit the whole amount if her brothers should die without sons. It was a very advantageous match for Utie, and it is thought Utie had arranged for the murder of his wife. Mary Utie was buried in a family plot near Spesutia Manor, since the first church to be established near Spesutie Island wasn't built until 1671. Nathaniel Utie died in 1675. The property remained in the Utie family until 1779 when Samuel Hughes purchased it. In 1802, William Smith bought the island, and his descendants would remain there for almost a century, though the War of 1812 brought some disruption.

Nathaniel Utie received license on May 7, 1658 to trade with the Indians for furs, and to arrest all persons who were trading in the upper part of the bay without license. On the 12th of July following he was commissioned captain of all forces between the coves of Patuxent River and the Severn Mountains, and was appointed to command as his own company all forces from the head of Severn River to the above mountains. In 1666, Nathaniel Utie was one of the commissioners appointed to effect an agreement between Virginia, North Carolina, and Maryland to suspend tobacco planting for a year, so as to drive the value up. Nathaniel lived at this time on Spesutie Island, and became the owner of considerable land on the Gunpowder and Sassafras Rivers. He was one of the most adventurous pioneers at the head-waters of the Chesapeake, and on account of the troubles with the Indians and the Dutch, the Provincial Council frequently met at his house for the purpose of investigating the facts, making treaties with the Indians, and trade relations. [22]

Figure 72 Map: Utie Family Spesutie Island Northern Portion at the mouth of Susquehanna River, Perkins, Uti Families. Cecil County North/Eastern (Chesapeake Bay), Mixon. Wilmington Delaware Upper portion between Delaware Bay and Chesapeake Bay; Bird, Epson Families. Bohemia River where the Utie's land was situated, which encompassed Spesutie Island was also home to the Susquehannough Indians.

"Moreover, there are records of Portuguese ships having sailed into Jamestown Bay as early as 1655, and since then there has been more or less settlement of Portuguese fishermen and sailors from Maine to Florida. Now it has been the history of the Portuguese race that wherever they settled they mixed in with the darker peoples forming the aboriginal populations of the countries occupied by Portuguese settlers, and this is the reason and cause of the Portuguese admixture among the tribes along the coast of the United States." James Mooney, Ethnologist, Smithsonian Institute. [23]

On the southern shore of the James River, according to the records, George Gibson, Thomas Gibson, Thomas Chivers/Chavis, 'Peter' Gibson, Thomas Busby, Robert Sweat and Adam Ivey are all found on Chippoakes Creek. John Utie Jr. born about 1619 London, was baptized in St. Andrew's Holborn Parish. He repatented his father's 1250 acres in 1638. In 1639 he assigned 100 acres of land to Thomas Gibson, land which Utie acquired in 1624 and named "Utopia" located at the head of Chippoakes Creek. York Co. VA records show *John Utie, Jr.* was deceased by 1647. William Knott, 312 Acres, Surry Co 28 Mar 1666, p. 482 (land patents).

---

[22] (Brugger 1988)
[23] (C. Hill n.d.)

112 acres on south side of James River on south side of Upper Chipoake Creek, bounded NW on land of Edward Oliver, N upon Wm. Thomas, E on George Gibson & SE on Mr. Fisher; 200 acres on south side of said River, Wly. on Jeremiah Clements, NW on Edward Oliver, Nly on Wm. Thomas, George Gibson & Edward Minter, Ely. on Wm. Gapins land & Mr. Thomas Busbie and SE on Mr. Richard Hill. (Pezzullo n.d.)

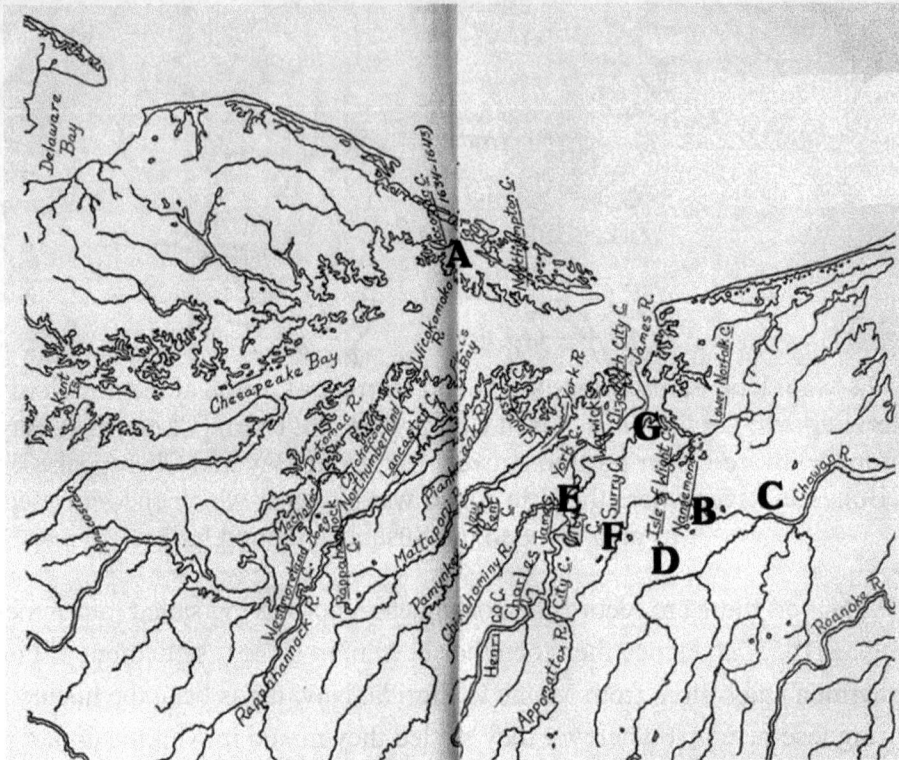

FIGURE 73MAP No. NECK OF THE VIRGINIAS

A. Accomack; Perkins, Jr., southern portion known as Talbots which once encompassed Accomack and North Hampton Counties between the Chesapeake and Delaware Bays, and home to the Rappahannock, and Nanticoke Indians

B. Nansemond; Home of the Nansemond Indians, Bass, Collins, (Wm., Tho., Jno.), Utie, Jr., Gibson (Gideon), Anderson, Brown.

C. Chowan; Home of the Chowanock Indians, Collins (Jno), Russell, Chavis, Stringer, Wise, Ash/Nash.

D. Isle of Wright; Bass, Anderson, Hardy, WM. Williams.

E. James City Co & Charles City Co.; Mayo, Sherrill, Parker, Bass/e, Utie, Gibson (Gibey), Weatherford.

F. Surry; Chavis, Sweat, Utie, Collins, Col Wm Brown (Cherokee Wars). 1630-1750.

G. Roanoke River; Thomas Goins/Goings, Hall, Strother, listed at Roanoke Island among the colonists who latter disappeared into the wilderness and assimilated with the Croaton later known as Lumbee Indians. Little else is known of the fate of these colonists. Not pictured is Specutie and northern portion of Chesapeake Bay, See Figure Above.

The Quiyoughcohannock were the first Virginia Indian tribe to make contact with the English in 1607 nearly at the time of arrival at Jamestown. Situated primarily in present-day Surry County, the Quiyoughcohannocks had four villages in the region of Upper Chippokes Creek. The Quiyoughcohannocks in 1608 South Carolina *Nathaniel Powell* and Anas Todkill southward in an unsuccessful attempt to locate survivors of the ill-fated colony on Roanoke Island. Upon arrival, the English observed a portion of an Indian ritual that would usher a young brave into manhood. The ritual was called the "huskanaw" (respectably). The colonists witnessed a portion of the festivities at the Quiyoughcohannock village in 1608. (Pezzullo n.d.)

We do not know if *Nathaniel Utie*, or *John, Jr. Utie* were the father of *Mary Utie* who married *Richard Perkins, Sr.* at Specutie 100 however, both Nathaniel and John, Jr. were reputed to have children among the settler women, slaves and Indian maidens, through trade with the Sesquehannough as well as the Quiyoughcohannocks Indians.

Figure 74 Photo: Unknown Perkins Cherry/Chary

Figure 75 Photo: Nancy Perkins (not pictured) mother of above pictured **Mary Polly Perkins** Nash & grandmother of **Absalom Perkins** she was listed in 1896 Cherokee applications as full blood Cherokee, though a spouse has never been identified for her, or parentage, she is buried at Glass Window Cemetery, what is left of the "Glass Window" trading post at Vernon Parish, Louisiana where the Groves/Ash/Nash built trade between No. Zulch, Madison Co., Texas just east of Crockett and Louisiana at the junction on the El Camino Real where it split north to Nacogdoches, and south to San Antonio. Now Hwy 21. This trail was once known as the Opelousas Beef Trail. It facilitated early Redbones into then Spanish Tejas where they invented and developed the Texas cattle culture. The trading post in Vernon Parish was the location of the famous Raw Hide Fight about 1850 occurred between the Redbones and the White Settlers. Mary Polly Perkins married James Ash/Nash and according to the mortality schedule 1850 Mary states James died of a knife wound. These could likely have been the result of the Rawhide Fight. Though he is not mentioned in any of the earlier reports.

There was a Fanny Nash found dead on the edge of Nacogdoches in early 1798, the result of a throat slashing. The report stimming from a condolette (official Spanish messenger) reports" among the Mississippi Territorial Papers, within the *Natchez Trace Collection*, located at University of Texas, at Austin. The condolette reported a "Fanny Nash" and a male companion were found hidden in low brush about 75' off the trail between Nacogdoches, and Natchitoches. Travelers noticed vulture's hoovering and went to investigate. The bodies being there for some days, the identity of the male companion was never given, just the remarks he was unidentifiable, and had suffered the same wounds.

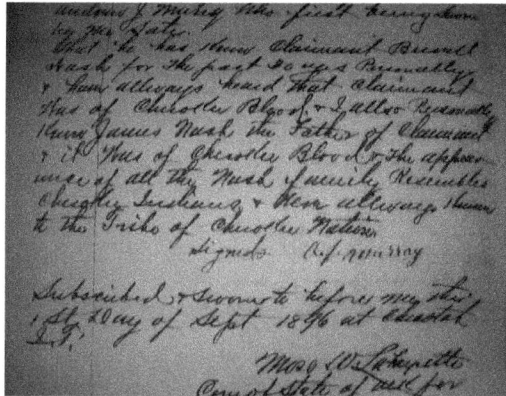

Figure 76 Document:1896 Cherokee affidavit of Perkins and Nash Family "Cherokee by blood" stating Nancy Perkins mother of Mary (pictured above) and wife of James Ash/Nash, and Thomas Ash/Nash were both "full blood Indian". Butler Nash (picture elsewhere here) Family self-migrated to Oklahoma, others family who applied remained in Texas, and forfeited head rights, forever.

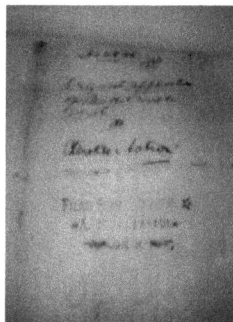

Figure 77 Document:1896 Cherokee Nation Rolls. Burrell Ash/Nash below self-migrated to Oklahoma. Brother to James II pictured below.

FIGURE 78 PHOTO: BURRELL ASH/NASH, SELF-MIGRATED TO OKLAHOMA.

FIGURE 79 PHOTO: JAMES II NASH FAMILY ELIZABETH DEARMOND

Figure 80 Photo: Missouri Lacey Goyens Ash/Nash, Ash/Nash. She was married to first cousins A. Ausberry and Guide E. Ash/Nash. Noted remarkable likeness to Pocahontas Doyle Thompson

FIGURE 81 PHOTO: JAMES II AND ELIZABETH DEARMOND NASH FAMILY IN FRONT OF THE HAND BUILT LOG HOME.

Figure 82 Photo:Emilie "Millie" Groves Daughter of James and Mary Polly Nash Groves. She married James F. Bass son of John and Delany Taylor Nelson Bass. **Figure 83** Photo: Frances Fannie Nelson Drake and husband Aaron N. Drake daughter of Amos Moses and Melissa Ashworth Nelson. Photo courtesy Robert Woolwine, a descendant.

Figure 84 Photo: Butler Ash/Nash and family with granddaughter self-migrated to Oklahoma in 1896. Cherokee Applications

The Bride's Family

Marie Rachel Drake born December 1806, her ancestry and heritage also steeped in the Redbone clan. Marie Rachel was the daughter of *John Aaron Jr.* born 1776 in St. Martinville Parish, Louisiana and died 1892 in Lafayette Parish, Louisiana and *Rosalie Abshire/Abcher* born 1782 in New Iberia, Iberia Parish, Louisiana and died 1871 in Lafayette, Lafayette Parish, Louisiana. The couple was married in May of 1800 in St Martinville, Attakapas Spanish Louisiana. They had at least the following children:

- *Mary Louisa Drake* born 1793, died 1828 married Unknown,
- *Charity Sarophina Drake* born about 1791 and died 1881, she married *Jeremiah Goin/Goings* (*Philip, Stephen, William*) and did not match, nor share an African haplo group assignment with the afore mentioned Redbone Going/Goyens/Sweat/Warwick/Powell/Williams and Perkins families, although we are

related both maternally and paternally. This family appears to originate in 1650s Colonial Virginia, and eastern North Carolina. The family appears to have been an example of a White forefather **William Goings** an indentured servant, who most certainly mixed with the Indian tribes where he was living, and migrated with the Mixed Blood fur and Indian trade around the Piedmont area of North Carolina. I believe this line that is closely related and Redbone descended were from the Welsh Neck of Shenandoah Valley and likely joined the families on their migrations into Cheraw, and PeeDee, South Carolina regions and are likely the family who has been very confused with the other William Goyens family. His descendants we suspect, and DNA is confirming, are Meherrin from Hertford and Bertie counties, with almost certainly a mixture of Nottoway, Chowan, and Coastal Algonquin, ancestry. However, their exact genetic match is of a Palestinian Arab origin. These families lived along the Natchez Trace and were infamous Indian Mixed Blood stand owners among the Chickasaw and Choctaw tribes. It was part of the agreement between the U.S. Congress and the Chickasaw and Choctaw Agencies; that only Indian Mixed Bloods could own and operate "stands" along the trace when the American government sought to enlarge the trail between Nashville, and Natchez, in order to facilitate settlements in the newly acquired territories. More about this family is also represented in the upcoming *Goins Book's*, South Texas Goins chapter by Gary J. Gabehart, and Marilyn Baggett Kobliaka whose Goings families were an exact yNA match for each other.

- *Angela Drake* born 1800
- *Francis Drake* born 1801
- *John Aaron Drake III* born 1805 in Louisiana and died 1892 in Calcasieu Parish, Louisiana and he married *Elizabeth "Betsy" Ashworth (Mary Perkins/James [3], Keziah Doyle/James [2], Catherine Smithe/James [1])* she was born about 1815 in St. Landry Parish, Louisiana
- *Marie Rachel*, Our Bride!
- *Sarah Celestine "Sally" Drake* born 1809 in Louisiana and married [1] *Thomas, Jr. Nash/Ash (Emily Slater/Thomas[3], Betsy Goins/Thomas Nash/Ash [2], Unknown/John Nash The Indian Trader at Ft. Blackmore among the Cherokee, Nottoway, Catawbas, Cheraws [1]) and* [2] *Nathan Perkins (Nancy Perkins/Unknown)*. *Sarah Celestine Drake Nash*

Perkins had at least one child with each husband. *Mary Elizabeth Nash* who married *Josiah Bass* (*Emily Groves/James F. Bass*) and *Absalom Richard Perkins* (*Nancy Perkins/Unknown*).

We found that *John Aaron Drake* lines of Virginia and Louisiana through the male line or Y-DNA descendants of Drake surname is actually very closely related to the Sir Francis Drake line of Cromwell's England. However, Sir Francis Drake was reputed to have no descendants at all, despite the fact that many claim him as their ancestor both here, and abroad. We found this group of "claimants" were very closely related to our lines, a known nephew of his *John Drake* ancestor of early Virgina Redbone families. They are not exact Y-DNA match but very closely related (within 1 genetic distance). We speculate these are actually the descendants, as suggested by Gary Gabehart "Mishiho" who married into the Ross lines of early Virginia Alqonquin Tribes of the Powhatan Indian Confederacy. This family is descended from the *John Drake* line who arrived at Virginia's James City about 1742 from England. *John Aaron, Sr.* was born 1750 in Elizabeth City, Virginia and died in August of 1813 in St Martin Parish, Louisiana. He married *Elizabeth Charity Chavis/Crieves* born about 1752 in King and Queen, Virginia and died in April of 1815 in St. Martin Parish, Louisiana. *John Aaron* was enumerated in Powhatan County, Virginia in 1779 at age 29 but married *Elizabeth Chavis* in St. Martin Parish the next year, 1800.

> *John Aaron Drake, Sr*. was born about 1750 in Elizabeth Co., Virginia and died in Louisiana. Though little is known of the ancestry of this couple they had at least three children;
>
> *Elizabeth Aurelise Drake* born 1776 and died in St. Landry Parish, Louisiana in about 1819, she married *Aaron Doyle* (*M. Mixon/John Joshua [3], E. Hill/Thomas[2], L. Hastings/Thomas[1],*)
>
> *Mary Louise Drake* born 1793 in Attakapas District, Louisiana and died 1828 in Louisiana, she married *Alexander Buxton* (*Jude*) born in 1793 South Carolina and died 1840 in Texas.
>
> *John Aaron Drake, Jr.* born about 1800 in St. Landry Parish, Louisiana and died about 1892 in Calcasieu Parish, Louisiana he married *Rosalie Abshire/Abcher*.
>
> "*Juaneromdraky*" translated John Aaron Drake, in the late 1820's, along with other Redbone family members were caught in Texas by the Spanish Officials, and there he

was charged with *"rounding up the King's Mustangs."* John Drake's band of wranglers and rough-en's were identified as "Coyote"[24] by the Spanish officials of Nacogdoches, Coahuila y Tejas. (Natchez Trace Colletion 1827).

Figure 85 Photo:1763 De Mestizo y d'India; Coyote [Note: the child has a stick raised above "fathers" head which we found a curious detail, most of the paintings have revel depictive scenes. This is a must have book for any researcher/descendant of early Colonial Mixed Bloods.[25]]

Sarah Celestine "Sally" Drake was born about 1809 and in 1829 was an orphan when applications were made for her marriage to [1] *Thomas Nash/Ash Jr.* They were only married about a year when Thomas Nash, Jr. obviously died about 1830, *Sarah next* married [2] *Nathan Perkins (R. Abshire/John Aaron Drake, Jr. ², C. Chavis/John Aaron Drake, Sr.¹)* they are the parents of Absalom Perkins pictured below.

---

[24] 1763 De Mestizo y d'India; Coyote Mexican Castes: Coyote= African, Spanish (White) + Indian. Some of the terms denoting the mix of races had zoological meanings. The lowest among the mixes of races were often denigrated with animal names like Lobo (Wolf) & Coyote.

[25] (Katzew 2004)

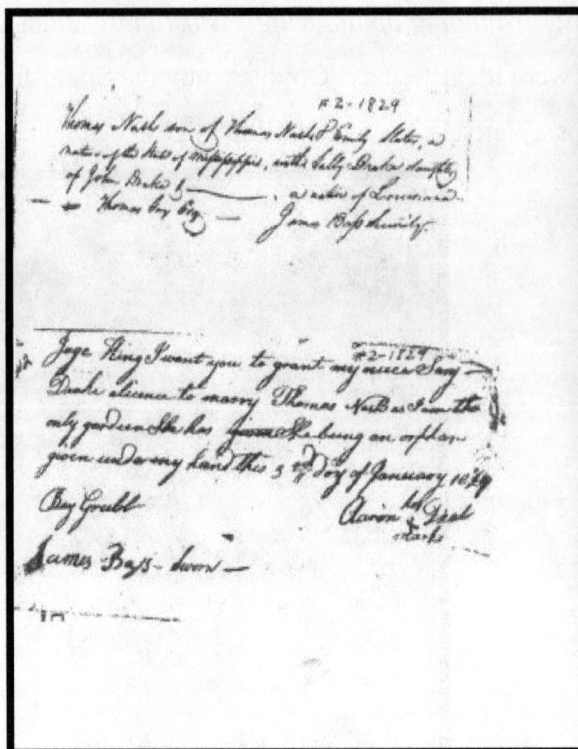

Figure 86 Marriage Document filed 1829 #1 and #2, Rapides Parish, Louisiana (Johnson, Drake Family Cousins 2005)

Paragraph #1 1829

Thomas Nash son of Thomas Nash & Emily Slater, a native of the State of Mississippi, with Sally Drake daughter of John Drake of _____, a native of Louisiana Thomas [Illegible] Esq.   James Bafs (Bass) surety.

Paragraph #2

Judge King I want you to grant my niece Sally Drake a license to marry Thomas Nash as I want only good, [illegible]…She being an orphan given under my hand this 3rd day of January 1829 Aaron X Drake (his mark) boy or illegible Grubb   James Bafs (Bass) Sworn

FIGURE 87 PHOTO: ABSALOM PERKINS SON OF SARAH CELESTINE DRAKE AND NATHAN PERKINS

FIGURE 88 ANN ELIZABETH DRAKE TURNBULL

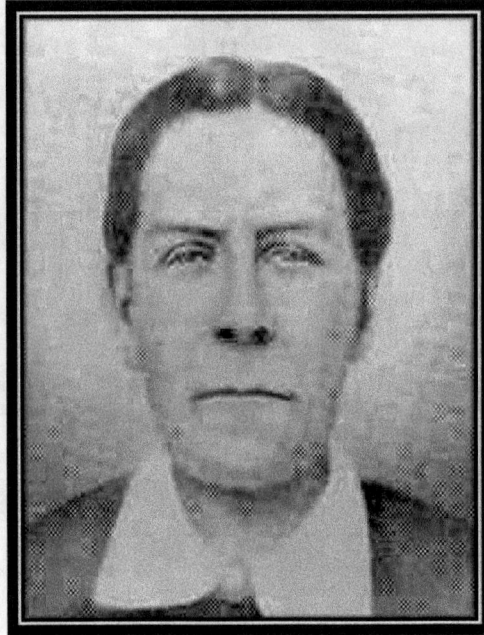

FIGURE 89 NANCY PERKINS GROVES (DAUGHTER OF UNKNOWN AND NANCY PERKINS)

Figure 90 Photo: Dr. Turner Brashears Turnbull & Angelico "Jerico" Perkins (Natchez Trace to Choctaw Nation Oklahoma). She was the daughter of Nicholas "Cader" and Angeline Brashear, she was born in St. Landry Parish, Louisiana in 1826 and died in 1893 Choctaw Nation, Indian Territory. She is the granddaughter of Joshua Perkins born 1795 in Pee Dee, SC and Mary Mixon born 1760 Cheraw, SC.

Turner & Jerico Perkins Turnbull. The couple became heavily, and politically involved with tribal affairs in Oklahoma and were instrumental in the Choctaws final removals.

They migrated with Marth Patsy Goins and Eli Crowder Family as well as James and Gipson Goings, both killed Mayhew Mission. The couple ran Turnbull's Stand along the Natchez Trace and was the maternal son of a Brashear. All descendants of Richard Perkins, Sr. Spesutie 100

.

FIGURE 91 PHOTOS: CHILDREN OF TURNER B. AND JERICHO PERKINS TURNBULL. L TO R TURNER B. JR. AND JULIA ANN TURNBULL

The Minister of the Gospel

Revd. Joseph Willis

The "Minister of the Gospel" who married the couple of our study, Reverend *Joseph Willis, Sr.* "Father of the Redbones" and "Apostle of the Attakapas" would also find his heritage and many descendants among the Doyle, Hill Redbone families. Reverend *Joseph Willis, Sr.* born about 1758 in Bladen, South Carolina and died in 1854 at 10 Mile near Calcasieu River, Vernon Parish, Louisiana. Willis was the offspring of the union between a Black and Cherokee Mixed Blood slave, and a prosperous White plantation owner, *Agerton Willis*, who freed his son of slave condition through his will, though Willis would in turn fight his uncles for partial inheritance and the courts for his freedom to become "The first Baptist Minister west of the Mississippi River" eventually being removed later by the Mississippi Baptist convention citing his "free colored" status as cause. Reverend Joseph Willis not only spread the Gospel among the

Redbones, but he also married among them. He was closely associated with *Tobias Gibson/Gypson* who settled many Redbone families around Vicksburg, Mississippi from PeeDee and Holestine Rivers (Warren, Perkins, Gibson, and Evans). Tobias Gibson/Gypson was also a progenitor forefather of many Redbones.

Reverend Willis was the only known enslaved Redbone progenitor; most had resisted slavery. "Brother" Willis, as he is referred to by the Redbones was first married to [1] *Rachel Bradford,* born about 1785 in Cheraw District, South Carolina in what is probably now Marlboro County. After the death of his first wife, he married about 1792 to [2] *Sarah Johnson* in Greenville, South Carolina. In 1800, he was enumerated in Woodville Mississippi, after selling his land in South Carolina the year previous. In 1836, he married [3] *Elvy Sweat*. Reverend Willis would have children with all his wives, ranging from birth years of 1792-1848. Willis's daughter with *Mary Bradford*, *Mary Willis*, she first married **Isaac** *Johnson*, and next, *Thomas Doyle,* born about 1770 in Pendleton District, South Carolina, the father of the groom. Doyle first married *Mary "Polly" Perkins* and died in Rapides Parish, Louisiana. A daughter born to this union was *Mary Doyle,* born 1857 in Opelousas Parish, Louisiana; she married *William Strothers* of the Indian Old Fields, Alabama north of Old Mobile.

Much has been documented on Joseph Willis, here and other sources. I will continue with the genealogical aspects of his life but resign he is a well-documented and highly respected Redbone Progenitor. I am also proud to be counted as a descendant of Willis, and his first wife Mary Bradford.

....*To Be Continued*

FIGURE 92 MAHALA NASH TURNER DAUGHTER OF THOMAS ASH/NASH (WILLIAM/H. PERKINS, THOMAS/E. SLATER) AND MARY POLLY SMITH. HER FATHER WILLIAM AND STEP FATHER AND UNCLE BEN ASH/NASH ARE MENTIONED ELSEWHERE IN THIS PAPER; HANNAH PERKINS ASH/NASH ASH/NASH WAS THE DAUGHTER OF NIMROD PERKINS AND BETSY WATERS (NOT LAUGHING WATERS).

Figure 93 Photo: Leonard Lemuel and Mary Groves Sweat

Figure 94 Photo: Ashworth siblings L to R Keziah, Hester, Louisa, and Joshua, children of James and Polly Perkins Ashworth, Burk, Angelina Co., Texas

FIGURE 95 PHOTO: BURRELL ASH/NASH PICTURED ELSEWHERE HERE, RECEIVES AWARD RECOGNITION FOR CONFEDERATE SERVICE IN THE CIVIL WAR.

Redbone Progenitor Family
John Theophilus Thompson & Alsey Butt Descendants

By Contributing Genealogist, family historians & photos Verna Thompson & Marilyn Baggett Kobliaka

FIGURE 96 PHOTO: DESCENDANT CHARLES THOMPSON

1-*John Theophilus Thompson* was born in 1710 in Tyrone, Ireland and died in Sep 1757 in Barbados at age 47. *John Theophilus* married *Alsey Butt*. *Alsey* was born in 1720 in Virginia and died in 1780 in Robeson Co., North Carolina at age 60. They had one son: *Theophilis.*

2-*Theophilis Thompson* was born in 1748 in Nash Co., North Carolina and died in 1805 in Robeson Co., North Carolina at age 57. *Theophilis* married *Sarah Elizabeth McLoftlin*. *Sarah Elizabeth* was born in 1752 and died in 1780 at age 28. They had three children: *John "Gozalo," James Lee*, and *Lemuel Burkett*.

General Notes: Described by family as "Scotch Irish Cheraw Indian" General Notes: http://search.ancestry.com/cgi-bin/sse.dll?db=flhg-settlersu pperga&h=428389&ti=0&indiv=try&gss=pt *Sketches of Some of the First Settlers of Upper Georgia, of the Cherokees*

3-*John "Gozalo*" *Thompson* was born in 1767 in Robeson Co., North Carolina and died in 1835 in Tennessee at age 68. *John "Gozalo"* married *Ahniswakie "Anna" Mann*, daughter of William Mann and *Wah Li Vann*, on 25 Feb 1792 in Orange Co., North Carolina. *Ahniswakie "Anna"* was born in 1773 in North Carolina and died in 1845 in Tennessee at age 72. They had 15 children: *John "Jack," Steven, Sahlie "Salley," Sarah, Charles, Millie Ann, Archibald,*

Nancy, Judith, Elizabeth "Lizzy," Lovenny, Ne Coo le, Isolier, James Jim, and *Alexander*.

4-*John "Jack" Thompson* was born in 1786 in Hardeman, Tennessee and died in 1845 in Alabama at age 59. John "Jack" married *Nana Merrell*. Nana was born in 1790 and died in 1815 at age 25. They had five children: *Charles, Alexander, Nancy, Elizabeth,* and *Sarah*.

5-*Charles Thompson* was born in 1807.

5-*Alexander Thompson* was born in 1809. 5-Nancy Thompson was born in 1811.

5-*Elizabeth Thompson* was born in 1814.

5-*Sarah Thompson* was born in 1815.

John "Jack" next married *Jennie Ann Vann*. *Jennie Ann* was born in 1787 in North Carolina and died in 1813 in Tennessee at age 26. They had two children: *Sarah Elizabeth* and *William.*

5-*Sarah Elizabeth Thompson* was born in 1790 and died in 1854 at age 64.

5-*William Thompson* was born in 1800 in Cherokee, Alabama and died in 1845 at age 45.

John "Jack" next married *Elizabeth Merrell* in 1815. *Elizabeth* was born in 1780 in Cherokee Nation, East. They had five children: *Margaret, John1, John, Richard "Dick,"* and *James*.

Figure 97 Photo: Tookah Tu-Ga Thompson

5-*Margaret Thompson* was born in 1812.

5-*John1 Thompson* was born in 1816 and died in 1845 at age 29. 5-John Thompson was born in 1817.

5-*Richard "Dick" Thompson* was born in 1818 and died in 1888 at age 70. Richard "Dick" married Elizabeth "Lizzy" A. Thornton on 25 Dec 1846 in Ft. Gibson, Muskogee, Indian Territory. Elizabeth "Lizzy" A. was born in Aug 1826 in Cherokee, Washington, Tennessee and died in May 1926 in Fort Gibson, Muskogee, Oklahoma at age 99. They had five children: *Mary J., Nancy, Margaret Emma, Sue Elizabeth*, and *Tookah Tu-Ga.*

6-*Mary J. Thompson* was born in 1847 and died in 1881 at age 34.

6-*Nancy Thompson* was born in 1848 and died in 1890 at age 42.

Figure 98 Photo: Margaret Emma Thompson Lipe

6-*Margaret Emma Thompson* was born in 1849 and died in 1926 at age 77. *Margaret Emma* married *Clarke C. Lipe* on 29 Aug 1873 in Ft. Gibson, Muskogee, Indian Territory.

6-*Sue Elizabeth Thompson* was born in 1851 and died in 1926 at age 75.

6-*Tookah Tu-Ga Thompson* (Figure 79) was born in Sep 1854 in Bayou Menard, Indian Territory and died in May 1939 in Ft. Gibson, Muskogee, Indian Territory at age 84. *Tookah Tu-Ga* married *William S. Nash/Ash/Ashes*, son of *Nathaniel Nash/Ash/Ashes* and *Sarah Smelser*, in 1878 in Illinois. William S. was born in Sep 1846 in New Orleans, Orleans Parish, Louisiana and died in Feb 1908 in Oklahoma at age 61.

General Notes: *WILLIAM SMELSER NASH*:

> 1880 Census [CN]: Illinois, 1298 1890 Census [CN]: Illinois, 1748 Biography: 1892, O'Beirne, Indian Territory, page 130
> Blood: Adopted White
> Occupation 1: 1890, Merchant Occupation 2: 1880, Clerk
> Starr's Notes: J083; b:9/10/1847

5-*James Thompson* was born in 1820.

4-*Steven Thompson* was born in 1789 in Hardeman, Tennessee. 4-Sahlie "Salley" Thompson was born in 1790.

4-*Sarah Thompson* was born in 1790 in Hardeman, Tennessee and died in 1850 in Benton, Lowdens, Alabama at age 60.

4-*Charles Thompson* was born in 1792.

4-*Millie Ann Thompson* was born in 1792 in Hardeman, Tennessee and died on 23 Oct 1858 in Sulfur Springs, Polk, Arkansas at age 66.

4-**Archibald Thompson** was born on 12 Apr 1793 in Tennessee, died in 1890 in Rosepine, Vernon Parish, Louisiana at age 97, and was buried in Occupy #1 Cemetery, Glenmora, Rapides Parish, Louisiana.

Noted events in his life were:

·   Petition Claim: 1811, in Mississippi.
·   He appeared on the census in 1820 in St. Landry Parish, Louisiana.
·   He owned land in 1820 in Opelousas.
·   He owned land in 1820 in St. Stephens, Mississippi.
·   He appeared on the census in 1830 in St. Landry Parish, Louisiana.
·   He appeared on the census in 1840 in Natchitoches Parish, Louisiana.

Archibald married **Mary Nancy Iles/Islands** on 12 Jun 1814 in Marion, Mississippi. **Mary Nancy** was born in 1796 in Halifax Co., North Carolina and died in 1860 in Caddo Parish, Louisiana at age 64. They had 12 children: **Susan, Nancy, Mary, William Frederick, John, Edmond, Dempsy, Ishom C., Thomas, Edward, Martha,** and **Lucinda**.

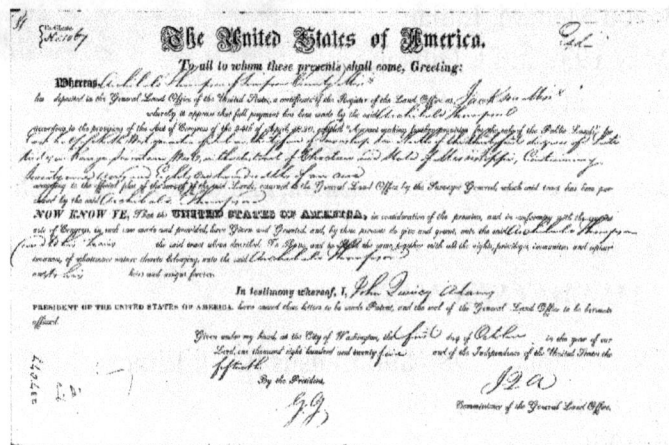

FIGURE 99 DOCUMENT: ARCHIBALD THOMPSON LAND CERTIFICATE LAND CERTIFICATE FOR OPELOUSAS DISTRICT, LOUISIANA

5-**Susan Thompson** was born in 1813.

5-**Nancy Thompson** was born in 1817.

5-**Mary Thompson** was born in 1819.

5-**William Frederick** Thompson was born in 1822 in St. Landry Parish, Louisiana and died in 1895 in Junction City, Claiborne Parish, Louisiana at age 73.

5-**John Thompson** was born in 1823.

5-**Edmond Thompson** was born in 1824 in St. Landry Parish, Louisiana, died on 20 May 1908 in Vernon Parish, Louisiana at age 84, and was buried in Occupy #1 Cemetery, Glenmora, Rapides Parish, Louisiana. Edmond married ***Martha Ann Howard. Martha Ann*** was born in 1835 in Catahoula Parish, Louisiana, died in 1900 in Rapides Parish, Louisiana at age 65, and was buried in Occupy #1 Cemetery, Glenmora, Rapides Parish, Louisiana. They're children: ***Eliza Jean, William, James F., Edmund, Hebe, Reba, Wesley, Enos F., Wade Hampton, Adah Keziah, Tennessee, James Wade***, ***Alexander, Martha E., Sophronia.***

6-***Eliza Jean Thompson*** was born in 1845 in Louisiana and died in 1912 in Shreveport, Bossier, Parish, Louisiana at age 67.

6-***William Thompson*** was born in 1847.

6-***James F. Thompson*** was born in 1848 and died in 1883 at age 35. 6-Edmund Thompson was born in 1850.

6-***Enos F. Thompson*** was born in 1854 in Rapides Parish, Louisiana, died in 1923 in Rapides Parish, Louisiana at age 69, and was buried in Occupy #1 Cemetery, Glenmora, Rapides Parish, Louisiana. ***Enos F.*** married ***Lydia Mancil*** on 22 Dec 1896 in Rapides Parish, Louisiana. Lydia was born in 1855. They had one daughter: Emma.

7-***Emma Thompson*** was born in Oct 1877 in Louisiana and died on 3 Aug 1947 in Rapides Parish, Louisiana at age 69. ***Emma*** married ***Camillus Ashworth***, son of ***Valentine Ashworth*** and ***Martha Ware. Camillus*** was born in 1871 and died in 1922 at age 51.

6-***Wade Hampton Thompson*** was born on 20 May 1858 in Louisiana and died on 21 Jan 1932 in Louisiana at age 73. ***Wade Hampton*** married ***Deliah Long*** in 1876 in Rapides Parish, Louisiana. ***Deliah*** was born in 1858 and died in 1895 at age 37. They had four children: ***Climson E., Martha, Edmond***, and ***Adra Kizzar.***

FIGURE 100 PHOTO: WADE H. THOMPSON

7-***Climson E. Thompson*** was born in 1877.

7-***Martha Thompson*** was born in 1879.

7-***Edmond Thompson*** was born in 1889 and died in 1987 at age 98. Edmond married ***Almarinda "Lydia" Doyle.*** She was the daughter of ***William Doyle*** and ***Celia Ann Ashworth***. Their Children were: ***Alexander, Cillia Ann, Marth Ann, Roselean, Artimese. .***

7-***Adra Kizzar Thompson*** was born on 2 Feb 1889 in Oakdale, Allen Parish, Louisiana and died on 22 Aug 1987 in Merryville, Beauregard Parish, Louisiana at age 98. ***Adra Kizzar*** married *Walter Russell Doyle/Dial Sr.*, son of *Henry Doyle/Dial* and *Martha Ann Drake*. *Walter Russell* was born on 31 Dec 1881 in Calcasieu Parish, Louisiana and died on 13 May 1944 in Beauregard Parish, Louisiana at age 62. They had five children: *Willie, John Jackson, Wade Hampton, Mae Belle,* and *Anna Belle.*

6-*Adah Keziah Thompson* was born in 1859 in Cravens, Rapides Parish, Louisiana

6-*James Wade Thompson* was born on 20 May 1858 in Rapides Parish, Louisiana and died in 1932 in Calcasieu Parish, Louisiana at age 74. *James Wade* married *Delia Honea* in Rapides Parish, Louisiana. Delia was born in 1858 in Vernon Parish, Louisiana and died in 1895 in Vernon Parish, Louisiana at age 37. They had one daughter: *Ebbie*.

7-*Ebbie Thompson* was born in 1876 in Vernon Parish, Louisiana and died in 1966 in Rapides Parish, Louisiana at age 90. *Ebbie* married *Ed Doyle/Dial*, son of *Jackson Doyle/Dial* and *Nancy Mancil*. *Ed* was born in 1873 in Rapides Parish, Louisiana.

James Wade next married *Eliza Jane Doyle/Dial*, daughter of *Jackson Doyle/Dial* and *Nancy Mancil*, on 21 Nov 1899 in Rapides Parish, Louisiana. Eliza Jane was born on 14 Jan 1880 and died on 16 Jan 1965 at age 85. They had nine children: *Ida Nedie*, *Dovie, Julious, James Fenwick, Lawson, Ernest, Lillie, Ed Lee,* and *Reeves*.

7-*Ida Nedie Thompson* was born on 5 Feb 1898 in Rapides Parish, Louisiana and died on 10 Sep 1985 in Vernon Parish, Louisiana at age 87.

7-*Dovie Thompson* was born in 1899.

7-*Julious Thompson* was born in 1900 in Rapides Parish, Louisiana and died in 1985 in Calcasieu Parish, Louisiana at age 85.

7-*James Fenwick Thompson* was born in 1903 in Rapides Parish, Louisiana and died on 11 May 1989 at age 86.

7-*Lawson Thompson* was born on 19 Jan 1906 and died on 23 Sep 1984 at age 78.

7-*Ernest Thompson* was born on 4 Feb 1909 in Louisiana and died on 2 Oct 1996 in Louisiana at age 87. 7-Lillie Thompson was born in 1912 and died in 2007 at age 95.

7-*Ed Lee Thompson* was born in 1915 and died in 1973 at age 58.

7-*Reeves Thompson* was born in 1918 and died in 1983 at age 65.

FIGURE 101 PHOTO: ADELINE MERICLE THOMPSON

6-*Alexander Thompson* was born in Aug 1861 in Louisiana and died on 17 Mar 1923 in Oakdale Cemetery, Allen Parish, Louisiana at age 61.

Alexander married *Adeline Mericle*, daughter of *Andrew Jackson Mericle* and *Louisa Ashworth,* on 16 Jan 1884 in Alexandria, Rapides Parish, LA. Adeline was born in 1864 in Alexandria, Rapides Parish, LA and died on 20 Jul 1950 in Shreveport, Bossier, Parish, Louisiana at age 86. They had two children: *Martha Louise* and *Joseph Marion*.

7-*Martha Louise Thompson* was born in 1890 and died in 1936 at age 46.

7-*Joseph Marion Thompson* was born on 28 Jun 1899 in Alabama and died on 11 Aug 1936 in De Ridder, Calcasieu Parish, La. at age 37. *Joseph Marion* married *Carrie Goins*, daughter of *William Mitchel Goins* (WW1 Draft card race "Indian") and *Nancy Perkins*. *Carrie* was born on 20 Mar 1902 in Texas and died on 10 Nov 1934 in De Ridder, Calcasieu Parish, Louisiana at age 32. They had six children: *Joseph, Talmadge, Hazel, Lee, Charles, Alston, Myrtle Marie, Ruby Irene, Robert Lee.*

Alexander next married *Pochahontas Doyle/Dial*, daughter of *Jackson Doyle/Dial* and *Nancy Mancil*, in 1892. Pocahontas was born on 2 May 1875 in Rapides Parish, Louisiana and died on 23 Dec 1964 at age 89. They had four children: *Wesley, Morrie, James*, and *Alvin Barney*

7-*Wesley Thompson* was born in 1894.

7-*Morrie Thompson* was born in 1902.

7-*James Thompson* was born in 1904.

7-*Alvin Barney Thompson* was born in 1916.

5-*Dempsy Thompson* was born in 1825.

5-*Ishom C. Thompson* was born in 1829.

5-*Thomas Thompson* was born in 1829.

5-*Edward Thompson* was born in 1831.

5-*Martha Thompson* was born in 1832.

5-*Lucinda Thompson* was born in 1834.

4-*Nancy Thompson* was born in 1796 in Hardeman, Tennessee and died in 1864 in Caddo Parish, Louisiana at age 68.

Figure 102 Photo: Right in long dark coat, Carrie Goins Thompson with father Wm Mitchel Goyens, her mother was Nancy Burgess. Young girl is probably sister Mary who married Rufus Ash/Nash, son of command and (3) Sena Goyens Ash/Nash

4-*Judith Thompson* was born on 29 Jun 1798 and died in 1840 in Smith, Texas at age 42.

4-*Elizabeth "Lizzy" Thompson* was born in 1803.

4-*Lovenny Thompson*.

4-*Ne Coo le Thompson*.

4-*Isolier Thompson*.

4-*James Jim Thompson* died in 1845. 4-Alexander Thompson died in 1845. 3-James Lee Thompson was born in 1780 and died in 1860 at age 80.

3-*Lemuel Burkett Thompson* was born on 10 Jun 1780 in Robeson Co., North Carolina and died on 16 Sep 1860 in Attala, Mississippi at age 80

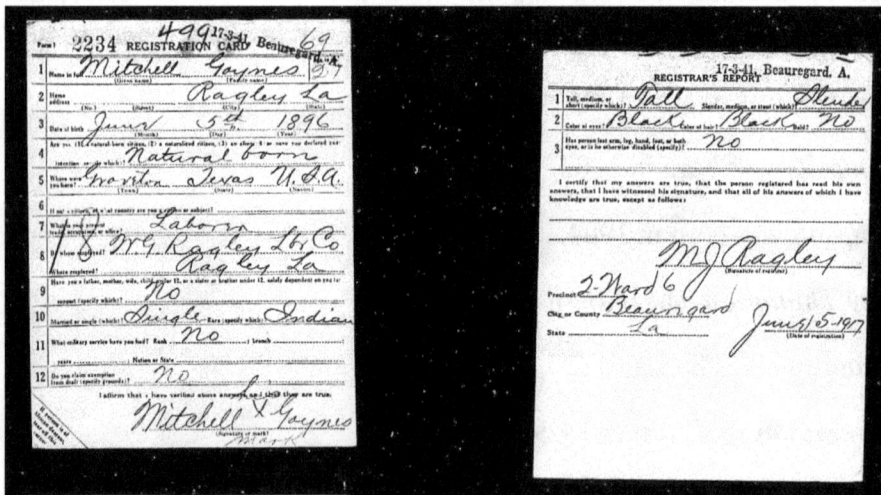

FIGURE 103 DOCUMENT: WM MITCHELL GOYENS WW1 MILITARY REGISTRATION CARD LISTS BORN IN GROVETON, TRINITY CO., TX. AND "INDIAN" AS RACE

Figure 104 Photo: Lee, Hazel & Joseph Talmadge Thompson

Figure 105 Photo: Charles Thompson

FIGURE 106 CHARLES AND WIFE

FIGURE 107 PHOTOS: **LEFT** RUBY THOMPSON DAUGHTER OF JOSEPH M AND CARRIE GOYENS THOMPSON, **MIDDLE**: HAZEL AND MARIE THOMPSON DAUGHTER OF JOSEPH M. AND CARRIE GOYENS THOMPSON, **RIGHT**: CARRIE GOYENS THOMPSON

FIGURE 108 PHOTOS: HANNAH IRENE GOINS BRANNON DAUGHTER OF ENIS AND JOSEPHINE NASH GOYENS AND RUBY THOMPSON DAUGHTER OF JOSEPH M. AND CARRIE GOYENS THOMPSON
FIGURES 109 PHOTO: CHARLES THOMPSON

FIGURE 110 PHOTO: CHARLIE (1892-1965) & ROSALEAN (1893-1980) THOMPSON JAMES (SON OF DAVID E. AND LYDIA ANN BASS JAMES)

FIGURE 111 PHOTO: FRANK JAMES (1919-1968) DIED ORANGE, ORANGE CO., TX. SON OF CHARLIE & ROSALEAN THOMASON JAMES

Redbone DNA Study

Presented at the Redbone Heritage Foundation Conference
By Stacy R. Webb, 2009
Nacogdoches, TX.
With updated results

In 2006 the Redbone Heritage Foundation began a DNA study of Redbone progenitor forefathers and mother's descendents. We mostly wanted to find biological kinship between common named surname lines within the families and establish Haplo group assignments in an effort to document migrations. Though our interrelatedness and lack of documentation caused us great genealogical nightmare, patterns are immerging which are answering more questions and allowing us to finally sort out familial lines and kinships.

Some surname lines we thought were related or "the same" in fact were not, and those we thought were a surname matched others among the Redbones with different surnames. Specifically, we found there are two separate male (Y-DNA) Goings and Goyens lines. One of the progenitors: ***Stephen*** and the other ***William or "Old Billy" Goings*** who returned identical Y-DNA (male) matches for one another.

Then there is the second line of the common spelling of Goyens line, that of ***Old Thomas Goyens***, who match several other surnames as presented below: The surname matches are ***Powell (Osceola)***, ***Williams*** (Old Thomas of Nacogdoches), ***Leonard C. Sweat*** of the Rawhide Fight, ***Wm. Berry Williams***, ***Reason Warwick*** and one genetic distance (very closely related) to the ***Richard Perkins*** line, a descendant of ***Old Jock*** and ***Mary Black***.

However, we are genetically related to one another on many genetic levels both these Goings and Goyens lines maternally. Neither of our known ***William Goings "Old Billy"*** (Stephen, James, Philip) nor the ***Thomas Goyens*** (m. Deliah Ash/Nash) line matched anyone else in any of the databases. There are no known matches among the Melungeon Goins project created by Jack Goins for either line of Redbone ***Goings,*** or ***Goyens.***

DNA has begun to unravel the mysteries surrounding the Redbones, their origins; interrelatedness and relationship to the various Mixed Ethnic Tribes of reputed Amerindian ancestry. Confirmation matches have been made for the female Goins line of Louisiana to the Melungeons of Tennessee and the Cherokee Nation, Tahlequah, Oklahoma. The female Ash/Nash lines to the Pee Dee and to the nomadic Gypsy Tribes of the world. Most specifically through the ***Mitchell, Nelson, Ash, Varner, Weaver, Drake, Ross, Allen/Alan*** maternal lines we matched to ***King Emil Mitchel*** (sister Queen Flora Mitchell) and to his wife ***Callie Marks***, the Queen of the Gypsy people. This family came from Brazil to the United States and worked for the United States government, assigned to bring thousands of persecuted Gypsies from South America, and Europe to America. These lines are extensively shared among many Native first American families and spans hundreds of other surname lines and tied modern Redbone descendants to the ancient Kalderash Gypsy royalty. This was a most exciting match, details to follow in subsequent issues and as developments arise.

Biggest Challenges

The biggest challenge facing the Redbone People/descendants at this time is the recognition of a cultural "tribal identity". Not in that we are seeking any sort of formal recognitions, just that it will move our research and understanding of our ancestors into a more appropriate reflective perspective. As in the case with any indigenous peoples, there are several but two sources in which an ethnologist will base a positive classification status of a people as "tribal" are: Do the people marry among one another; and' do the people migrate together? The answer for both these questions for all Redbone families is a resounding YES. Therefore, it would be of great benefit to our people, researchers, descendants, genealogist, DNA studies and scholars; is to adjust the course of research and identity toward a more tribal approach than a singular family unit.

Pedigree Chart

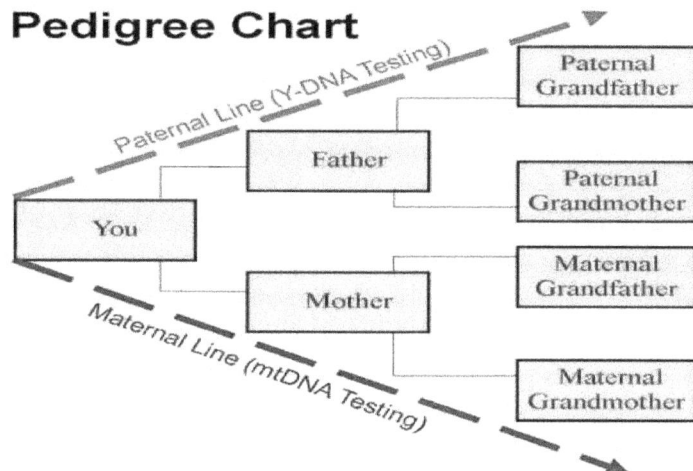

Presented here are the results of some of our comparisons. The tests were performed by various Y- and Mt-DNA companies. However, we used exclusively DNATribes for Autosomal though others later have used different companies. Our DNA study is ongoing and we encourage anyone interested to donate your results.

The second large hurdles come in the form of establishing and documenting the genealogical interrelatedness; considering world and North American migrations, ethnic and cultural struggles, war, death and assimilations. Now that DNA is proving without a shadow of doubt, that in fact we are related to several of the various other remnant Indian Mixed Blood families with other "monikers" and geographic locations: era and generational interrelatedness; we must begin digging beyond our geographic locations of our most immediate generational kin. Though it is always nice to know those most closely related to us we must move our research forward back to our tribal connections filling in the gaps, which are many along the way.

In an attempt to reconstruct our true and historically accurate heritage, we must examine our people, their struggles and final victory of full acceptances of origins and mixture. I would also like to make explicitly clear; we are not finding any DNA results associated with "African slave" element among our collective results. We do see a Moorish, Moroccan and Berber type admixture heavily with Turk and Portuguese Guinea "Goan" (India), Spanish (Iberian), and Gypsy element DNA comparisons among our people. These ancestors would, of course, have been "Slavic" or among the traditional Ottoman Empire and European Colonial Indentured "Crom[26]-wellian[27] " period mixture (Welsh, Irish, White & European and Gypsy (Italy, Spain,

Portugal, France outcasts), also known as "white slavery" through the indentured and convict slave element.

Slave traders, Countrymen, Indian trader and Spanish explorer and or Portuguese "adventurer" type admixtures similar to a Phoenician maritime sort of admixture among the majority of the families. We are also seeing strong hits among the Canary Islander people in Texas and South America. These ancestors arrived on these shores an already heavily mixed folk then immediately mixed heavily with most all Native Indigenous tribes of America, and would be considered "outlanders" settling the American frontiers, living on the remotest of White settlements. That being said, we fully expect that there are, were and will be discovered such folk as the runaway slave element however, as of yet, we have not found anything similar to that among the DNA results. We hope to finally put to bed, so to speak the origins, and there are many, once and for all with a new perspective and pride in our Redbone heritage. Each family will be examined, the best that we can utilization of genetic genealogy which is an evolving science. We attempt to keep up with current discoveries in science of DNA interpretations coupled with further DNA testing and will report those in future issues of the Redbone Chronicles.

---

[26] Crom·well (krŏm'wĕl', -wəl, krŭm'-), Oliver 1599-1658.
English military, political, and religious figure who led the Parliamentarian victory in the English Civil War (1642-1649) and called for the execution of Charles I. As lord protector of England (1653-1658) he ruled as a virtual dictator. His son Richard (1626-1712) succeeded him briefly as lord protector (1658-1659) before the restoration of the monarchy under Charles II.

[27] Crom•wel•li•an (krɒmˈwɛl i ən, krʌm-)adj of, pertaining to, or characteristic of the politics, practices, etc., of Oliver Cromwell or of the Commonwealth and Protectorate. [1715–25]

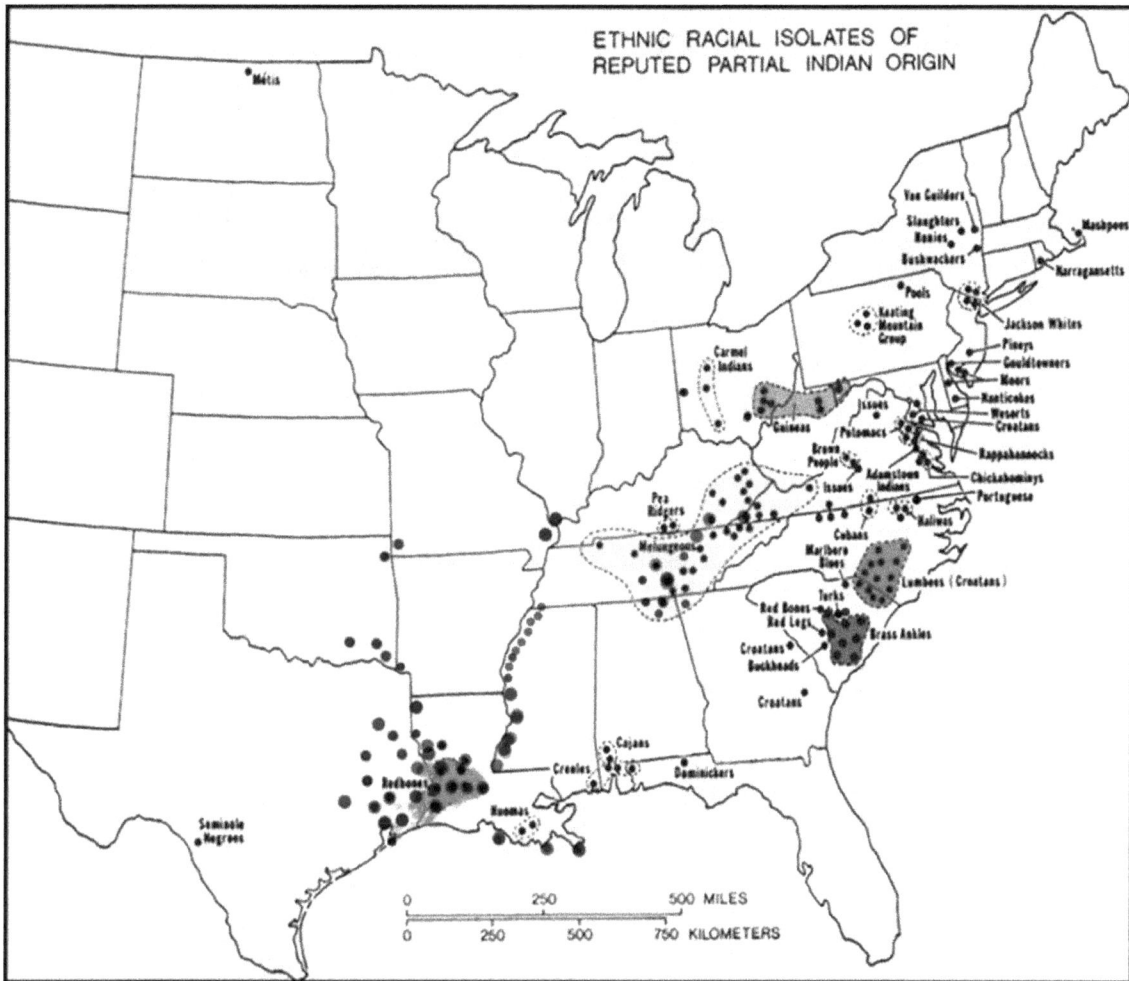

FIGURE 112 MAP: ETHNIC RACIAL ISOLATES OF REPUTED PARTIAL INDIAN ORIGIN. PRESENTED 2006 CONFERENCE OF THE PEOPLE KNOWN AS REDBONES, NATCHITOCHES, LOUISIANA BY STACY R. WEBB. NOT PICTURED HERE IS THE GROUP WHO WENT OUT WEST TO THE ROCKIES AND MIXED AMONG THE NORTH WESTERN INDIANS OF CHIEF JOSEPH'S PEOPLE OF NEZ PIERCE (BRIDGES, WEAVER, SIZEMORE, WILLIAMS, ASH/NASH), AND THE BASQUE PEOPLE.

REPUBLICAN BULLETIN, No. 9.

THE ISSUE.

WHITE SLAVERY.

THE EXTENSION OF SLAVERY IS THE QUESTION NOT ONLY OVER **FREE SOIL**, BUT OVER **FREE MEN**. DO YOU DOUBT IT? READ THE WORDS OF THE HIGHEST AUTHORITIES IN THE SOUTH.

The *Richmond* (*Va.*) *Enquirer*, the oldest Democratic paper in the Old Dominion, a most able supporter of Buchanan for the Presidency, and of the Cincinnati Platform, speaks thus on this question. We take its own forcible words.

"Until recently, the defence of Slavery has labored under great difficulties, because its apologists, (for they were mere apologists,) took half way ground. They confined the defence of slavery to mere *negro* slavery; thereby giving up the slavery *principle*, admitting *other forms* of slavery to be *wrong*.

The line of defence, however, is now changed. The South maintains that SLAVERY IS RIGHT, NATURAL, AND NECESSARY, AND DOES NOT DEPEND UPON DIFFERENCE OF COMPLEXION. THE LAWS OF THE SLAVE STATES JUSTIFY THE HOLDING OF WHITE MEN IN BONDAGE."

Another leading press of the Democratic party, and a worthy organ of Mr. Buchanan, published in South Carolina, sustains the views we have quoted from the Enquirer. It uses this plain, straightforward language on the subject :—

"Slavery is the natural and normal condition of the laboring man, whether *white* or *black*. The great evil of Northern *free* society is, that it is burthened with a SERVILE CLASS OF MECHANICS AND LABORERS, UNFIT FOR SELF-GOVERNMENT, and yet clothed with the attributes and powers of citizens. Master and slave is a relation in society as necessary as that of parent and child; and the Northern States will yet have to introduce it. Their *theory of a free government is a delusion.*"

But there is still broader ground on the subject of society, taken by the *Richmond Enquirer*. It says, in a recent number :—

"Repeatedly have we asked the North, 'Has not the experiment of universal liberty FAILED? Are not the evils of FREE SOCIETY INSUFFERABLE? And do not most thinking men among you propose to subvert and reconstruct it?' Still no answer. This gloomy silence is another conclusive proof, added to many other conclusive evidences we have furnished, THAT FREE SOCIETY, IN THE LONG RUN, IS AN IMPRACTICABLE FORM OF SOCIETY."

Another paper, published in Virginia, the *South Side Democrat*, a journal distinguished for its faithful support of Mr. Buchanan, says :

FIGURE 113 DOCUMENT: REPUBLICAN BULLETIN, No. 9 THE ISSUE WHITE SLAVERY: THAT SLAVERY IS RIGHT, NATURAL AND NECESSARY, AND DOES NOT DEPEND UPON DIFFERENCES OF COMPLEXION. THE LAWS OF THE SLAVE STATES JUSTIFY THE HOLDING OF WHITE MEN IN BONDAGE.

236

Y-DNA Comparisons of Surname Descendants & Haplo Assignment Research

Donor	Pedigree	Details	Origin	Haplo group[28]	Subclade[29]	Markers Compared	Genetic Distance	Autosomal[30]
Descendant Of Albert Goins	James Goings	Stephen Goings [31]	SC-Ms-La	H[32]1a DYS 425= null	M82	29	0	

---

[28] Genetics, a set of similar haplotypes inherited together, or a group who shares a set of similar haplotypes, used to understand genetic lineages, origins, and migration patterns. Haplogroupings are ten of thousands of years old and are only a guide from your furthest most distant ancestor, to you.

[29] In genetics, a **subclade** is a subgroup of a haplogroup. Subclades are often referred to in genealogical DNA tests of mitochondrial (femle) DNA haplogroups and human Y(male)-chromosome DNA haplogroups, where they represent subbranches of major branches on the human family tree.

[30] Autosomal is a genealogical DNA test that looks at a person's genome at specific locations. Results give information about genealogy or personal ancestry. In general, these tests compare the results of an individual to others from the same lineage or to current and historic ethnic groups. They are intended only to give genealogical information and possible migration.

[31] (Robert Goings vs. Choctaw Nation n.d.)

[32] Haplogroup H (M69) is a Y-chromosome haplogroup. This haplogroup is found at a high frequency in India. It is generally rare outside of the Indian subcontinent but is common among the Roma people, particularly the H-M82 subgroup. It is a branch of Haplogroup F, and is believed to have arisen in India between 20,000 and 30,000 years ago. Its probable site of introduction is India since it is concentrated there, but it may also have arisen in Iran or the Middle East. It seems to represent the main Y-haplogroup of the indigenous paleolithic inhabitants of India, because it is the most frequent Y-haplogroup of lower castes and tribal populations (25-35%), especially those of Dravidian origin. On the other hand, its presence in upper castes is quite rare (ca. 10%) (Cordaux et al. 2004, Sengupta et al. 2006, Thanseem et al. 2006). Very low frequencies of the Haplogroup H are found among populations of Pakistan compared to the frequency of this haplogroup among Indian populations. A recent study of Y-chromosome variation among populations of Pakistan found Haplogroup H1-M52 Y-chromosomes in only 2.5% of a sample of the general Pakistani population (16 out of 638 individuals), and this haplogroup was also found at similar frequencies among ethnic Pashtuns (4/96 or 4.2%) and Burusho (4/97 or 4.1%). Surprisingly, Haplogroup H1-M52 was found at a much higher frequency among this study's sample of Kalash (9/44 or 20.5%) (Firasat et al. 2007).Haplogroup H has been found very rarely outside of the Roma and populations of the Indian subcontinent, including approximately 6% (1 out of 17 individuals) of a sample of Kurds from Turkmenistan, 4% (2/53) of Iranians from Samarkand, 2% (1/56) of Uzbeks from Bukhara, 3% (2/70) of Uzbeks from Khorezm, 2% (1/63) of Uzbeks from the Fergana Valley, 4% (2/45) of Uzbeks from Samarkand, 12.5% (2/16) of Tajiks from Dushanbe, and 2% (1/41) of Uyghurs from Kazakhstan (Wells et al. 2001). The subclade H1a-M82 has also been found in 2.0% (3/150) of a sample of the population of Iran, but only in the southern parts of the country (Regueiro et al. 2006). (India 2010)

Descendant of Wm Moses & Charlotty Nelson	William Goings	Stephen Goings [34]	SC-Ga-Al-TX	H1a	M82	29	0	
Descendant of Philip & Oti Montroe	Philip Goings (1) Luchia Lawson, (2) Oti Montroe, (3) Keziah Ash/Nash	Stephen Goings [35]	UNK-Ms-Ga-La-Al-S.Dakota (Sioux), OK(Chickasaw/Choctaw), TX	H1a	M82	29	0	FIGURE 114 PG. 1 GOINS/GOINGS AUTOSOMAL RESULTS, DONOR DESCENDANT PHILIP & OTI MONTROE Figure 116
Descendant of Jeremiah & Sarophina Drake	Philip Goings SAA	1770 IT Ms. Territory	Ms-La-TX	H1a	M82	37	0	Same as above
Descendant of Frank Goins (Sioux)	Gibson "Gip" Goings SAA	Stephen Goings	Ms-Forced Removal-Dakota-OK	H1a	M82	29	0	Same as above
Descendant John "Bit Nose" Goings & Nancy Johnson	Descendant John Henry Goings	Dean's Stand Natchez Trace –La.	SC/TN-Ms-La	H1a	M82			Same as above
Descendant of Murchison/Goings	Daniel Harmon/Murchison	Murchison	Moore Co., NC	R		29	No Match	On File
Descendants of	Wm Thomas		EM-236					See

---

[33] H and sub clades appear to primarily be found in the Middle East and South Asia. The only known H* population of Europe are the Roma / Romany Gypsy people who are confirmed to be in Y Haplo Group H1a - M82. By some estimates the Romany version of Y Haplo Group H1a - M82 maybe only 2000 years old. The Romany version of H1a - M82 is identified through marker 425 = 0 null. No other M82 population so far has been identified as carrying M82 with the 425 = 0 null marker mutation outside the Romany Gypsy population. (DNA, H-Y Haplo 2014)

[34] Ibid.

[35] Ibid.

Wm. Collins Goyens	m. Deliah Ash/Nash		La-OK-	DYS 390=21[37]				citation no. 32
Descendant Wm. Simon Goyens Orphan nephew of Wm Goyens of Nacogdoches and Hadley m. Lucy Beulah Cline.	Stephen Breakinridge (1795-1896) m. Adeline Sampson	Goyens	Ark-Mo-La-Tx	EM-2/DYS 390=21		29	0	
Descendant of Powell/Osceola	Wm. Billy Powell "Osceola" (1803-1838) 3 wives 1 was a Thompson	Unknown "half-bred" and Ann Polly Moniac Coppinger (1769-1838)	Ga-Fl-SC-died Ft Moultrie-family escaped in Ark	EM-2/DYS 390=21		29	0	
Descendant of Leonard C. Sweat (1813-1861) m. Elizabeth Burgess	Wm Sweat (1720-?)	Robert Sweat (1670-1696) s/o Margaret Cornish Gaweean Sweat (w/o John) (1610-1718)	Va-NC-Ga. Ala-Ms-OK-La-Tx.	EM-2/DYS 390=21	Z1704	29	0	
Descendant of Reason Warwick	Reason O. Obediah Warwick (1770-1819) m. Anna Lee NC-Ga-Al-Ms	Reason W. Warwick (1760-?) Sampson, NC-Ga.	Sampson NC-Ga.-Ms-AL-TX.	EM-2/DYS 390=21		29	0	
		Anthony Jr. Williams 1686 Isle of						

[36] In human genetics, **Haplogroup E-V38** is a human Y-chromosome DNA haplogroup. It is the phylogenetic term for the series of unique sequence variants on the human Y-chromosome. It is often found in African males and their descendants and is heritably passed in lineage from father to son. Geneticists study these variants in populations to find the evolutionary lineage to a common male human ancestor. It can also be referred to in phylogenetic nomenclature by names such as **E1b1a** (although the exact definition of phylogenetic names can vary over time). E-V38 has two basal branches, E-M329 (formerly E1b1c) and E-M2 (formerly E1b1a), the former is almost exclusively found in Ethiopia. The E-M2 branches are the predominant lineage in Western Africa, Central Africa, Southern Africa, and the southern parts of Eastern Africa. E-M2 has several subclades, however many members are included in either E-L485 or E-U175.

[37] (Zahi Hawass Published 17 December 2012)

	(1816-1886) m. Martha (maybe nee Gibbes) Sweat	Wright d 1752 Duplin, NC to William Williams (1736-1795) m. Mary Ward (1739-1800) Ga.					
Descendants of Richard Perkins	Richard	Perkins		EM-2/DYS 390=21		37	1	
Ashworth	James Ashworth			R-M269		29	0	
McWilliams	James Ashworth			R-M269		29	0	See Figure Y & Mt-DNA **Autosomal Testing** Results **Figure 118**
Ashworth		England[38]		I-M253		37	No Match	
Herron	Unknown	Unknown		R-M269		37	2	
Descendant of		Thomas						See Y & Mt-

[38] (DNA, Ashworth Surname Group n.d.)

[39] Ancestor **E-P2** Descendants **E-M2, E-M329** Defining mutations L222.1, V38, V100 Y-DNA haplogroup E would appear to have arisen in Northeast Africa (Egypt /Libya) based on the concentration and variety of E subclades in that area today. But the fact that Haplogroup E is closely linked with Haplogroup D, which is not found in Africa, leaves open the possibility that E first arose in the Near or Middle East and was subsequently carried into Africa by a back migration.E1b1 is by far the lineage of greatest geographical distribution. It has two important sub-lineages, E1b1a and E1b1b. E1b1a is an African lineage that probably expanded from northern African to sub-Saharan and equatorial Africa with the Bantu agricultural expansion. E1b1a is the most common lineage among African Americans. E1b1b1 probably evolved either in Northeast Africa or the Near East and then expanded to the west--both north and south of the Mediterranean Sea. Eb1b1 clusters are seen today in Western Europe, Southeast Europe, the Near East, Northeast Africa and Northwest Africa[39]. This haplo E-M2 is shared also with Egyptian King Tutankhamun, the boy king of ancient Egypt, as well as the older King Ramesses which is identified through DYS 390=21. Only in the **Goyens** did DYS=21.

[40] **EP-2** is found in the U.S. with a rate of 17.66%, African Americans 62.1%, European Americans 0.9%, Hispanic Americans 5.8% (Please keep in mind that Hispanic peoples are a mixture of Native American with a Spaniard/White European a direct mixture from pre through Colonial eras, collectively classified as "Mestizo" in modern terms of DNA) Native Americans 1.3%, Asian Americans 1.6%

Manuel Ash/Nash (1) Nancy Simmons (1844-1880)	James (1813-1850) m. Mary Polly Perkins (1820-1870)	Ash/Nash/Ashes b. (1753-1850) Chowan, NC						DNA Autosomal Testing Results Figure 118
Descendant of Manuel Ash/Nash (2) Matilda Sweat Mason	James (1813-1850) m. Mary Polly Perkins (1820-1870)	Thomas Ash/Nash/Ashes b. (1753-1850) Chowan, NC		E-M2	M329	29	0	
Descendant of William Ash/Nash	William Nash	Nash		E-P2			1	N/A

Mt-DNA Matches & Haplo Grouping Research

	Redbone Mt-DNA by Surname Haplogroup Assignments Mt-DNA Genetic Matches
H-Helina	**Haplo H "Helina"** Haplogroup H represents a female ancestor who lived in the Middle East upto 28,400 years ago. Some surviving daughters then went to Europe, and some stayed in the Middle East. Haplo H is the most common and most diverse maternal lineage in Europe, in most of the Near East and in the Caucasus region. The Saami of Lapland are the only ethnic group in Europe who have low percentages of haplogroup H, varying from 0% to 7%. The frequency of haplogroup H in Europe usually ranges between 40% and 50%. The lowest frequencies are observed in Cyprus (31%), Finland (36%), Iceland (38%) as well as Belarus, Ukraine, Romania and Hungary (all 39%). The only region where H exceeds 50% of the population is Asturias (54%) and Galicia (58%) in northern Spain, and Wales (60%). Jemina **Sinnes Goin** Spanish "Peg" Unknown wife of Vardy Collins (Biddy)-Musgrove-Coles-Wilson-Doyle-Hill-Goins (Louisiana, male Y-DNA see above James Goings) Lucy **Goins**, b. 1820 and d. 1902 Moore County, NC Sarah **Taylor,** b. 17 Feb 1826, Arkansas, d. 10 Mar Mary Muscgrove Mary Ann **Evans** abt 1814, Polk County, Tennessee Sarah Milly **Williams**, b. 1790 and d. 1884 Anna **Drake** b. 1792 NY d. 1870 Nancy **Johnson** 1810- TN Elvira **Mullins** Rebbeca **Collins**; Sneedsville, Tennessee Martha Patty **Johnson** 1780-1854 **Nelson** Minerva **Moore** Elizabeth **Croley/Crowley** bc1806 Powell Valley, TN Mary **Mimms** Catherine **Collins**-b. abt. 1805 VA or TN **Sweat,** 1795 Sarah Ann **Bean,** 1828
I-Iris	**Haplo I1a1b-** A similar view puts more emphasis on the Persian Gulf region of

	the Near East
	Haplogroup I-Iris dates to ~25 ka ago and is overall most frequent in Europe, but the facts that it has a frequency peak in the Gulf region and that its highest diversity values are in the Gulf, Anatolia, and southeast Europe suggest that its origin is most likely in the Near East and/or Arabia. It is noteworthy that, with the exception of its northern neighbor Azerbaijan, Iran is the only population in which haplogroup I exhibits polymorphic levels. Also, a contour plot based on the regional phylogeographic distribution of the I haplogroup exhibits frequency clines consistent with an Iranian cradle... Moreover, when compared with other populations in the region, those from the Levant (Iraq, Syria and Palestine) and the Arabian Peninsula (Oman and UAE) exhibit significantly lower proportions of I individuals... It should be noted that this haplogroup has been detected in European groups (Krk, a tiny island off the coast of Croatia (11.3%), and Lemko, an isolate from the Carpathian Highlands (11.3%)) at comparable frequencies to those observed in the North Iranian population. However, the higher frequencies of the haplogroup within Europe are found in geographical isolates and are likely the result of founder effects and/or drift... it is plausible that the high levels of haplogroup I present in Iran may be the result of a localized enrichment through the action of genetic drift or may signal geographical proximity to the location of origin. **Goans, Goins, Gowen, Nelson, Mayo, Patterson, Mitchell, Allen, Foster** (Beaufort, SC), **Daly**, Brown (Brethitt, KY), **Griffith/Griffin** (1795, Patrick Co., Va.), **Combs, Cunningham, Butler** (1867 Robeson Co., NC), **Harper** (1748), McGowan (1808-1849), Shores (Robeson, NC 1804), Hollis, McCoy, **Lockhart** (1806), **Bennett** (1818-1880), **Stowe** (Louisiana Freedman 1825-1860), **Frances Allen** (1868, Cherokee, NC), **Howard** (1769-1872, Maryland), **Hodge, Williams, Dean** (1785, Georgia), **Bell, McCloud, Young, Stewart, Anderson** (La. & Ga.), **Williams, Water/s** (1848-1875, KY), **Robinson, Moore** (TN).
J, J1b	**Haplo J assignment group Jasmine** originates in the Middle East some 30,000-50,000 years ago. Many subclades of J were also born there, but eventually, some began the slow migration to Europe bout 10,000 years ago. Haplo J is found today in its highest frequency Arabia at 25% among Bedouin and Yemeni. Haplo T assignment familial group is also closely related to Haplo J. Mary Lowery Annie Eliza E/**MANUEL** born 1830s Stokes Co., N.C. to KY Elizabeth **Hall-Mullins**, b.1820, Dickenson Co., VA Mary Ellen **Tucker** Nancy **Taylor**, born 1788, Maryland Nancy Jane **Hill**, born 1813 Barren County, KY. Mary **Scott**, born 1820 Edgefield Co., S.C.

	Edward **Tipton**, born 25 Jan 1618, died 1696 Anne **Bradshaw**, born 1660, died 1742 Maryland Mahala Ester **Varner**, born 1826, died 1870 Elizabeth **Cloud**, born 1730 Pennsylvania, died 1785 Sage **Collins**, born mid-1800s, died early-1900s. Nancy Jane **Kelly Boyd**, born 1880, died 1973 North Carolina Sarah **Hall**, born 1851 Thomas **Dixon**, born 1700, died 1763 Nancy Lucinda **Bowels**, born 1816, died 1919 Matilda **Williams**, **Byrd**, **Ross**, born 1820 in KY. Died 1905, Arkansas Mary **Davis**, born 1799 Mary Louise **Lawson** b. 1797 d. 1870 Mariah **Berry** South Carolina 1824-1867 Susan **Thompson / Thomson** Amelia **Nichols**, b. 1768 Orange, NC, USA Cynthia Ann **Ware**, 1849-1876 **J1b,** a distinct enclave of ancient Mt-DNA: The mitochondrial haplogroup J contains several sub-lineages. The original haplogroup J originated in the Near East approximately 50,000 years ago. Within Europe, sub-lineages of haplogroup J have distinct and interesting distributions. Haplogroup J1b is found distributed in the Near East and southern Iberia (Portugal, Spain and Basque Lands including France, Italy and Egypt), and may have been part of the original colonization wave of Neolithic settlers moving around the Mediterranean 6000 years ago or perhaps a lineage of Phoenician traders. Land of Alan now modern Portugal and Spain. We also remark that this rare haplo assignment is shared with several religious groups associated with the Mennonite Order of the United States and Mexico. This is wholly accounted for an ancestry of the Austria-Switzerland and or known as Mixed Blood "Black-Dutch" lineage. It is also seen on occasion among the Acadian female lines also a direct result with Germanic Tribes who conquered the converso tribes to Christianity known as the Vikings, who later were given Normandy France from whence the Acadians migrated. Norseman=Normandy, or "Norsemen's Land." **Simmons/Symons, Allen, Mitchell, Nelson, Meador/Metoyer, Cooper, Banks, Cole, Stringer**.
C,A,C1c **Native** **American** **(East Asian)**	**Haplogroup C assignment Group** is believed to have arisen somewhere between the Caspian Sea and Lake Baikal some 60,000 years before present. It is a descendant of the haplogroup M. **Distribution** Haplogroup C is found in Northeast Asia (including Siberia). In Eurasia, Haplogroup C is especially frequent among populations of arctic Siberia, such as Yukaghirs and Nganasans. Haplogroup C is one of five Mt-DNA haplogroups found in the indigenous peoples of the Americas, the others being A, B, D, and X. The subclades C1b, C1c, C1d, and C4c are found in the first people of the Americas.

	C1a is found only in Asia. **A** David **Weaver**-Nancy **Weatherford** Maria Victoria de **Chaves** y Otero, b. 1735 d. 1784 **Goins**, Ash/Nash **Mummy Juanita** The mummy "Juanita" of Peru, also called the "Ice Maiden", has been shown to belong to mitochondrial haplogroup A **C** A-ma-do-ya **Moytoy,** 1640, Cherokee Nation East **Hall**, Maria Ana Augustina Alcantara-Alamos, Son, Mx 1758 **Scott**, Unknown **Anderson**, Tafoya Maria de Hinojos New Mexico **Rogers**, Unknown **Bell**, Quiles **King** **Gallegos**, Unknown **Torres,** Consuelo Rodriguez **Castro**, Amelia **Monocayo** 1862, Meenie V. **Perry** born 1896 died 1930, Tennessee **C1c** Nancy **Ward,** born circa 1738, (Cherokee) Monroe Co., TN **Sewell**, Unknown **C1d** **Perkins**, Maria **Petra** de la **Garza** **C5c1a** **Berry** Minerva **Kaiser**, b. 1891 **Williamson**, Nancy **Bridges**, Georgia 1790 Thompson, Omia Shade
Loa1 Matches	**Rebecca Ash/Nash** Haplo has East African Origin as well as migrations in East Africa, North Africa and South East Africa. Haplogroup **L0a1** is found at 4% among Cushitic Speakers and 6% among the Amhara Ethiopians, it has frequencies of 4% among the Tigrais and 5% among the Ethiopian population. It can be seen at 3% with Yemenis and 10% of Mozambique population. Matches: **Mary M D'Armand** b. 1820 TN, and d. 1881 Fannin County, TX Family history describes her as a red-headed French woman. She was married 1843 to Abner B. Raney. **Mary McQueen,**1905

Angelina Rossi 1850 Camporeale Sicily
Euphemia Whitehead, b. 1878
Ella Finley,b.c. 1845 VA and d. 1931 Arkansas
Mary Frances Russell, born 1834, Illinois, US
Jefferys b.1901 and d.1973
Collins, Unknown wife of Samuel born 1802 Tennessee

John Nash, Indian trader assigned to give gifts, and trade with the Indians on Rye Cove to Cumberland River, Tennessee. In 1778 he bought a "Warrior Squaw" on Powell Mountain from a "Peddler" near Fort Blackmore. She was of Shawnee, and Lanape tribes; possibly from the same group as Cornstalk's sister Nonhelema, a famous British loyalist. The family later removed to Ohio then to the Carolina's where later the DNA shows up among the Pee Dee Indians. They traveled with **Harmon**, and **Pryor** families as well as the **Nash**, and **Ashworth** families. Cornstalk was a famous Indian maiden who warned that many of the Eastern Coastal Indians had removed to Ohio and had forged alliances with the British there. We believe that some of our families were in fact Tories who removed to Ohio (**Cherry**) and later rejoined their dislocated relatives in Missouri/Arkansas, Louisiana Territory and Texas.

Three Ethiopian samples showed neither L0a1- nor L0a2-defining mutations and thus remain unclassified at the L0a level.

One of them even lacked the 16188 transversion characteristic of L0a but shared both its defining coding-region mutation at np 12720 and the 16148 mutation in HVS-I. Control-region sequences of the L0f type have been found so far at marginal frequencies only in East Africa, with the highest incidence (3/12) among the Iraq population of Tanzania

The phylogeny of the L0 clade in Ethiopians lends further credence to the idea that East Africa is the most likely source of Haplogroup L0a variation
In addition Haplogroup Loa1 can be found among the Egyptian Population of Lower Egypt Alexandria

In a study on the Population of Brazil, also yields the following ethnics groups related to your Haplo assignment
Haplogroup Loa1: Mbundu, Cabinda, Santiago, Bakaka, Bassa, Daba, Ewondo, Fali, Kotoko, Mafa, Podokwo, Tupuri, Uldeme, Afar-Ethiopians, Amhara-Ethiopians, Tigrai-Ethiopia-Eritrea, Balanta, Beafada from Guinea Bissau, Bijagó, Djola, Fula Preto, Mancanha, Mandinga, Mansonca,
Nalu, Papel, Nairob, Turkana, Sena, Tswa, Forros, Mandenka, Limba, Loko, Temne, Nubians

FIGURE 114 PG. 1 GOINS/GOINGS AUTOSOMAL RESULTS, DONOR DESCENDANT PHILIP & OTI MONTROE

DNA TRIBES

Part B: Your High Resolution Native Population Match Results

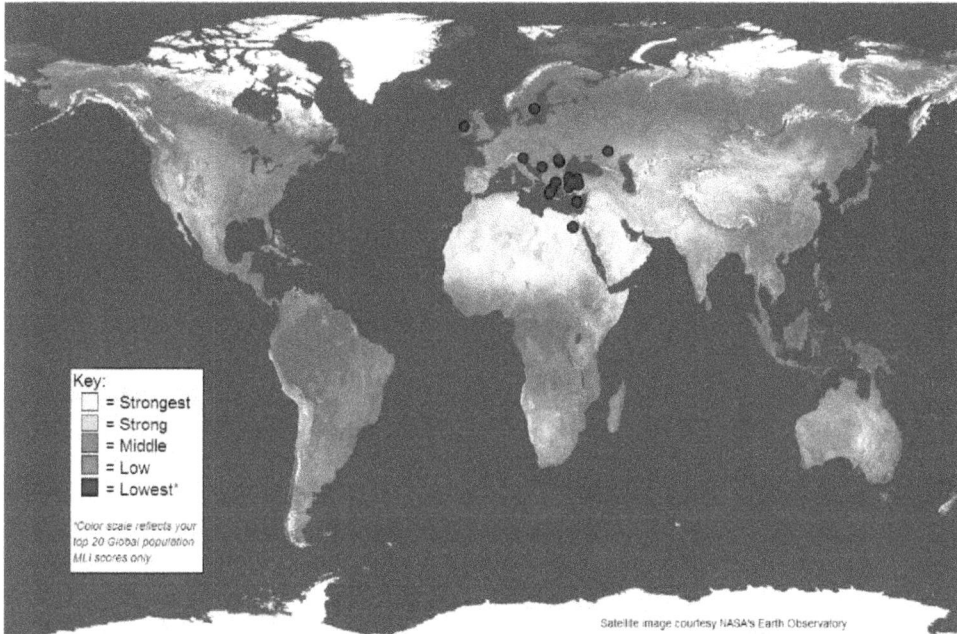

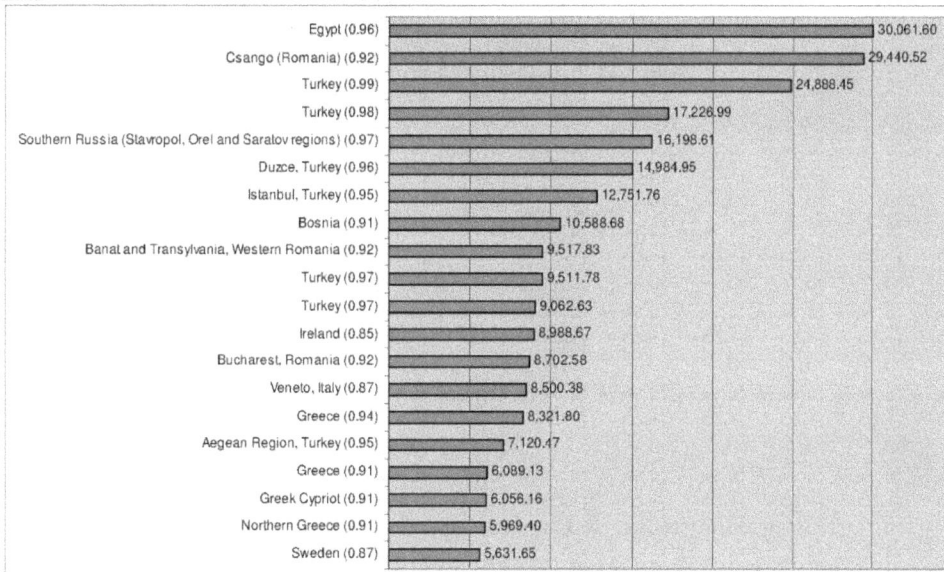

Key:
- ☐ = Strongest
- ☐ = Strong
- ☐ = Middle
- ☐ = Low
- ☐ = Lowest*

*Color scale reflects your top 20 Global population MLI scores only.

Satellite image courtesy NASA's Earth Observatory

Population	Score
Egypt (0.96)	30,061.60
Csango (Romania) (0.92)	29,440.52
Turkey (0.99)	24,888.45
Turkey (0.98)	17,226.99
Southern Russia (Stavropol, Orel and Saratov regions) (0.97)	16,198.61
Duzce, Turkey (0.96)	14,984.95
Istanbul, Turkey (0.95)	12,751.76
Bosnia (0.91)	10,588.68
Banat and Transylvania, Western Romania (0.92)	9,517.83
Turkey (0.97)	9,511.78
Turkey (0.97)	9,062.63
Ireland (0.85)	8,988.67
Bucharest, Romania (0.92)	8,702.58
Veneto, Italy (0.87)	8,500.38
Greece (0.94)	8,321.80
Aegean Region, Turkey (0.95)	7,120.47
Greece (0.91)	6,089.13
Greek Cypriot (0.91)	6,056.16
Northern Greece (0.91)	5,969.40
Sweden (0.87)	5,631.65

DNA Tribes Genetic Ancestry Analysis

FIGURE 115PG. 2 GOINS/GOINGS AUTOSOMAL RESULTS

DNA TRIBES *what's your tribe?*

Part C: Your High Resolution Global Population Match Results

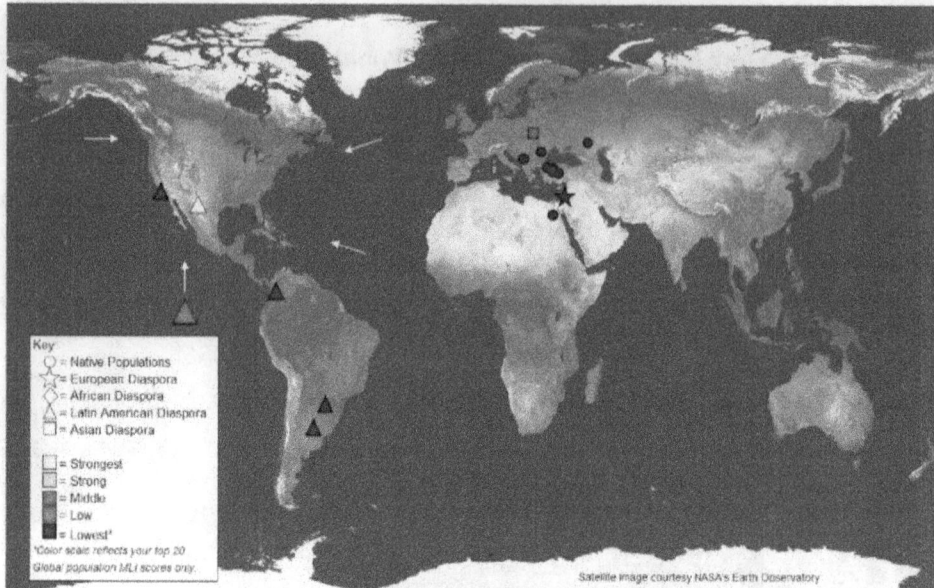

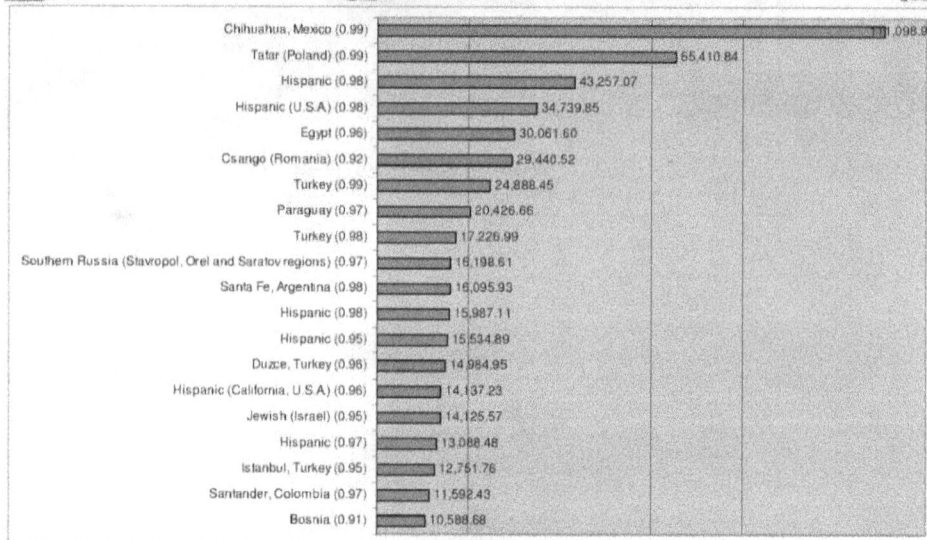

Key:
- = Native Populations
- = European Diaspora
- = African Diaspora
- = Latin American Diaspora
- = Asian Diaspora

- = Strongest
- = Strong
- = Middle
- = Low
- = Lowest*

*Color scale reflects your top 20
Global population MLI scores only.

Satellite image courtesy NASA's Earth Observatory

Population	Score
Chihuahua, Mexico (0.99)	1,098.90
Tatar (Poland) (0.99)	65,410.84
Hispanic (0.98)	43,257.07
Hispanic (U.S.A) (0.98)	34,739.85
Egypt (0.96)	30,061.60
Csango (Romania) (0.92)	29,440.52
Turkey (0.99)	24,888.45
Paraguay (0.97)	20,426.66
Turkey (0.98)	17,226.99
Southern Russia (Stavropol, Orel and Saratov regions) (0.97)	16,198.61
Santa Fe, Argentina (0.98)	16,095.93
Hispanic (0.98)	15,987.11
Hispanic (0.95)	15,534.89
Duzce, Turkey (0.96)	14,984.95
Hispanic (California, U.S.A) (0.96)	14,137.23
Jewish (Israel) (0.95)	14,125.57
Hispanic (0.97)	13,088.48
Istanbul, Turkey (0.95)	12,751.76
Santander, Colombia (0.97)	11,592.43
Bosnia (0.91)	10,588.68

DNA Tribes Genetic Ancestry Analysis
www.dnatribes.com - Customer support: support@dnatribes.com

7/4/2008 - Page 9 of 10

FIGURE 116 PG.3 GOINS/GOINGS AUTOSOMAL MATCHES

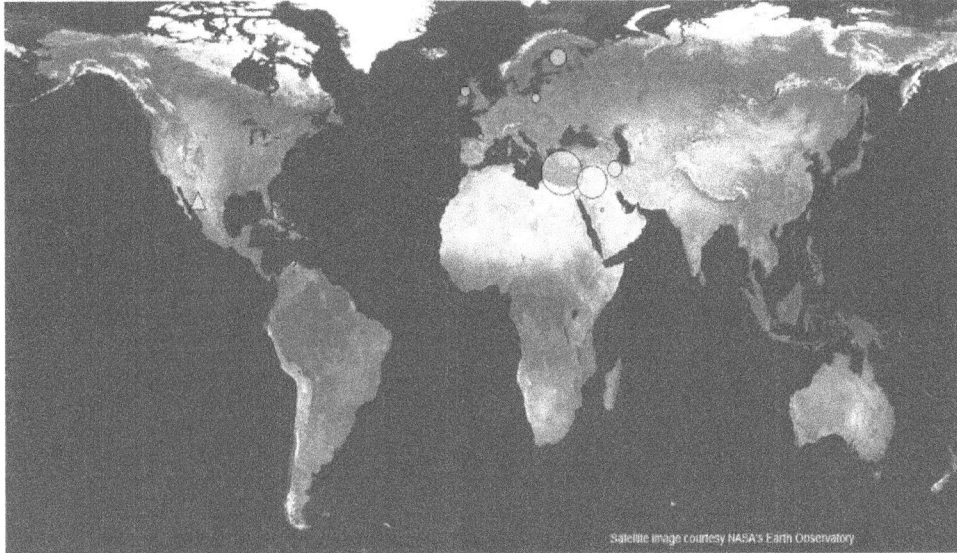

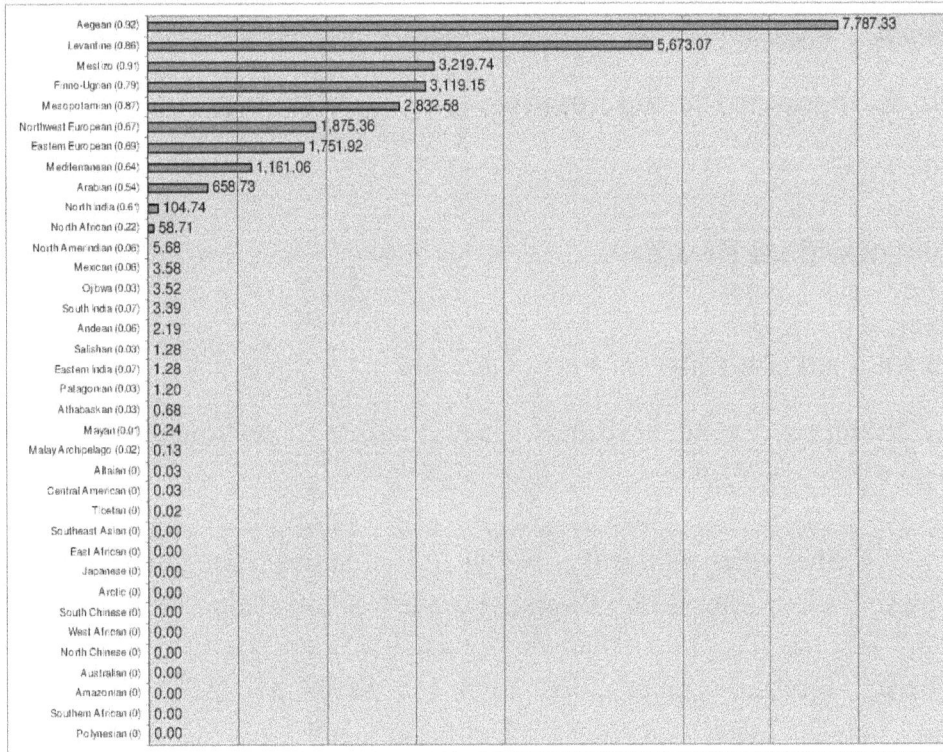

DNA Tribes Genetic Ancestry Analysis

FIGURE 117 MATCH GOYENS TO KING RAMESES III E-M2 WITH DYS 390=21

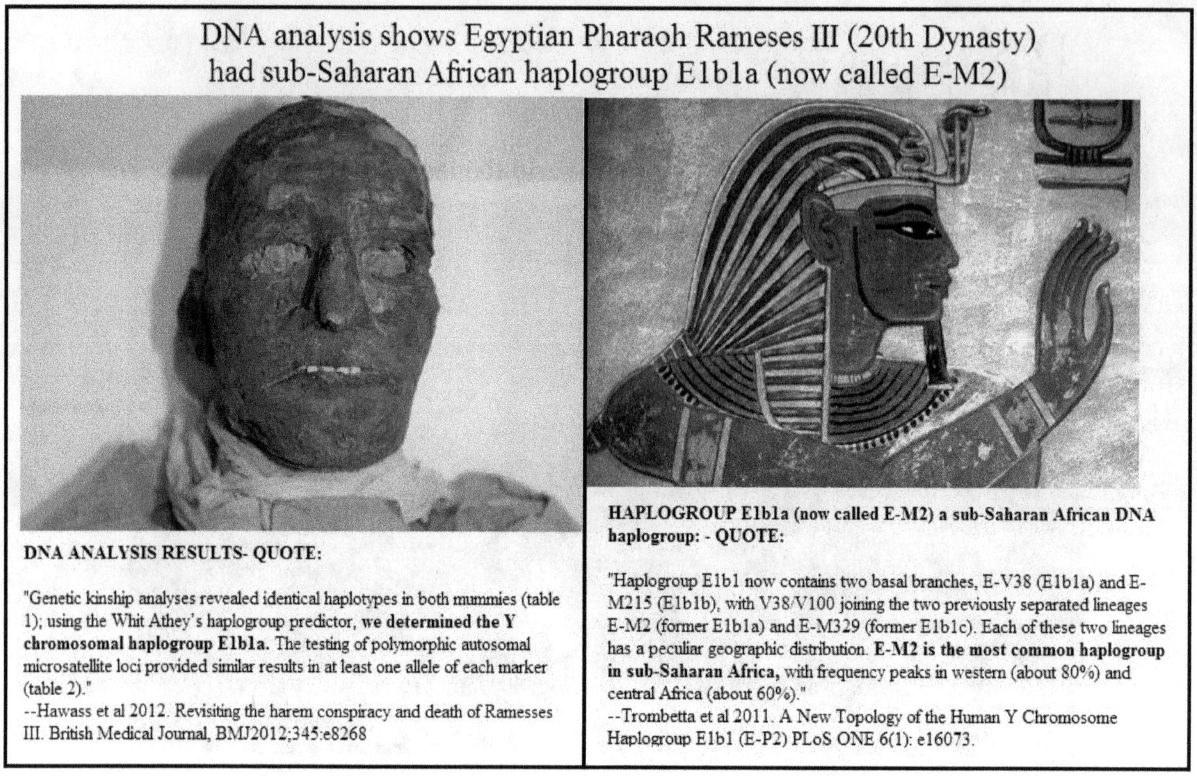

DNA analysis shows Egyptian Pharaoh Rameses III (20th Dynasty)
had sub-Saharan African haplogroup E1b1a (now called E-M2)

DNA ANALYSIS RESULTS- QUOTE:

"Genetic kinship analyses revealed identical haplotypes in both mummies (table 1); using the Whit Athey's haplogroup predictor, **we determined the Y chromosomal haplogroup E1b1a.** The testing of polymorphic autosomal microsatellite loci provided similar results in at least one allele of each marker (table 2)."

--Hawass et al 2012. Revisiting the harem conspiracy and death of Ramesses III. British Medical Journal, BMJ2012;345:e8268

HAPLOGROUP E1b1a (now called E-M2) a sub-Saharan African DNA haplogroup: - QUOTE:

"Haplogroup E1b1 now contains two basal branches, E-V38 (E1b1a) and E-M215 (E1b1b), with V38/V100 joining the two previously separated lineages E-M2 (former E1b1a) and E-M329 (former E1b1c). Each of these two lineages has a peculiar geographic distribution. **E-M2 is the most common haplogroup in sub-Saharan Africa,** with frequency peaks in western (about 80%) and central Africa (about 60%)."

--Trombetta et al 2011. A New Topology of the Human Y Chromosome Haplogroup E1b1 (E-P2) PLoS ONE 6(1): e16073.

Y & Mt-DNA Autosomal Testing Results

Figure 118

Nash Male Autosomal Results

Most Distant known ancestor
Thomas Ash/Nash b. 1750s Chowan, North Carolina

My Expected Results were (from prior knowledge): English, Native American, Irish, German, Cherokee Indian

My Actual DNA Tribes Analysis Results: **Native Match** Strong/Strongest and Respective MLIs were: Mazatlán City, Mexico 8.9 Basque (Basque County, Spain) 6.4 Pakistan 4.2 Spain 4.1 Portugal 3.7 Toscana, Italy 3.4 Strathclyde, Scotland 3.2 Tamil (India) 3.1 Northern Portugal 2.9 Veneto, Italy 2.6 Andalusia, Spain 2.6 Turkey 2.4 Piedmont, Italy 2.4 Austria 2.4 Kurdish (North Iraq) 2.1 Italy 2.1 Lombardia, Italy 1.9 Marmara, turkey 1.9 Bavaria, Germany 1.9 Italy 1.9

My Actual DNA Tribes Analysis Results – **Global Match** Strong/Strongest and Respective

MLIs were: Rio Negro, Argentina 15.4 Hispanic 14.6 Mexico 14.5 Hispanic (U.S.A.) 14.1 Costa Rica 12.0 Hispanic 10.1 el Salvador 9.9 Mazatlán City, Mexico 8.9 Bogota, Columbia 8.1 Caucasian (U.S.A.) 7.1 Valley of Mexico 6.8 Mendoza, Argentina 6.6 Basque (Basque country, Spain) 6.4 Santa Fe, Argentina 6.2 Mestizo (Ecuador) 6.2 Chubut, Argentina 5.9 central Mexico 5.2 Hispanic (U.S.A.) 5.1

My Actual DNA Tribes Analysis Results – World Region Match Strong/Strongest and Respective MLIs were: Mestizo 6.29 Central Amerindian 4.73 Northwest European 2.35 Mediterranean 2.24 India 2.08 Asia minor 1.97 north African 1.76 eastern European 0.89 Japanese 0.53 northeast Amerindian 0.49 Arabian 0.48 Finno-Ugrian 0.36 Mongolian 0.36 north India 0.17 India tribal 0.10 Athabaskan 0.04 southeast Asian 0.03 Salish 0.03 Chinese 0.03 Malay archipelago 0.03 Tibetan 0.02 Polynesian 0.01 Amazonian 0.01

Female Ash/Nash Autosomal Results

Most distant known maternal ancestor on the direct female line:
Name: **Kila Ashe; Kizzah Nash/Ash-Emily Slater, Davis**
Year Born: About 1826
Year Died: Unknown
PEE DEE INDIAN SOUTH CAROLINA, **ASH**
Matching Mutations
HVR1 HVR2
1. 16223T Not Tested 2. 16290T 3. 16291T 4. 16319A 5. 16362C 6. 16519C
Tested with: Genographic Project/Family Tree DNA/Sorenson Labs
Results
Shoshone Peguese

Additional information: My family descends from several tribes that resided in the Anson County area on the border between North Carolina & South Carolina that lived along the Pee Dee River. These tribes were called Pee Dee and the other tribe the Keyauwee. This is the line my maternal ancestors descend from. I also descend from the Chowanoc Indians who lived further North in Gates county NC.
Our people and their descendants are still living in the Carolinas well and strong. I am a tribal member of the MCDC Pee Dee Indian Tribe, McColl SC.

A Haplogroup is believed to have arisen in Asia some 30,000–50,000 years before present. Its ancestral haplogroup was **N**. Its highest frequencies are among Indigenous peoples of the Americas (Native American), its largest overall population is in East Asia, and its greatest variety (which suggests its origin point) is in East Asia.

Male Ashworth Autosomal Results

Autosomal **Haplo Assignments- R1b1a2 (R-M269)**
Native Population Matches:

Albanian (Kosovo, Albania) (0.4), Csango (Romania) (0.21), Serbia and Montenegro (0.26), Macedonian (0.24), Calabria, Italy (0.21), Banat and Transylvania, Western Romania (0.2), Istanbul, Turkey (0.21), Bucharest, Romania (0.19), Greece (0.2), Northern Greece (0.2), Spain (0.16), Slovenia (0.14), Vienna, Austria (0.15), Austria (0.16), Slovenia (0.16), Toscana, Italy (0.15), Netherlands (0.15), Emilia-Romagna, Italy (0.15), Andalusia, Spain (0.1), Flemish (0.14), Northwest European (0.07), Mediterranean (0.06), Levantine (0.07), Eastern European (0.06), Australian (0.23), Mesopotamian (0.04), Eastern India (0.1), Finno-Ugrian (0.03), Arabian (0.01), North African (0.01). South India (0), Mestizo (0), Malay Archipelago (0.02), Altaian (0), Tibetan (0), Southeast Asian (0), South Chinese (0), North Chinese (0), East, African (0), Japanese (0), West African (0), Polynesian (0), Southern African (0), Arctic (0), Andean (0), Mayan (0), Mexican (0), North Amerindian (0), Salishan (0), Patagonian (0), Central American (0), Athabaskan (0), Ojibwa (0), Amazonian (0)

Global Population Matches:
Albanian (Kosovo, Albania) (0.4), European-Aboriginal (mixed) (Western Australia) (0.61), European-Aboriginal (mixed) (Western Australia) (0.5), European-Aboriginal (mixed) (Northern Territory, Australia) (0.68), Csango (Romania) (0.21), Serbia and Montenegro (0.26), European-Aboriginal (mixed) (South Australia) (0.38), European-Aboriginal (mixed) (Riverine Region, Australia) (0.28), Indian (Malaysia) (0.27), Macedonian (0.24), Calabria, Italy (0.21), Banat and TransylvaniaWestern Romania (0.2), European-Aboriginal (mixed) (Northern Territory, Australia) (0.51), Istanbul, Turkey (0.21), Palestine (0.2), European-Aboriginal (mixed) (Queensland, Australia) (0.37), Bucharest, Romania (0.19), Greece (0.2)

World Region Matches:
Northwest European (0.07), Mediterranean (0.06), Levantine (0.07), Eastern, European (0.06), Australian (0.23), Mesopotamian (0.04), Eastern India (0.1), Finno-Ugrian (0.03), Arabian (0.01), North African (0.01), South India (0), Mestizo (0), Malay Archipelago (0.02), Altaian (0), Tibetan (0), Southeast Asian (0), South, Chinese (0), North Chinese (0), East African (0), Japanese (0), West African (0), Polynesian (0), Southern African (0), Arctic (0), Andean (0), Mayan (0), Mexican (0), North Amerindian (0), Salishan (0), Patagonian (0), Central American (0), Athabaskan (0), Ojibwa (0), Amazonian (0)

Female Ashworth Autosomal Results

Furthest suspected ancestor Catherine Smyth Choctaw Nation, Mississippi

Europe (Northeast European)	Finnish	53.37% ±6.58%
Native American (Central American)	Maya	17.98% ±0.61%
Middle East	Palestinian, Bedouin	28.65% ±5.97%

Daughters of Eve

7 Daughters & 27 Step Daughters

Dr. Wallace's mitochondrial DNA lineages are "haplogroups" but known as "daughters of Eve," because all of the lineages are branches of the trunk that stems from the mitochondrial Eve.

Dr. Wallace is now exploring the root of the mitochondrial tree. In the March 2000 American Journal of Human Genetics, he and colleagues identify the Vasikela Kung of the northwestern Kalahari Desert in southern Africa as the population that lies nearest to the root of the human mtDNA tree. Another population that seems almost equally old is that of the Biaka pygmies of Central Africa.

The 7 European & American Daughters of Eve

Prof. Sykes and Oxford University researchers in England have identified seven ancestral matriarchal groups from which all Europeans appear to be descended. Every European can trace his or her evolutionary history back to the seven ancestral mother groups, also referred to as the Seven European Daughters of Eve. Sykes et al obtained buccal cells from 6,000 individuals and analyzed the samples using the mitochondrial DNA (mtDNA) analysis. It is known that mtDNA mutates at a very slow rate, such as 1 mutation in every 10,000 generations or 20,000 years. So they figured that the women would have lived between 8,000 and 45,000 years ago. What is amazing is that all seven of the genetic groups appear to be descended from the Lara clan, one of three clans that still exist today in Africa. This is called the African Eve theory. It was proposed in the late 1980's by Allan Wilson, Mark Stoneking and others. The African Eve theory states that all humans share a common African ancestor. Migration routes of the 7 daughters are at this site: **http://www.oxfordancestors.com** As of 2002, there are believed to be 36 distinct genetic groups worldwide.

From Patrick Guinness, "In mtDNA, there are a maximum of 14 mutations between all humans (so far). From the middle of them, there are 26 mutations between humans and neanderthals, and more when you look at the great apes. The experts say that we and neanderthals had an ancestor ~250,000 years ago."

The Seven European Daughters of Eve matriarchal groups correspond to Dr. Wallace's lineages above, and were given names by Prof. Sykes:

- **Helena:** (Greek for "light")This clan's descendants are the most numerous in Europe, having started 20,000 years ago from a hunting family in the Dordogne region of the ice-capped Pyrenees in southern France. As the climate warmed, Helena's descendants trekked northward to what is now England, some 12,000 years ago. Members of this group are now present in all European countries.

- **Jasmine:** (Persian for "flower") Her people had a relatively happy life in Syria 10,000 years ago, where they farmed wheat and raised domestic animals. Jasmine's descendants arrived in Europe too late to experience the hardships of the Ice Age. Her clan brought agriculture into Europe.

- **Katrine:** (Greek for "pure") lived 15,000 years ago near Venice. Her clan ventured north, but many are still to be found in the Alps. The 5000 year old IceMan was one of her descendants. Today most of Katrine's clan live in the Alps.

- **Tara**: (Gaelic for "rock") This clan settled in Tuscany in Northern Italy about 17,000 years ago when the hills were thick with forests. After the Ice Age, her clan moved into France and trekked across the dry land that was to become the English Channel into Ireland.

- **Ursula:** (Latin for "she-bear") lived about 45,000 years ago in Northern Greece. She was slender and graceful and hunted with stone tools. Her clan spread across Europe including Britain and France.

- **Valda**: (Scandinavian for "ruler") Originally from the hills of northern Spain, Valda and her immediate descendants lived 17,000 years ago and shared the land with Ursula's clan. They spread out after the Ice Age, some of her clan becoming the Saami or Lapps of northern Finland and Norway.

- **Xenia**: (Greek for "hospitable") lived 25,000 years ago on the plains beneath the Caucasus Mountains on the eastern edge of the Black Sea. As the Ice Age ended her clan spread to Europe and across Asia to America. [As Dr. Wallace discovered, the X pattern is a rare European lineage and is also among the northern Native Americans such as the Ojibwa and Sioux.]

The 27 Step Daughters of Eve

Oxford geneticist Bryan Sykes, author of <u>*The Seven Daughters Of Eve: The Science That Reveals Our Genetic Ancestry*</u> just might have what it takes to become another <u>Carl Sagan</u> or <u>Louis Leakey</u> – that rare scientist with both the scientific skills and genius for self-promotion needed to make himself a household name.

Most importantly, though, Sykes has grasped a simple fact about population genetics that resounds emotionally with the average person, yet has largely eluded most learned commentators. Namely, *genes are the stuff of genealogy*. Each individual's genes are descended from some people, but not from some other people. Thus, Sykes discovered, people often feel a sense of family pride and loyalty to others, living and dead, with whom they share some DNA.

Further, if you read between his lines, you can readily understand why – despite all the propaganda that "race does not exist" – humanity will never get over its obsession with race: Race is Family. A racial group is an extremely extended family that is inbred to some degree.

In fact, people are so interested in tracing their family connections that Sykes has gone into business for himself. He started a for-profit firm OxfordAncestors.com. "Discover your ancestral mother," he advertises. For $220 he'll trace your DNA (actually, a particular set of your specialized mitochondrial DNA) back to one of the seven Stone Age women who are the ancestors in the all-female line of 95% of all white Europeans.

BUT, if you happen to be from a non-European race, well, Sykes has got 27 other matrilineal clans sketchily worked out for you. Still, the Eurocentric, cashocentric Sykes tends to treat those non-Caucasian ancient mothers as if they were The Twenty-Seven Stepdaughters of Eve.

Specific mitochondrial haplogroups are typically found in different regions of the world, and this is due to unique population histories. In the process of spreading around the world, many populations—with their special mitochondrial haplogroups—became isolated, and specific haplogroups concentrated in geographic regions. Today, we have identified certain haplogroups that originated in Africa, Europe, Asia, the islands of the Pacific, the Americas, and even particular ethnic groups. Of course, haplogroups that are specific to one region are sometimes found in another, but this is due to recent migration.

A, B, C, & D: Haplogroups A, B, C, & D. Native American mtDNA Haplogroups. Also see mtDNA Haplogroup X.

F: Mitochondrial haplogroup F Information.
The Evidence of mtDNA Haplogroup F in a European Population and its Ethnohistoric Implications

H: Mitochondrial haplogroup H is a predominantly European haplogroup that participated in a population expansion beginning approximately 20,000 years ago. Today, about 30% of all mitochondrial lineages in Europe are classified as haplogroup H. It is rather uniformly distributed throughout Europe suggesting a major role in the peopling of Europe, and descendant lineages of the original haplogroup H appear in the Near East as a result of migration. Future work will better resolve the distribution and historical characteristics of this haplogroup. Bryan Sykes in his Seven Daughters of Eve book named this mtDNA haplogroup Helena.

HV: Mitochondrial haplogroup HV is a primarily European haplogroup that underwent an expansion beginning approximately 20,000 years ago. It is more prevalent in western Europe than in eastern Europe, and descendant lineages of the original haplogroup HV appear in the Near East as a result of more recent migration. One of the dominant mitochondrial haplogroups in Europe, haplogroup HV pre-dates the occurrence of farming in Europe. Future work will better resolve the distribution and historical characteristics of this haplogroup.

I: Principally a European haplogroup, haplogroup I is detected at very low frequency across west Eurasia with slightly greater representation in northern and western Europe. Given its wide, but sparse, distribution, it is likely that it was present in those populations that first colonized Europe. This hypothesis is supported by the estimate its age—approximately 30,000 years. Bonnie Schrack in her mtDNA Haplogroup I project named this mtDNA haplogroup Iris.

J*: The mitochondrial haplogroup J contains several sub-lineages. The original haplogroup J originated in the Near East approximately 50,000 years ago. Within Europe, sub-lineages of haplogroup J have distinct and interesting distributions. Haplogroup J* — the root lineage of haplogroup J — is found distributed throughout Europe, but at a relatively low frequency. Haplogroup J* is generally considered one of the prominent lineages that was part of the Neolithic spread of agriculture into Europe from the Near East beginning approximately 10,000 years ago. Bryan Sykes in his Seven Daughters of Eve book named this mtDNA haplogroup Jasmine.

J1b1: The mitochondrial haplogroup J contains several sub-lineages. The original haplogroup J originated in the Near East approximately 50,000 years ago. Within Europe, sub-lineages of haplogroup J have distinct and interesting distributions. Haplogroup J1b is found distributed in the Near East and southern Iberia, and may have been part of the original colonization wave of Neolithic settlers moving around the Mediterranean 6000 years ago or perhaps a lineage of Phoenician traders. Within haplogroup J1b, a derivative lineage haplogroup J1b1 has been found in Britain and another sub-lineage detected in Italy. Further research will better establish the relationship of these two geographically distant, yet evolutionarily related, haplogroups. Bryan Sykes in his Seven Daughters of Eve book named this mtDNA haplogroup Jasmine.

K: The mitochondrial super-haplogroup U encompasses haplogroups U1-U7 and haplogroup K. Haplogroup K is found through Europe, and contains multiple closely related lineages indicating a recent population expansion. The origin of haplogroup K dates to approximately 16,000 years ago, and it has been suggested that individuals with this haplogroup took part in the pre-Neolithic expansion following the Last Glacial Maximum. Bryan Sykes in his Seven Daughters of Eve book named this mtDNA haplogroup Katrine.

L1: Haplogroup L1 is found in West and Central sub-Saharan Africa. Some of its branches (L1d, L1k, L1a, L1f) were recently re-classified into haplogroup L0 as L0d, L0k, L0a and L0f. Haplogroup L1 arose with Mitochondrial Eve and haplogroup L0 is an offshoot. The descendants of haplogroup L1 are also African haplogroups L2 and L3, the latter of which gave rise to all non-African haplogroups. Haplogroup L1 is believed to have first appeared in Africa approximately 150,000 to 170,000 years ago.

L2: Haplogroup L2 is native to sub-Saharan Africa, where it is present in approximately one third of all people. It is believed to have arisen approximately 70,000 years ago from the line of haplogroup L1.

L3: Haplogroup L3 is confined to Africa and emigrant African populations. It is most common in East Africa. However, L3 is also the haplogroup from which the macro-haplogroups M and N are believed to have arisen. These two haplogroups are ancestral to all haplogroups outside Africa, and are believed to represent the initial migration by modern humans out of Africa.

M: Haplogroup M cluster has been characterized as generally of east Eurasia—a geographic region that includes south Asia, east Asia, and Australasia. One of the two deep roots of the mitochondrial tree of haplogroups found in Asia, haplogroup M dates to approximately 70,000 years ago. Interestingly, one of the sub-haplogroups of the M cluster, haplogroup M1, is found primarily in northern Africa, suggesting either a very early divergence from the root of haplogroup M or even migration back to Africa after the original dispersal into Eurasia. Future work will further document the historical distribution of this root haplogroup and closely related haplogroups within the M cluster.

N: Haplogroup N. The N superhaplogroup has been characterized as pan-Eurasian. Haplogroup N is one of the two major trunks emerging from the original African root, and dates to approximately 65,000 years ago. Interestingly, several sub-haplogroups of the N cluster—haplogroup N1 and derivative lineages—have been detected in the Near East, suggesting either early divergence near the root of haplogroup N or subsequent migrations back towards western Eurasia following the original dispersal into east Eurasia. Future work will further document the historical distribution of this root haplogroup and closely related haplogroups within the N cluster.

N1c: N1c specific mitochondrial haplogroups are typically found in different regions of the world, and this is due to unique population histories. In the process of spreading around the world, many populations—with their special mitochondrial haplogroups—became isolated, and specific haplogroups concentrated in geographic regions. Today, we have identified certain haplogroups that originated in Africa, Europe, Asia, the islands of the Pacific, the Americas, and even particular ethnic groups. Of course, haplogroups that are specific to one region are sometimes found in another, but this is due to recent migration.

T: Haplogroup T is believed to have lived around 17,000 years ago in Nothern Italy. Tara's people would have come from the Near East, and her descendents spread all over Europe. Bryan Sykes in his Seven Daughters of Eve book named this mtDNA haplogroup Tara.

T1: MtDNA Haplogroup T1 Project

U2: Mitochondrial haplogroup U2.
Cyndi Rutledge's mtDNA Haplogroup U2 Project

U5: The mitochondrial super-haplogroup U encompasses haplogroups U1-U7 and haplogroup K. Haplogroup U5, with its own multiple lineages nested within, is the oldest European-specific haplogroup, and its origin dates to approximately 50,000 years ago. Most likely arising in the

Near East, and spreading into Europe in a very early expansion, the presence of haplogroup U5 in Europe pre-dates the expansion of agriculture in Europe. Haplogroup U5a1—a lineage within haplogroup U5—arose in Europe approximately 30,000 years ago, and is mainly found in northwest Europe. In the context of its rather ancient origin, the modern distribution of haplogroup U5a1 suggests that individuals bearing this haplogroup were part the initial expansion tracking the retreat of ice sheets from Europe. Bryan Sykes in his Seven Daughters of Eve book named this mtDNA haplogroup Ursula.

U6: The mitochondrial super-haplogroup U encompasses haplogroups U1-U7 and haplogroup K. Bryan Sykes in his Seven Daughters of Eve book named this mtDNA haplogroup Ursula.

U7: The mitochondrial super-haplogroup U encompasses haplogroups U1-U7 and haplogroup K. Haplogroup U7 has a Near Eastern origin approximately 30,000 years ago. Within Europe, it occurs at low frequency in the Caucasus. Bryan Sykes in his Seven Daughters of Eve book named this mtDNA haplogroup Ursula.

V: Bryan Sykes in his Seven Daughters of Eve book named this mtDNA haplogroup Velda.

W: Haplogroup W is a "daughter" of N and a "sister" of R, I, X, & A.

X: Haplogroup X is found in Europe and Asia, and is believed to have migrated to the Americas about 15,000 years ago, making up a very small component of the Native American population. Bryan Sykes in his Seven Daughters of Eve book named this mtDNA haplogroup Xenia.

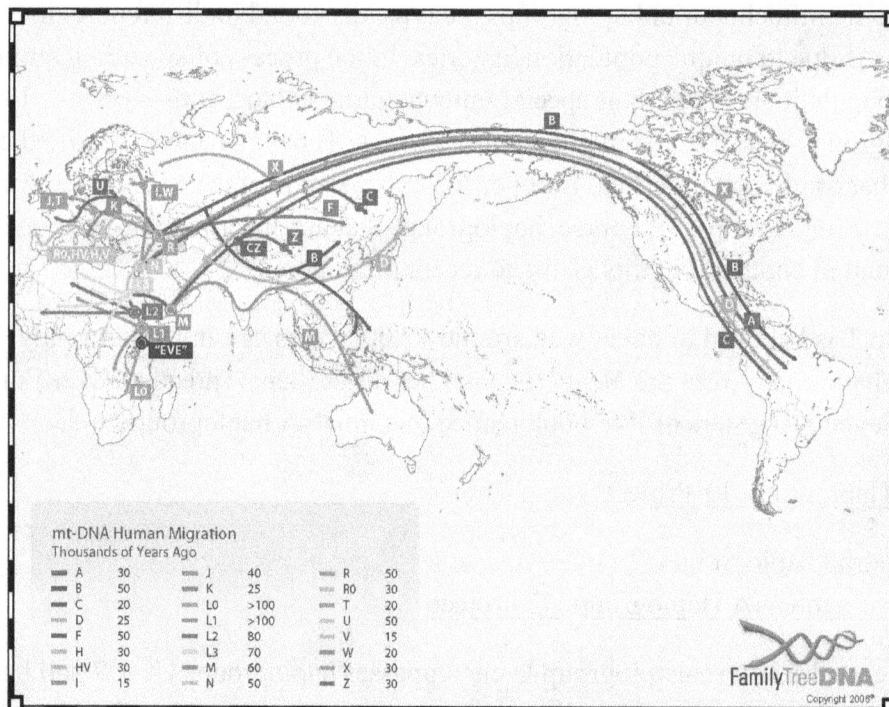

mt-DNA Human Migration
Thousands of Years Ago

A	30	J	40	R	50		
B	50	K	25	RO	30		
C	20	L0	>100	T	20		
D	25	L1	>100	U	50		
F	50	L2	80	V	15		
H	30	L3	70	W	20		
HV	30	M	60	X	30		
I	15	N	50	Z	30		

FamilyTreeDNA
Copyright 2006

A great deal of work has been done on other parts of the world in the past decade and it is very clear that there are plenty more clans than just the 7 Daughters of Eve in Europe. The precise definition of what makes a clan depends on having a very good sample of different countries. The present estimate is that there are at least 30 clans in the rest of the world of equivalent standing to the seven European clans. Fourteen of them in are found in Africa, six in Eastern Asia and four in Native Americans. But some parts of the world have been only very sparsely studied so far and they just don't know what to expect. For instance, it shouldn't be a surprise if they find several completely new clans among native Australians.

Population y

Update on the high rates of "Aboriginal Australian", Paupua New Guinea and Tasuman (Australasian) DNA comparison hits among the Redbones and the theories we had understood to be attributed to our Romani (Gypsy/Egyptian) heritage, perhaps are Native first family connections instead.

Recently, a DNA study was made in a remote people hidden in the Amazonian jungles of South America. In an article published at Smithsonian.com July 21st 2015 by Helen Thompson titled *A DNA Search for the First Americans Links Amazon Groups to the Indigenous Australians* takes aim at the theory just one migration wave of founding fore parents settled the Americas. The overall held theories of first American's arrival and disbursement of the past perhaps are not correct. The hotly debated topic for decades received a new twist in 2008 when DNA findings of an ancient group of humans in Oregon were released. The study results showed that the remains had genetic ties to modern Native Americans. Then in 2014, a genetic test of 12,000 year old human remains found in an underwater cave in Mexico also had genetic ties to modern Native Americans. Genetic study of the findings, have since proven that both of the ancient remains revealed genetic linkages to Eurasia adding to the findings of a single founding migration of first Americans. A second smaller migration, only 6,000 years ago show a stronger resemblance to the modern populations of Canadian tribes, linked to a third migration.

Though coauthor of the study, David Reich, a geneticist at Harvard University found evidence to support the migration theories, after close study of the genomes from cultures in Central and South America, Pontus Skoglund, a researcher at Riech's lab noticed that the Suri and Karitiana people of the Amazon had stronger ties to the indigenous groups of Australia (Aboriginal), New Guineans and Andaman Islanders, than that of Eurasians. A newer sampling was taken, though these are hard to come by because of weather conditions and remote location of the Suri, Karitiana and Xavante people of the Amazon. After sifting through the genomes however, the study did confirm that these South American Indians are genetically more closely related to the Australasians than the Siberian people (migration from Eurasians).

The DNA that link the two groups had to arrive from somewhere, because they have about the same, in common with Australians and they do with New Guineans, the researchers think that they share a common ancestor tens of thousands of years ago in Asia but that DNA does not still exist in Asia. Therefore, the belief is that each group have an ancient common ancestor, one part of the family went north through Siberia, while the other migrated south to New Guinea and Australia. They have dubbed this population "Y" for ypykuera, or "ancestor" in Tupi, a language spoken by the Suri and Karitiana.

Details of Population "y" arrival are not understood at this time, and a common migration period coinciding one another, was not ruled out. However, the scientists believe the lineage of Eurasian settlers is very old and that somewhere along the migration paths they probably mixed with the lineages of Population y. The Amazonian tribes remain isolated from most other South American Indian groups, thus, the signal remains stronger in their DNA.

The results line up with studies of ancient skulls unearthed in Brazil and Colombia that bear stronger resemblance to those of Australasians than the skulls of other Native Americans. Based on the skeletal remains, some anthropologists had previously pointed to more than one founding group, but others had brushed off the similarities as a byproduct of these groups living and working in similar environments. Bones can only be measured and interpreted so many ways, while genes usually make a more concrete case. "The problem so far was that there has never been strong genetic evidence to support this notion," says Mark Hubbe, an anthropologist at Ohio State University who was not affiliated with the latest study. But even genetic evidence is subject to skepticism and scrutiny. Cecil Lewis Jr., an anthropological geneticist at the University of Oklahoma, cautions that Amazonian groups are low on genetic diversity and are more susceptible to genetic drift[41]. "This raises very serious questions about the role of chance … in creating this Australasian affinity," he says.

Another group led by Eske Willerslev and Maanasa Raghavan at the University at Copenhagen reports in *Science* today that Native Americans descend from just one line that crossed the land bridge no earlier than 23,000 years ago. While they didn't look at Amazonian groups in-depth, the team did find a weak link between Australasians and some South American populations, which they chalk up to gene flow from Eskimos. However, there is a problem: Evidence of Population y doesn't persist in modern Eurasian groups, nor does it seem to show up

---

[41] **Genetic Drift**. Variation in the relative frequency of different genotypes in a small population, owing to the chance disappearance of particular genes as individuals die or do not reproduce.

in other Native Americans. If Aleutian Islanders or their ancestors had somehow mixed with an Australasian group up north or made their way south to the Amazon, they'd leave genetic clues along the way. "It's not a clear alternative," argues Reich.

Both studies therefore suggest that the ancestry of the first Americans is a lot more complicated than scientists had envisioned. "There is a greater diversity of Native American founding populations than previously thought," says Skoglund. "And these founding populations connect indigenous groups in far apart places of the world."

Two samples Autosomal DNA results common among the Redbone test study showing high hits to Australasian populations; see figures 96 & 97. According to Lucas at Tribes DNA, this a most common admixture of the the Redbone people. Though initial findings of our Redbone DNA study attributed these high resolution hits among the Redbone people to the Australasians, Papua New Guinea to be stimming from an ancient migration from India to Australia (respectively). The known Gypsy or Romani DNA among our families having their origins in India thus the comparisons to Australiasian. However, a new twist in that research of recent years, leads us to believe this could also be Native American, rather than the understood migration from India.

In a recent article from Archeology.org titled *Aboriginal Australian Y-Chromosomes Dated Back 50,000 Years*; published the 29th of February 2016 explains further a recent genome findings. A team of scientist from Cambridge, England at the Wellcome Trust Institute and La Trobe University study sequencing in the Y (male) chromosomes of 13 Aboriginal Australian men. The study showed that the Aboriginal Australian DNA dated to some 50,000 years to the arrival time of the first humans on the continent. It had been suggested by previous studies that another wave of people arrived in Australia from India between four and five thousand years ago. Though even the archeological evidence prove this migration path from India coincides with the introduction of the Dingo populations and stone tools. However "the data shows that Aboriginal Australian Y-chromosomes very distinctly different Indian ones these results refute the previously Y-chromosome study, this excluding this part of the puzzle as providing evidence for a prehistoric migration from India. Instead, the results are agreement with the archeological evidences about when people arrived in this part of the world," Anders Bergstrom of the Wellcome Trust Sanger Institute said in a press release.

Thus, we have developed the concept these comparison markers are actually ancient first American as opposed to the known hits from India which would follow the Gypsy tribes of the world. Further research is needed and follow ups will be published in subsequent issues of the Redbone Chronicles.

FIGURE 119 RESULTS: AUTOSOMAL TESTING AUSTRALASIAN HITS COMMON AMONG REDBONE DNA RESULTS

Part C: Your High Resolution Global Population Match Results

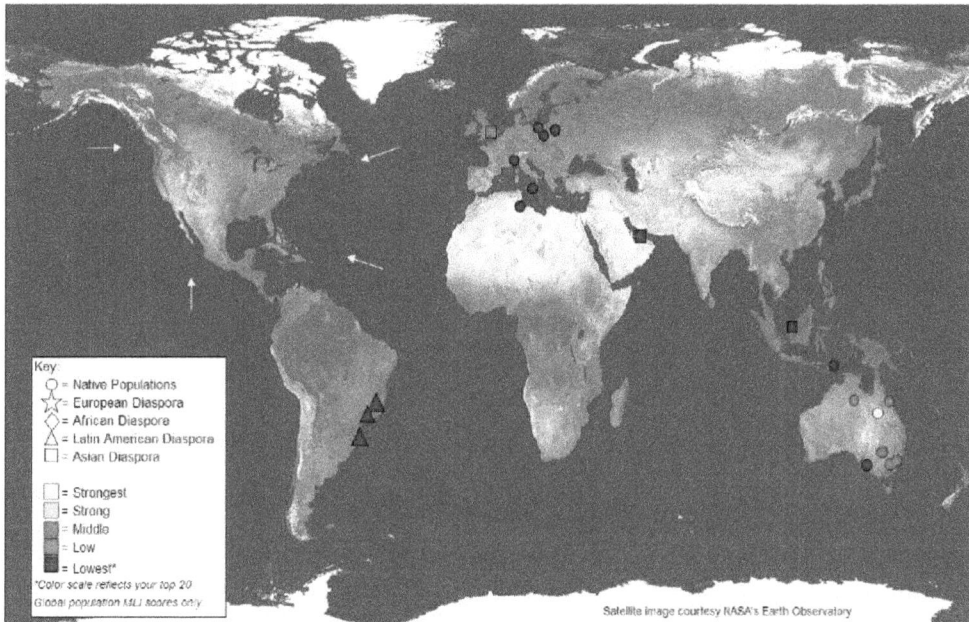

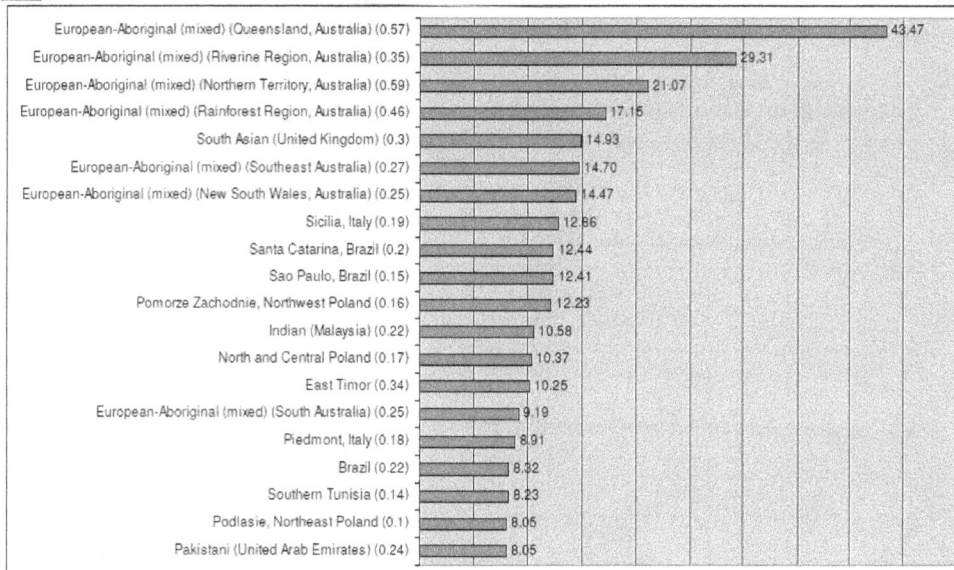

Population	Score
European-Aboriginal (mixed) (Queensland, Australia) (0.57)	43.47
European-Aboriginal (mixed) (Riverine Region, Australia) (0.35)	29.31
European-Aboriginal (mixed) (Northern Territory, Australia) (0.59)	21.07
European-Aboriginal (mixed) (Rainforest Region, Australia) (0.46)	17.15
South Asian (United Kingdom) (0.3)	14.93
European-Aboriginal (mixed) (Southeast Australia) (0.27)	14.70
European-Aboriginal (mixed) (New South Wales, Australia) (0.25)	14.47
Sicilia, Italy (0.19)	12.86
Santa Catarina, Brazil (0.2)	12.44
Sao Paulo, Brazil (0.15)	12.41
Pomorze Zachodnie, Northwest Poland (0.16)	12.23
Indian (Malaysia) (0.22)	10.58
North and Central Poland (0.17)	10.37
East Timor (0.34)	10.25
European-Aboriginal (mixed) (South Australia) (0.25)	9.19
Piedmont, Italy (0.18)	8.91
Brazil (0.22)	8.32
Southern Tunisia (0.14)	8.23
Podlasie, Northeast Poland (0.1)	8.05
Pakistani (United Arab Emirates) (0.24)	8.05

FIGURE 120 RESULTS: AUTOSOMAL TESTING AUSTRALASIAN HITS COMMON AMONG REDBONE DNA RESULTS

Part C: Your High Resolution Global Population Match Results

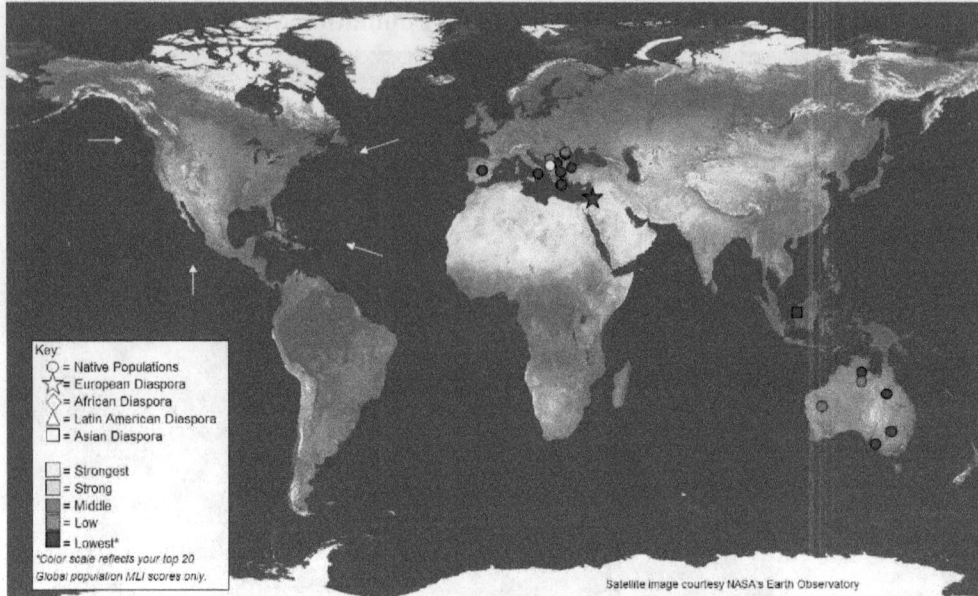

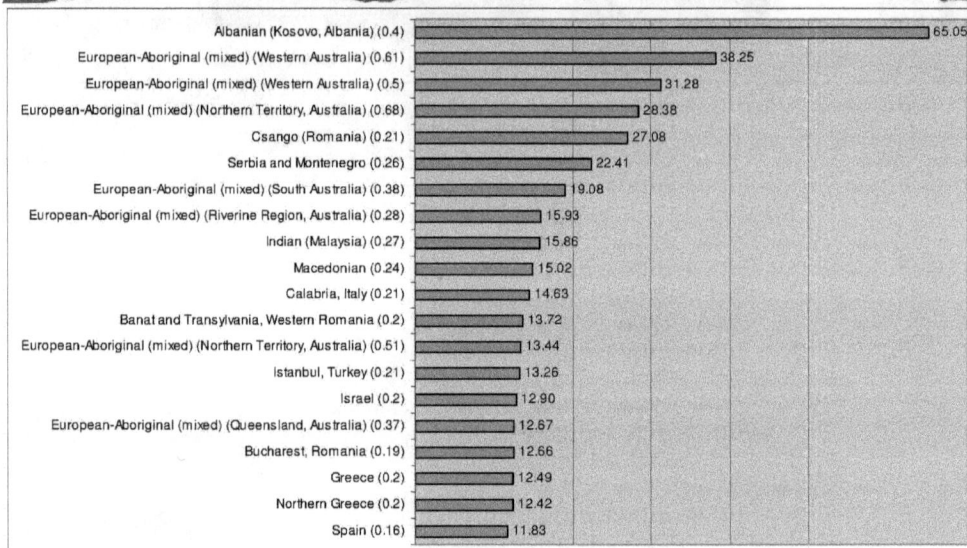

Population	Score
Albanian (Kosovo, Albania) (0.4)	65.05
European-Aboriginal (mixed) (Western Australia) (0.61)	38.25
European-Aboriginal (mixed) (Western Australia) (0.5)	31.28
European-Aboriginal (mixed) (Northern Territory, Australia) (0.68)	28.38
Csango (Romania) (0.21)	27.08
Serbia and Montenegro (0.26)	22.41
European-Aboriginal (mixed) (South Australia) (0.38)	19.08
European-Aboriginal (mixed) (Riverine Region, Australia) (0.28)	15.93
Indian (Malaysia) (0.27)	15.86
Macedonian (0.24)	15.02
Calabria, Italy (0.21)	14.63
Banat and Transylvania, Western Romania (0.2)	13.72
European-Aboriginal (mixed) (Northern Territory, Australia) (0.51)	13.44
Istanbul, Turkey (0.21)	13.26
Israel (0.2)	12.90
European-Aboriginal (mixed) (Queensland, Australia) (0.37)	12.67
Bucharest, Romania (0.19)	12.66
Greece (0.2)	12.49
Northern Greece (0.2)	12.42
Spain (0.16)	11.83

DNA Tribes Genetic Ancestry Analysis
www.dnatribes.com - Customer support: *support@dnatribes.com*

6/11/2008 - Page 9 of 10

Index

www.ingramcontent.com/pod-product-compliance
Lightning Source LLC
Chambersburg PA
CBHW080327270326
41927CB00014B/3118